The Lost Art of the
Good Schmooze

The Lost Art of the Good Schmooze

Building Rapport and Defusing Conflict in Everyday and Public Talk

DIANA BOXER

 PRAEGER

AN IMPRINT OF ABC-CLIO, LLC
Santa Barbara, California • Denver, Colorado • Oxford, England

Library of Congress Cataloging-in-Publication Data

Boxer, Diana, 1948-
  The lost art of the good schmooze: Building rapport and defusing conflict in
everyday and public talk / Diana Boxer.
      p. cm.
  Includes bibliographical references and index.
  ISBN 978-0-313-38341-0 (hard copy : alk. paper)—ISBN 978-0-313-38342-7
(ebook) 1. Social interaction. I. Title.
  HM1111.B68   2011
  302.3'46—dc22   2010049790

ISBN: 978-0-313-38341-0
EISBN: 978-0-313-38342-7

15 14 13 12 11   1 2 3 4 5

This book is also available on the World Wide Web as an eBook.
Visit www.abc-clio.com for details.

Praeger
An Imprint of ABC-CLIO, LLC

ABC-CLIO, LLC
130 Cremona Drive, P.O. Box 1911
Santa Barbara, California 93116-1911

This book is printed on acid-free paper ∞

Manufactured in the United States of America

This book is dedicated to my father, Ben Boxer—
master of the lost art of the good schmooze

Contents

Acknowledgments

Many people supported me in the writing of this book, and I wish to express my sincere gratitude to all of them. My husband, Joseph Cook, put up with my long hours at the desk; moreover, he not only read and meticulously commented on parts of the manuscript, but he also urged me to take iced tea breaks, eat meals, and even get away for recreational activities. He deserves my heartfelt thanks. My dear friend Angel Kwolek-Folland not only gave me feedback on earlier drafts, but also fed me at her home time and again during the book's preparation. Thank you, Angel, for urging me to watch Gator football when I felt that I should have been writing. My research assistant, Caroline Kennelly Latterman, proofread each chapter, told me what worked and what did not, and did a lot of tedious work on endnotes and the bibliography—all while preparing for her own wedding. My lovely daughters, Marin Feldman Xavier and Brooke Feldman; their husbands, Ricardo Xavier and Scott Hinzman; and my wonderful stepsons, Alexander and Zachary Cook, gave me the family nurturing so needed during this project. These grown children provided endless data on family schmoozing. Finally, my thanks to my editor at Praeger, Valentina Tursini, who tolerated my frequent e-mail queries and still always provided positive and encouraging words.

Introduction

Schmoozing is great! IMHO [in my humble opinion] the act of schmoozing is to converse about life itself—the good, the bad, and the ugly. It's a heartfelt interaction with others, not just something to while away the time. Unfortunately, it's become a lost art. If more people schmoozed on a daily basis, I believe there would be less stress in the world.

Claire Heifech on Facebook, 2009

What exactly is it that makes for smooth interactions for some people but awkward interactions for others? Why are some people able to chat easily, not only with friends but even with total strangers, and through these chats build social relationships? Why are some people able to effortlessly make small talk at work, with those higher in the hierarchy as well as lower? What makes for smooth and successful talk in all spheres of life and how does this success impact our lives? These are some of the questions addressed in this book.

The meaning of schmoozing is widely recognized by residents of certain large cities in the northeastern part of the United States (e.g., metropolitan New York). In fact, the person responsible for the previous quote is from my hometown, Hillside, New Jersey—just 14 miles from New York City. A cartoon that appeared recently in the *New York Times*[1] depicts the four New Yorkers who are now serving on the Supreme Court (this was just as Elena Kagan was about to undergo confirmation). Scalia, Ginsburg, Sotomayor, and Kagan are shown schmoozing in their native tongue—New York dialect. The gist of their exchanges shows native pronunciation, but the schmoozing is about ordinary social talk. This includes Scalia and Ginsburg discussing whether a certain bus line runs in "Elmhoist" (Elmhurst, Queens), and Kagan asking Sotomayor, "Yungry? Jeat jet?" Clearly, this is a stereotypical conception, but such are the topics of schmoozing. It is just about ordinary chatting—not necessarily about the kinds of important topics normally expected of Supreme Court justices.

Outside of the New York metropolitan area, the meaning of schmoozing is often construed differently. For example, when I ask the students in my linguistics classes here in the southern United States to tell me the meaning of schmoozing, they typically answer that it means "sucking up." Some will answer, "You know, schmoozing up." It is the *up* part of the two-word verb that gives away the new meaning. Schmoozing up and sucking up have negative connotations. They imply talk for direct benefits or networking for personal gain.

Any Internet search with the keyword *schmoozing* yields results that indicate its new meaning—what I refer to in this book as bad schmoozing. The description of schmoozing from *The Free Dictionary* yields the definition: "To converse casually, especially in order to gain an advantage or make a social connection." When the synonym *chatter* is used, it is often preceded by the adjective *idle*. *The Urban Dictionary*, perhaps the quintessential source for the most current usages, refers to schmoozing as "the pointless evening pursuit of kissing important butts to better one's employment prospects," and "making ingratiating small talk—talk that is business-oriented, designed to both provide and solicit personal information but avoids overt pitching." To be sure, overt pitching is too obvious. The new sense of schmoozing cannot be construed as sucking up, lest it be rendered unsuccessful.

The original meaning of schmooze derives from Yiddish, and means to pass the time chatting. The results are simply warm feelings of interacting. The benefits are indirect. When you get warm feelings from someone who interacts with you, you are likely to want to spend more time with that person. The more time spent with each other, the more likely that something will ensue—a friendship, an exchange of goods and/or services, offers and favors, and so on. The meaning of schmooze as it has evolved into present-day usage overlooks the step of establishing a relationship simply for the sake of human interaction. In our modern world, we tend to want to skip this stage. Indeed, perhaps we rush through it with our ultimate goal in mind—getting something out of the interaction. Thus, in our haste to get things done, to multitask, good schmoozing has become a lost art.

The press has of late used the notion of *schmooze* in the way most Americans now perceive it. As many will recall, a few years ago there was a large-scale lobbying scandal in Washington centering on Jack Abramoff. The press referred to him as the consummate schmoozer. This use of the term drives home the realization that schmoozing has devolved into something far from its original meaning. It has taken on a negative connotation. I did a commentary for National Public Radio's program *All Things Considered* on January 30, 2006, titled, "The Etymology of Schmooze." I reproduce it here to offer some background regarding how a term can undergo what linguists call *semantic derogation*: evolution from a positive to a negative denotation.

Michele Norris, host: Lobbying reform has moved up the Congressional agenda thanks in no small part to the Jack Abramoff scandal. Abramoff pleaded guilty to fraud and tax evasion charges, which he did while exploiting his position as an influential lobbyist. For a long time, lobbying in Washington has had a bad reputation, and the scandal has made that reputation even worse. And according to commentator and linguist Diana Boxer, it has also damaged the perception of another long-standing practice in the Capitol.

Diana Boxer: Jack Abramoff is sullying the good schmooze. Nobody denies that schmoozing is at the heart of lobbying. But the term has acquired a bad rap, and this latest ethics debacle is a nail in the coffin for what used to mean something positive.

The word *schmooze* derives from the Yiddish *shmuesn*, which in turn derives from Hebrew *shemuah*, meaning "rumor." Its earliest written reference dates to 1897, when it appeared in *The New York Times Weekly Magazine* in the sentence, "He loves dearly to stop and chat (*schmoos*, he calls it)."

When the term was borrowed into American English, it originally meant to have a warm conversation—to shoot the breeze—to pass the time chatting. As with English, German borrowed Yiddish *shmus*, and, while it now means something like "to kiss or neck" in German, its early evolution took on a change to resemble "empty flattery."

To be sure, it's always been just a short step from schmoozing to flattery or "sucking up." But, used to be, when we schmoozed, we felt good about just chatting and building rapport. We came away from the experience having opened or strengthened a relationship. It wasn't about networking or gaining favor.

Good schmoozers, in the original sense of the term, may get what they want or need. But the benefits are indirect—they stem from the warm feelings of just interacting.

Unfortunately, the meaning of schmoozing has come to serve the twin masters of what linguists call *interaction* and *transaction*. Mostly, unfortunately, transaction. Today schmoozing means chatting, with benefits. We could view the sleazing of schmoozing as evolution. Linguists no longer insist that we uphold the traditional meanings of words. Instead, we view language evolution as a natural process. We neither judge the changes nor mourn them.

But when language change reflects degradation in cultural values, the issue at hand is something much more serious. Schmoozing becomes an activity that serves only the purpose of the highest bidder. For lobbyists like Abramoff, "don't schmooze, you lose" becomes the motto.

We should mourn the schmooze because it no longer serves the good of the community. The schmooze on Capitol Hill has made friends with the bribe, and that's a sad place to be.

GOOD SCHMOOZE, BAD SCHMOOZE

As seen in the NPR commentary, the word *schmooze* comes from the Yiddish language and literally means to have a satisfying verbal exchange that makes the participants feel good just "shooting the breeze." In essence, it means using talk to lubricate interactions with others through knowing what to say at the right time.

Given this literal meaning, we can easily understand how it is just a short distance between shooting the breeze and sucking up. The closest notion to schmoozing in English is *small talk*. But that notion is also not so positive—its importance is diminished by being referred to as *small*. In fact, small talk is a big thing that is largely underappreciated in the United States. This is where it all becomes murky. The good schmooze transpires without "sucking up." It builds relationships and defuses conflict in our everyday talk.

Small talk is a big thing because people who are good at it get close to others. This is no small thing, to be sure. Getting close to others brings social satisfaction and sometimes unforeseen opportunities. Of course, small talk or schmoozing can be carried too far, and when this happens, others may begin to suspect one's intentions. This is where the fine line is drawn. What I want to convey here is how to reclaim the lost art of the good schmooze without having it be construed as sucking up.

Perhaps the confusion derives from the way our culture has evolved. In our preindustrialized society, small talk was an important part of the fabric of everyday social interaction. This continued to be true during our industrial revolution and beyond. But when we became a technologized, consumer-oriented society, things began to change. Volumes have since been written about such phenomena as "The Me Generation." At that point the concept of networking leapt into popular media, and schmoozing became virtually synonymous with networking. Therefore, when I ask people their conception of schmoozing, most tell me it is about networking or glad-handing for personal advancement.

An example from real life illustrates the fine line between the good schmooze and sucking up or networking. This happened several years ago in one of my own classes at the university:

Jamie was a new graduate student. It was the first day of class during the fall semester, when new students were just arriving and getting to know each other and their professors. The specific graduate course that I was teaching met for three hours once a week in the late afternoon. I introduced the material for the first hour or so and then told the students to take a 10-minute break. As students were filing out of the room to grab a drink or snack (it was nearing dinnertime), Jamie came up to the front of the room toward where I was standing, all the while holding up an academic journal opened to a particular page. Jamie said:

Jamie: I can't believe I get to take a course with the person who
        wrote this.
Me: [I'm immediately engaged] Oh, have you read that?

A conversation naturally ensued in which we got to know each other a bit in the short break. After the class we continued our discussion. I found out that Jamie was going to have trouble taking the course. She had a job in her hometown, a two-hour drive from the university. What happened?

It is true that the opening statement may be perceived as flattery, or sucking up. It is also true that ego boosting has a lot to do with how we

xvi   Introduction

react to individuals. Nonetheless, it is possible that Jamie's statement was one of genuine delight in being there. Either way, the conversation proceeded.

Me: So, where do you teach?
Jamie: I teach English as a second language (ESL) at the community college in Jacksonville.
Me: Well, did you know that I'm responsible for the ESL instruction on this campus?
Jamie: Really? Do you think I might be able to teach here? If so, I'd be able to study here full time.

After getting to know each other better and after I had a chance to check Jamie's credentials, she became a teaching assistant. This in turn provided her with free tuition as well as a stipend. It was a win-win situation that would not have come to this successful conclusion had Jamie not come up during break to schmooze. She turned out to be an excellent ESL teacher.

No doubt this example leads one to ask if indeed Jamie was flattering to get what she wanted. Some may even go further and perceive her verbal behavior as groveling. One is always suspicious, and it is hard to prove otherwise without getting to know a person better. It seemed that it was not obsequious. Jamie's personality was warm and sweet, and she was genuine. She was an outstanding scholar/teacher and became successful in her career.

The examples from real verbal exchanges offered in the following chapters ought to demonstrate that the art of schmoozing is merely about showing interest in others that in turn piques their interest in you. This is true in all spheres of life. The good schmooze aids in navigating through social interactions, where what is at stake is making friends. It also comes in handy in workplace interactions, where the stakes involve moving up the career ladder. But the intent is never simply to flatter, network, or grovel.

Perhaps it is worth disambiguating these notions. We have already discussed networking—chatting with people in order to have them get to know who you are and to be impressed with you in some way. Through their positive impression, they may potentially give you something (e.g., a job). Groveling is more blatantly networking. I consider this bad schmoozing. It carries with it a sense of begging—not an acceptable way to get what you want. Flattering, of course, may be part of groveling and networking—and it is usually blatant insofar as it attempts to make the addressee feel good about some attribute.

Jamie is a good example of a master of schmoozing. The question clearly arises, was she flattering, groveling, networking, or simply schmoozing? Four years after our original encounter in the example just given, Jamie completed her doctorate in linguistics under my mentorship. In other words, she proved herself to be more than capable of doing what had to be done to accomplish that difficult task. She was a relatively bright individual, but no more intelligent than most who enter our graduate program. When she was about to complete her degree, she went on the job market, as most young academics do. Her credentials were interesting enough for her to be interviewed, which is the first important step. Beyond that stage, however, the art of the good schmooze is more often than not what gets the person the foot in the door and eventually the job offer.

The edge of competing when the competition gets tough often depends on who has the most winning "personality." Personality, it is widely agreed, depends to a great extent on talk. When Jamie was interviewed, she presented herself exactly as who she was—a warm, caring, and intelligent person who is also motivated and capable. The attributes of "warm" and "caring" are what came through in the good schmooze. More than being "motivated" and "capable" (which are the requisite qualities any employer is seeking), the person who comes through knowing the lost art of the good schmooze is likely to get the prize. In this case, the prize was the job offer.

The art of talk is practiced in settings where we are most comfortable with others (e.g., family contexts) to more formal situations where we may feel more hesitant to assert ourselves by "greasing the wheels of interaction" (e.g., at school or work). Considering what we know about the art of the good schmooze in everyday talk, it is possible to become more happy and successful in all aspects of life. Given all of this, it seems worth recapturing the good schmooze in one's worlds of verbal interactions.

THE LOST ART

The study of the art of talk is derived from the field of linguistics. Linguistics is the science and art of language. It is the analysis not only of how language is *structured*, but it is very much about how language is actually *used*. This subfield of linguistics, referred to as *discourse analysis*, is closely related to what we call *pragmatics*. Linguists have struggled with an adequate definition of the term *pragmatics*, but to put it most simply, the notion refers to what is actually meant by what is said or written. It is the study of language as it is used by real, live people for their own purposes. For example, if we are native speakers of a particular language (e.g., American English), we know that when someone says, "Isn't it hot in here?" it might mean that person would like the window opened or the air conditioning turned up or down. It depends on the context. The meaning is implied, and is usually evident from how and when it is said and to whom.

We use language for many purposes: to socialize children, to let a spouse know how we feel, to try to get a student to comply with the rules of school, to ask for a raise, to let potential friends know that we would like to get to know them better, and so on. Some of us are skilled at using language to achieve these purposes. Indeed, it is a marvel to listen to those who are adept at the art of the good schmooze and to see how it can gain at least the interest of those participating.

DISPLAYING IDENTITIES THROUGH TALK

Our choices in how we use language have to do with how we perceive ourselves, in essence, who we are and how we display our underlying and shifting identities. These identities have to do with multiple factors—as speakers of a particular language, as members of particular communities, and as individuals in particular settings. At any moment in time, we may want to display that we are from a particular religious congregation, a member of a specific tennis club, or merely that we are from an English-speaking place.

Imagine that you are in an airport in a foreign country due to a layover between flights. You find yourself in the restroom and a stranger who looks somewhat like you in dress and features is washing her hands at the sink. Here is the way the actual interaction happened between two American women, strangers to each other, in an airport in England. We will simply call them A and B:

A: Gee, that water's hot!
B: Yeah, you'd think they'd have just one faucet you can adjust.

B realized that A was complaining about the sink having two sepa-rate faucets, one hot and one cold. In such a situation, identifying each other as having shared membership in some place, B responded in such a way as to let the stranger know that she understood and agreed that the British system was outdated. She perfectly commiser-ated. This, in turn, had the possibility of opening up a conversation in which a momentary solidarity was established. This sort of brief rapport is common among strangers in a strange place. That is to say, the fact that both speakers were American in a foreign country gave them a built-in solidarity that made it more likely for them to talk to each other. How did they identify each other as American? One can only surmise that there were signals—deriving from clothing, perhaps. Maybe they overheard the accent prior to the opener.

So, you strike up a conversation, based on a common complaint, and who knows? The relationship could build into something previously unforeseen. At the very least, it could serve as a temporary, fleeting bond. Perhaps you are from neighboring cities. Perhaps you attended the same school. The fact is that if you become involved in the talk you will seek commonalities through the talk; the talk, then, has the poten-tial to lead to a friendship. If you never responded in the first place, it would go nowhere.

In the following pages, it should become clear that through our moment-to-moment language choices, our very identities are devel-oped and displayed through language use. We display who we are or how we want to be perceived by selectively offering bits and pieces of relevant information about ourselves within the context of any inter-action. Are we young mothers? If so, we are certain to open conver-sations with others who share this identity on the playground. Are we busy professionals? We are sure to display this identity somehow with those who engage us. Whether it is family-related, work-related, socially-related, or school-related, our talk displays who we are in any particular situation.

Some engage in identity display in such a way as to alienate others. This is true, for example, when we cross over the line of schmoozing to boasting in social interactions. The art of the good schmooze is an art indeed. The good schmooze means telling others about yourself, displaying that you are a person worthy of further interaction, without overstating the case. Exaggeration and grandstanding usually backfire. The skill is to be able to express an interest in others through mutual sharing of attributes or spheres of interaction.

An example from public life can be seen in Tavis Smiley's TV interview with Barack Obama on October 18, 2007. Obama was beginning his campaign, and the interview centered on one of his recently published books:

Smiley: [introducing his guest] His most recent *New York Times* best seller is *The Audacity of Hope: Thoughts on Reclaiming the American Dream*. The book comes out in paperback November the sixth, as if there is anybody in America who does not have it in hardback already.

Smiley: [to Obama] I was just reading. You sold over a million copies of that book.

Obama: We did alright.

Smiley: Isn't that amazing?

Obama: Well, you know, almost as much, as many books as you sell, Tavis.

Smiley: Get outta here. Good to see you, man. [extends hand, they give a casual shake/low five]

Obama: You doin' alright?

Smiley: Yeah, I'm hangin' in, you alright?

Obama: I'm doin' fine.

Skill at drawing others out is typically more successful at building relationships and good will than talking about oneself. In this previous interaction, Obama turns the focus off of himself and on to Smiley by reminding the audience that the interviewer himself is a successful published author. The immediate bond is evident. Not only do the two men share a common racial identity, but they are both also authors of best-selling books. They go on, in this brief segment of the clip, to display their sharedness through verbal means (e.g., using truncated, informal words *outta*, *doin'*) as well as nonverbal means (e.g., low five). Obama does the good schmooze through identity display with both Smiley and with the viewing audience. The viewers see him as a "regular guy," a person who can be informal, with whom one might want to have a warm chat—not just a member of an elite, high-echelon stratum of society.

Of course, good schmoozers display their own identity as well as draw others out. However, the balance is delicate. To illustrate this important difference, the next example shows how schmoozing misfired in a business/social situation. The setting here is a bed and breakfast, one of those fashionable inns that offer an alternative to the modern hotel or motel. Such places of lodging feature not only a more charming atmosphere for overnighters, they also offer a homier feeling replete with friendly conversation, especially over breakfast. In a recent experience at such an inn during a short vacation, I was taken aback by the kind of talk produced by the owners. Since the conversation was not recorded, but overheard, I will not attempt to reproduce it here in detail but rather to simply provide an overview.

A middle-aged couple sat down at the candle lit table for their three-course breakfast, while the innkeeper (we'll call him Bob) proceeded to try to engage them in talk while serving the food. He asked the customary questions about where they live and work, which is a typical opener that seeks to establish common ground. By doing this, he was right on target with beginning the schmooze.

As the couple offered small snippets of information about themselves, they began to tell of a recent trip to visit their daughter, who was a medical resident in a West Coast city. On that note, Bob took this information as an invitation to pontificate on his views about the current state of managed health care in the United States. This might have been all well and good had he practiced the important feature of schmoozing that is known as good turn-taking and turn-giving. Bob did not do this. Instead, he held forth on the subject to the extent that the guests could not manage to insert any replies at all. What resulted was really a monologue in which they must have felt trapped having to endure the self-serving talk of a total stranger over breakfast. From their silence and their facial expressions, it was clear that they were turned off. What is the likely result of this kind of lack of skill at schmoozing? It would not be at all surprising to discover that Bob lost their business. While I did not take the liberty of asking the couple how they felt, who would want to return knowing they would have to suffer such talk?

Feeling trapped is not what *interlocutors* (co-conversationalists) seek in a conversation; indeed, this kind of one-way talk is the opposite of satisfying and causes us to feel we need to escape. Just like obvious sucking up, it has a negative result. A good innkeeper knows that the art of the good schmooze is part of what attracts people to these types of inns. Guests who seek anonymity choose a more impersonal type of lodging to begin with. Indeed, Bob's attempt at schmoozing seriously failed. Rather than make the guests feel like they wanted to return, it probably made them want to run away. This is an example of how *not* knowing the art of schmoozing can not only cost you friends, but cost you business opportunities as well. Clearly, from this example, the art of schmoozing is important in all spheres of life.

DOMAINS

In sociolinguistics, we call the various spheres of interaction *domains* of talk. A domain refers to a sphere of life in which verbal and nonverbal interactions occur. The domains discussed in this book are the following: friendship (social life), family (home life), employment (work life), and education (school and college life). I also include a chapter on cross-cultural interaction, since the United States has become a multicultural country in which our everyday talk must take into account different ethnic, national, and racial norms of interaction.

The chapters in this book provide examples of the good schmooze in ordinary conversational interaction and sequences of schmoozing taken from public life. That is, we examine conversational interactions from the public sphere, including political interactions as well as examples from television, radio, and film media. These provide rich information on how public and media figures do the art of the good schmooze, providing iconic examples that shape our ordinary, everyday interactions.

Counterexamples from public and private life offer a framework for seeing just how the good schmooze can backfire. Confrontational discourse that leads to conflict talk is the flipside of the good schmooze. Each chapter provides real examples of good and bad schmoozing.

How we use language to interact with family members, friends, acquaintances, teachers, peers, coworkers, and colleagues determines how others perceive us. This, in turn, affects how well we fit into groups, how harmonious our relationships are, and ultimately, how much we achieve a feeling of belonging. This belonging is a part of a sense of membership—without it, we are left with isolation and alienation. Our interactional competence impacts greatly on our lives.

"I'LL BE YOUR BEST FRIEND": SCHMOOZING IN SOCIAL LIFE

Chapter 1, schmoozing in social life, explores in detail how we use language to make friends and successfully (or unsuccessfully) interact with other individuals and in groups. This is the domain of face-to-face interaction with people we are getting to know, people we already know and with whom we have a friendship, and strangers thrown together into contexts of immediate interaction. How we build solidarity has consequences for consolidating our membership and ultimately our sense of well-being.

Schmoozing in social interaction entails knowledge of how to engage in speech acts. This is a sociolinguistic term referring to such verbal phenomena as greetings, requests, refusals, compliments, apologizes, praise, and so on. When speech acts are carried out successfully in social interaction, it can lead to the building of social relationships.

Why is it that some people are skilled at making friends while others are just unable to do so with ease? What are the factors that constrain successful social interaction? What does the term *successful* mean, anyway, when focusing on social life? These are all issues to be explored in the analysis of face-to-face interactions in the social domain.

To offer one small example of how speech acts can be used to lubricate social interaction, we can examine an actual sequence of conversation on complimenting. In the following exchange, two women, slightly acquainted, are standing in a corridor waiting to enter an office. Since they are just killing time, Maria opens a conversation with Jasmine by offering her a simple compliment:

Maria: That's a really pretty sweater.
Jasmine: Oh, this old thing? I got it on sale.
Maria: I really like the way the color looks on you.
Jasmine: Well, it hasn't worn very well. That's what you get for shopping for bargains. I got it at X store.
Maria: Really? That's one of my favorite places to shop. You can really find some good buys.

For women, this conversation probably resonates quite faithfully with their personal experience. In fact, women often open conversations based on simple appearance compliments—those focusing on clothing, hair, and so on. As it happened, Maria and Jasmine had a conversation based on this opener in which they went on to find out that they both live near X store, in fact in adjacent neighborhoods. This discovery naturally led to other disclosures—that they each had two children who went to the same school and that they both had similar criticisms of the school system. This opener led to the beginnings of a friendship. Through a simple compliment/response sequence, a mutual solidarity was established.

Note that there was no straightforward "thank you" given here as a response to the original compliment. In fact, counter to our native speaker intuition that compliments are typically followed by an expression of gratitude, "thank you" is rarer than we think in such a context. Moreover, a simple "thank you" with no further information (such as "I got it on sale") may serve to close a conversation prematurely. Many women know, below the level of consciousness, that giving more information about a complimented item has the potential to lead to a good schmooze.

A considerable amount of empirical data is available on social talk. Chapter 1 delves more deeply into the art of social schmoozing. It culminates with an in-depth study of joking and teasing in social interactions. Examples of transcribed conversational exchanges from political interactions and media talk shows that highlight social schmoozing are interwoven with everyday social conversations.

"ALL IN THE FAMILY": SCHMOOZING WITH LOVED ONES

The family is our sanctuary. It is the place where we are meant to feel most comfortable—where we are able to let down our guard and just be ourselves. Unfortunately, the simple fact that we are dealing with the ones we love most is inextricably intertwined with the fact that we care passionately about our loved ones and their well-being. These two basic facts are what Georgetown sociolinguist Deborah Tannen refers to as the conflict between connection and control.[2]

The mismatch between wanting to be supportive with family members and wanting what is best for them often causes us to talk in ways that are critical, or that contradict rather than support. For example, we tend to give advice or even contradict when commiseration is sought. In a large research project that culminated in my 1993 book, *Complaining and Commiserating*, I noted that we tend to give advice to family members when, under similar circumstances with acquaintances or even strangers, we would commiserate. Consider the following conversation between a wife and husband. The wife, Amy, has just returned home late from her work as a paralegal. Her husband,

Richard, has been waiting for her return so that they can figure out what to have for dinner. As she enters, the conversation begins:

Richard: Hey, you're finally here!
Amy: Wow, what a long one!
Richard: Busy day?
Amy: I had to stay late because my boss is totally under the gun. She has extra cases so the burden falls on me for the background work. ... [Amy goes on to a list of extra jobs she had to do that day].
Richard: It's time you put a stop to this. It's not even for your career, it's for hers. ... [goes on to complain and give her advice].
Amy: I was just telling you about my day!

Richard has fallen into the familiar trap of wanting to solve what he sees as Amy's problems at work. But from Amy's perspective, she was just responding to Richard's question, "Busy day?" In fact, when asked to analyze what went awry in this interaction, both partners felt they misunderstood the other's point of view. Richard thought that Amy's relating all that went on during her workday was complaining. Amy insisted she was not complaining but merely telling Richard about her workday. To be sure, Amy said that she is very happy with this job, and that she feels fulfilled by the work. She would have liked a supportive response from Richard, indicating that he understood and was there for her.

Had Richard been conversing with a friend, colleague, or even a stranger, he probably would not have responded by giving advice. Rather, it is likely that he would have said something akin to, "I know what you mean" or "work is getting more and more demanding." That type of response indicates commiseration and support, which validates the other's sentiment. Richard replied as he did this because of his vested interest in Amy's well-being. After all, if his wife is happy, it makes for a happier life for him. Therefore, he wants her to solve what he perceives to be a problem. Within families, we see this kind of interaction over and over again. With those we love most, it is most difficult to just stand back and give supportive responses. This is true for partners as well as children.

Role expectations for children, women, and men are revealed in the analysis of family schmoozing. How family members speak and are spoken to, expectations for participation, turn-taking, getting and holding the floor, and relevant topics for discussion are all important discourse phenomena in family interactions. These issues are always a reflection of power dynamics among family members. Chapter 2 outlines in detail the importance of schmoozing, and schmoozing to everyone's satisfaction, in families. The chapter interweaves schmoozing examples (and conflict examples) from everyday familial exchanges and from public and media interactions. The conversational exchanges illustrate how the good schmooze does (and does not) take place in families. The chapter culminates with an in-depth view of nagging (or how not to schmooze) in the familial domain.

"I REALLY NEED THIS JOB": SCHMOOZING IN THE WORKPLACE

The U.S. workplace has become steadily more diverse. With more women, different ethnic groups and various racial groups having increased access to a wider range of jobs, the analysis of schmoozing in the workplace is increasingly important for workplace satisfaction. Here is where we see the fine line between good schmoozing and networking.

As we have seen, networking is an example of a kind of talk that can serve to positively enhance one's image or, conversely, when done unctuously, can backfire. To be sure, brownnosing is not positive. Getting to know someone through positive interaction is what leads to good connections. In networking, there is a delicate balance, and this is what makes it so tricky and why so many of us are not good at it.

Here is an example. In the following sequence, two academics are found face-to-face at a conference. Dr. Carrie Daniels, who is relatively new at her job, has read much of what Dr. James Wolfson has written and is very excited (and nervous) to meet him:

Carrie Daniels: I'm a great admirer of your work.
James Wolfson: Well thank you very much.
Carrie Daniels: I'm from the University of Z.
James Wolfson: Oh, never been there. Excuse me [and walks away].

Anyone would agree that this attempt at networking seriously flopped. What could Carrie have done differently? This is not an easy question to answer, since the alternatives depend heavily on emotional states (e.g., nervousness) and the interlocutor's willingness to schmooze. Clearly, some of this is out of our immediate control. For example, Dr. Wolfson is perhaps simply a rude person. More likely, however, is that he has many close colleagues at the conference with whom he would prefer to converse. What Dr. Daniels needed to do, particularly as a new scholar in the field, would be to say something specifically intelligent about Dr. Wolfson's work that might have the potential to engage him in conversation. The balancing act here would be to display her insights without appearing to grovel. This is a tough one. Here is a hypothetical example of how this could be done:

Carrie Daniels: Dr. Wolfson, I'm Carrie Daniels from Z University. I want to tell you that I've admired your work, and I'm particularly interested in your theory of X.
James Wolfson: Well, thank you very much.
Carrie Daniels: Yes, I've found that the theory works out very nicely in my data. I've collected [and goes on to tell about her data], and it patterns out almost 100 percent of the time. I believe you were right on target. Very compelling!
James Wolfson: Well, that's always good to know. Theories like this one always need to stand up to real tests. What specifically are you investigating on the whole?

[They go on to exchange information about each other.]

Note how the addition of a bit of further information about a specific area of interest in Wolfson's work is the key ingredient in taking the networking to a successful beginning. It is precisely that which makes the interaction go further into an exchange that naturally leads to more disclosures about Carrie's areas of interest. This has the possibility of forging a long-lasting professional relationship.

Chapter 3, on workplace schmoozing, goes beyond networking to take up many aspects of talk in work life. The chapter discusses the use of humor in the workplace as well as talk in service encounters (in stores, businesses, and general errands). It culminates with an in-depth look at bragging and boasting in one workplace setting, a brokerage house. As in the other chapters, examples from the media and from public/political work life are interwoven with those from spontaneous workplace interactions.

"I NEED TO GET INTO THIS COURSE": SCHMOOZING IN EDUCATIONAL INTERACTIONS

More and more U.S. citizens are spending an increasing number of years as students. In fact, the average age of graduate students in my department is early thirties. As it is no longer easy to get ahead in one's career without advanced training, it has become increasingly important to learn the art of the good schmooze in the education domain.

Chapter 4 discusses doing the talk of higher education. Recall the example earlier, where Jamie was attending a graduate course the first day of the semester. That conversation between Jamie and the professor demonstrated how a potential student was able to schmooze her way to a teaching assistantship and eventually a PhD.

The chapter on schmoozing in education focuses on such notions as *face*.[3] Most people are familiar with the notions of *saving face* and *losing face*. Here we delve into *presenting face*. Chapter 4 includes discussions and examples of teacher schmoozing and student schmoozing. The chapter includes an in-depth analysis of examples from advising sessions. The focus is on how the good schmooze forms part of getting a foot in the door rather than the door in the face.

"YOU'RE NOT FROM HERE, ARE YOU?": SCHMOOZING CROSS-CULTURALLY

It is no longer safe to assume that people with whom we come into contact share our norms and values for talk. The United States is not a melting pot, and perhaps never was one. This concept may, in fact, be mythical. It is more realistic to view our present-day society as a salad bowl. That is to say, we do not mix peoples from all over and end up with soup—a blending of widely diverse characteristics into a new and different whole. The mix is made up of different kinds of people who retain their diverse characteristics. The salad retains the varied features of the many that make it up, resulting in an interesting conglomeration.

This is the sphere of talk with perhaps the most inherent dangers of misunderstanding, misinterpretation, and misconception. The fact is that people who come from different communities, whether they are different countries, different ethnic or racial groups, or even different regions of the same country, are bound to hold different norms for speaking.

For example, in some societies (especially in developing countries), it is considered a compliment to tell others that they have gained weight. In most U.S. communities, we would not say anything at all like this, at the risk of insulting. Examples of different rules and norms of appropriate speech behavior abound. This mismatch of norms is what leads us to perceive others as rude, impolite, or just weird. The following is an example from real data to show how this can play out.

This conversational exchange took place between two students who were conversation partners in a language program. Bonnie was a native speaker of North American English, and Itoko was a young Japanese woman in the United States studying the English language. Bonnie had studied Japanese and had spent some time in Japan, so she was interested in conversing regularly with Itoko. In this way, they each got practice in their second language. The conversation took place after they had met several times and had gotten to know each other somewhat. Here Bonnie is telling Itoko about her recent trip to Japan:

Bonnie: My plane trip to Japan was pretty difficult. I mean, it wasn't direct from New York to Tokyo or anything. I had to go to Toronto.

Itoko: Mm hmm.

Bonnie: I had to go to Toronto and then I had to spend a night in a hotel in Toronto, and then I had to get to the airport again the next day, and go to Vancouver and switch planes, and I was really tired …

Itoko: Yeah?

Bonnie: And then when I got to Tokyo after I had been traveling for 20 hours I had to catch a cab into Tokyo station …

Itoko: Uh huh.

Bonnie: Then get another cab and find my way, you know, and I had to explain to the taxi driver where my hotel was because he didn't know where it was.

Itoko: Right, uh huh. Where did you stay?

[a few exchanges later about the hotel]

Bonnie: It's so funny. I sit here going on and on and you just say
         "uh huh." It's like I'm in an interview or something [both
         laugh].

In her last statement, Bonnie expressed dissatisfaction with Itoko's
lack of participation in the conversation. Even though Bonnie was
somewhat familiar with Japanese linguistic norms, she still felt frustrated. What Itoko was doing was following Japanese rules of speaking
in giving a lot of supportive moves to Bonnie, in the form of short
replies such as "uh huh."

These types of minimal responses are expected in Japanese interaction, and show that the listener is interested and is relinquishing a turn.
It is a part of the Japanese code of politeness. In English, however, we
do not use minimal responses nearly as much. When we do it as much
as the Japanese without other responses, it seems weird. In fact, Bonnie
was expecting Itoko to take more substantive turns in the conversation,
just like Americans are expected to do. When she did not, Bonnie had
to carry the burden of talk by herself. Really all that Itoko needed to
do might have been to say something like "oh, no," perhaps followed
by a brief question, instead of "uh huh."

Since Bonnie and Itoko knew each other fairly well and met regularly to converse, it was safe for them to discuss the way the conversation was going. Imagine if they had been strangers who were trying to
get to know each other. No doubt Bonnie would have abandoned the
attempt to schmooze. Moreover, she may well have thought her Japanese interlocutor rude, or at the very least, too shy to interact. Taking
the case further, this is the way that cultural stereotypes are born. The
dangers are great indeed.

THE LOST ART OF THE GOOD SCHMOOZE

Recapturing the lost art of the good schmooze can benefit ordinary
speakers in ordinary verbal interactions in all areas of life. Clearly,
the benefits to accrue range from making friends, having more satisfactory relationships with family members, getting ahead at school
or work, and understanding your fellow citizens of the world. These
are immediate and personal. The larger picture includes general

harmony. Harmony begins at home but extends to understanding between diverse peoples. The potential benefits, therefore, are vast.

Each of these chapters illustrates face-to-face interactions within a domain or cross-culturally, and what the findings imply for our happiness, success, and sense of belonging.

NOTES

1. Jeff Danziger, "CartoonArts International," *New York Times*, May 16, 2010.

2. For further reading about talk among adult family members, see Deborah Tannen, *I Only Say This Because I Love You* (New York: Random House, 2001).

3. Penelope Brown and Stephen C. Levinson, *Politeness: Some Universals in Language Use* (Cambridge: Cambridge University Press, 1978). For a detailed description of "face," see Erving Goffman, *The Presentation of Self in Everyday Life* (New York: Doubleday Dell Publishing Group, Inc., 1959).

CHAPTER 1

The Good Schmooze in Social Interaction

> During the Samuel Johnson days they had big men enjoying small talk;
> today we have small men enjoying big talk.
>
> Fred Allen

Social schmoozing is the backbone of friendship. It often seems mundane and effortless on the surface, but in fact it is extraordinary work. We build connections by sharing personal disclosures. The more we share or divulge about ourselves, in a give and take of interaction, the more we learn to understand others' meanings. It is a circular process. Schmoozing builds connections, but we cannot build these connections without some commonalities.

Here is how it is circular: We open relationships with others we do not know well or at all. How do we do this? There has to be some even small commonality to act as the springboard. It starts with finding what this springboard could possibly be. It is intuitive to many. When standing out in the cold, rainy weather waiting for a bus, the commonality is braving the elements. If two people are wearing the same shoes, tie, or hat, the commonality is an item of clothing—something worth a comment as a conversational opener. Sitting next to a passenger on an airplane, one cannot help but notice what that person is reading. The possible opener is clear: reading taste. The more that is disclosed, the more we are able to build commonalities with others.

Schmoozing is as important with strangers—perhaps more important even—as it is with friends and acquaintances. With people we already know, we have at least some knowledge of what to use as a small talk opener. Imagine being at a party. Some people dread having to make small talk while standing around eating tidbits or having a drink. This is the typical party scene in our culture (other cultures may center parties on music and dancing, making it easier). But in this sort of scene, we have to know how to open talk, and typically schmoozing gets the conversation going.

The normal tendency is to gravitate toward someone we know. Unless we are exceptionally outgoing, many do not feel comfortable opening conversations with complete strangers except when introduced by a mutual acquaintance. You get your drink or nibbles and look around the room. You may have arrived on the early side, and in so doing, you do not yet see any of the friends you expected to be there. You spot someone you recently met but do not know very well. What do you do? Do you walk across to the opposite side of the room in avoidance behavior? It might be tempting, but where will it get you? To the wall to join the wallflowers.

Let us propose instead that you buck up your courage and take the plunge. You walk over to the acquaintance and start schmoozing. What you say depends on what you already know about the person. Starting with some common knowledge is the easiest way. Perhaps you know that the other person plays golf. Perhaps s/he is a member of your political party, a community group you know of, your church, has children the same ages as yours, and so on. The list is endless. What do you know about them that is a possible opener? This is the obvious starting point—to find something in common, based on what you already know about a person, and start the schmooze. We will analyze numerous examples in this chapter on social talk on how this is done. These ordinary conversational sequences, taken from real social interactions, should serve as good illustrations, as in the following example.

Jeff is a rather shy person in general, but he is intent on meeting new people. Life as a computer programmer is very isolating, and it is hard to meet people outside of work. Social networking Web sites are one thing, but meeting people face to face is where social life really gets going.

Jeff gets his drink, turns around and looks, and sees a small group of people that includes a familiar face. It takes a minute to dredge up where the face is from. Jeff soon places it—it's the receptionist at his gym. He knows neither of the other two people talking to her. Jeff walks over to the small group and says hi to the woman:

Jeff: I knew yours was a familiar face. The gym, right?
Woman: Exactly. Good memory. You look familiar, too. I'm Cindy.

Jeff: Now I can put a name with the face. I'm Jeff.
Cindy: These are my friends Paula and Greg.
Jeff: [greeting with a handshake, nod of the head, or smile—it all depends on the age group and social circle] Do you guys go to the gym too?

Jeff used several strategies to open the talk. First, he got up the courage to walk over to the group. Recognizing one of the people helped him to think of something to say. He dug into his repertoire to find something to use as the opener, and this was the place where Cindy worked. Jeff now had a springboard for conversation.

After Cindy's introduction of herself by name, this was Jeff's cue to say something else. It was nothing terribly witty, just a tidbit that showed he had something to say—he could now put Cindy's name with her face.

Jeff was on the way to schmoozing. He did this by presenting himself, then allowing those whom he just met to present who they are. He asked a simple question, "Do you guys go to the gym, too?" This set the stage for commonalities to be established. It also showed Paula and Greg that Jeff was turning the floor over to them to talk about themselves. This is an important part of schmoozing in social interactions.

Nobody likes a conversation hog. The key to positive social talk is getting people to talk about themselves. Most people love to talk about themselves and will tell you who they are if given the slightest opportunity. A simple opener and short exchange has the potential to lead to friendships. At the very least, it has the possibility of making for an interesting party in which people get to know one another.

Talking to complete strangers may be more or less threatening than the above scenario. Of course, one has to be careful, but if we never talked to strangers, we might miss opportunities. The following is a recent conversation I had that took place at Home Depot. I was doing a quick errand for electrical wall plates and asked the clerk to direct me to the appropriate aisle. As I looked through the available styles, a man just to my right opened a conversation:

Man: [to me]: The cheaper ones are over there [pointing farther down the aisle].
Me: Oh, I want the expensive ones [with a joking tone].

Man: I'm in the business and so always go for the cheap.
Me: Those who built my house obviously had the same idea.
      Now I'm trying to find something that looks better.
Man: I hear you.

At this point, I could have pursued the conversation further. It seemed obvious that the gentleman opened the conversation with more than just a passing interest in letting me know where else to look for wall plates. I could have taken him up on the conversation, making it more of a "getting to know you" exchange than an exchange about home-improvement products. Since I had little interest, I let the conversation go to further transaction (information exchange) rather than interaction (shooting the breeze).

Me: Seems like they don't have much of a variety. Since you're
      in the business, can you tell me where else I can go for a
      better selection of these?
Man: You might try a lighting store.
Me: That's an idea. I think I'll do that. Thanks.
Man: Good luck with it.

The simple exchange could have opened a friendship if that was desired by both parties. Nonetheless, my willingness to respond to the man's opener gave me valuable information based on his work expertise. I proceeded to the nearest lighting store and found what I was looking for. My errand was accomplished. The simple schmoozing exchange helped me in a small aspect of my day's agenda.

In contrast to the previous transaction, the interactional aspects of schmoozing enable us to amass further information about others that leads to more comfortable schmoozing with them. We get to know their opinions, lifestyle, and beliefs. Knowing these things, we are able to choose appropriate topics for further talk. The more we find out, the fewer details are needed to feel commonality. We may even finish each other's sentences!

This happens all the time with close friends, as in the following sequence of conversation. I was at my friend Maria's house many years ago when the doorbell rang. Maria and I were graduate students together at the time and meeting to discuss some issues coming up in the course we were both taking. Her neighbor Kira was just dropping by to deliver something that she had borrowed. Maria introduced us and we chatted for a bit:

Me: Were you baking with this borrowed pan?
Kira: Birthday cake for my son. I couldn't find my cake pan.
Me: I'm impressed!

[Maria and I speak simultaneously, as if on cue]:
Me: I don't bake.
Maria: She doesn't bake.

Maria's utterance came at the same moment as my own and said the same thing. This is like finishing my sentence. We had built enough of a relationship for this to occur. By saying virtually the same thing at the same time, we are displaying how much we know about each other. In so doing, we are showing our acceptance of each other's foibles. That I don't bake makes me different from Maria—and Kira, for that matter. They have baking in common, and that display strengthens their bond. What Maria and I have in common is something else—we're both linguists. So, I don't bake—it's not important in our friendship because we share other things. We display that for Kira. But also we increase our bond as friends.

We are really only able to finish each other's sentences because of our shared knowledge about each other. Maria knew enough about me to tease me, in front of Kira, about the fact that I don't bake. She is displaying for her neighbor that while she likes baking, she has friends who enjoy other things. Maria is highlighting for me that she is a person talented at things domestic.

Knowing how to do social schmoozing means getting at the real meaning of what people say. This is not always easy. Being good at it involves some tuning in to how people present themselves. In other words, we are dealing with identity display, both our own and theirs. We learn about the multiple identities of people through this kind of schmoozing. We understand the displays—albeit subconsciously.

Doing the social butterfly thing depends largely on where, when, and with whom we are talking. The aim of social schmoozing is to create, affirm, and reaffirm friendships. In short, by displaying who we are, we establish a rapport or solidarity with others. Some use the display for one-upmanship. This can lead to conflict. One-upmanship alienates, but solidarity displays work. We display solidarity or rapport by finding commonalities. This leads to a relationship. The friendship may lead to formation of a social network—membership in a group or community. A circle of friends equals a social life. Social life leads to recreation and leisure. Balance leads to happier lives. It seems logical.

Some would say we have lost this balance in our lives. We work more and more, finding it hard to fit everything in. But even grownups need to play. We all need friends to play with. Schmoozing leads to friendships.

SAYING HELLO AND GOODBYE

Greetings and partings are an important part of schmoozing. Even greetings on the run have the potential to lead to conversations. These small exchanges can have big impacts on one's life. While it may be somewhat counterintuitive, partings can also be rapport-inspiring when done in the spirit of positive schmoozing.

"HEY, HOW ARE YA DOIN?" OPENERS

Probably the most widely used schmoozing opener is the greeting "How are you?" or some variation on this formula. Most of us know that this expression is just a greeting and not a question about health. Other societies have similar greetings, such as the question "Have you eaten?" in Chinese. Again, it is a reflection of what is valued in a particular society. Because we know that "How are you?" is a greeting rather than a request for detailed information, we tend to say "fine" regardless of the context—even if we are sick and at the doctor's office!

We know that is just the beginning of conversation, if there is time. If not, the greeting can be on the run. But if time permits—and this depends largely on what is expected in different communities—a conversation will ensue. For many people who come from large urban areas, greetings on the run are the rule. We live a fast-paced life and do not have much time for schmoozing. But, in other areas, schmoozing takes high priority.

This is sometimes difficult to get used to. I personally went through culture shock when moving from a large northeastern city to a small, southern college town. I was taken aback to realize that you cannot just rush through the checkout line in stores, for example. You have to wait until other people ahead of you in line finish chatting. Then you have to at least exchange pleasantries when it is your turn. If you don't do this, you are the one who is weird. A recent example will illustrate this kind of shooting the breeze:

Jane has gone down her country driveway to fetch the mail. She sees George, the letter carrier, driving up and waits for him. They've known each other for eight years now, ever since Jane moved into this rural neighborhood. But it's not often that they come face to face. Jane and George greet each other simultaneously with a "Hey, how're you doin?"

Jane: I haven't seen you in a while. Not usually out here when you come by.
George: True. How do you like this beautiful weather?
Jane: Nice, but a bit cool for boating.
George: Yeah, do you fish?
Jane: No, but my husband does.
George: So what do you do on the boat?
Jane: Oh, I love the snorkeling—but it's too cold for that now. Need to go to the Keys for that.
George: I don't like it much when it gets up beyond 80.
Jane: Hey, you're living in the wrong place! By the way, you're coming later and later these days. What's up?

They continue to talk about the mail delivery getting later and later. George tells of how people keep saying fewer folks are using the U.S. Postal Service, but he is seeing more and more mail every day. He used to be done by 3:30 P.M. Now he is lucky if he gets home by 6 P.M.—and he only gets paid for eight hours. Jane asks what time his workday begins, and George tells her 7 A.M. She's aghast that he works an 11-hour day! She closes by saying, "Well, you'd better move on or you'll never get home." George replies, "My horses will be wondering what happened to me."

Even though George had a lot more mail to deliver, he did not hesitate to stop and chat with Jane. After all, he does not get to see his "customers" all that often in this rural area. So, that means George

gets done later and later the more he participates in schmoozing. Is it
worth it? It must be. It makes work life more like social life, and that
is a good thing.

We can analyze more closely at how the conversation went from
greetings as openers to other topics. The greeting really was not
the opener here. If they were both in a big rush, they would have
stopped at the greeting. The opener was George's comment about
the beautiful weather. It's always safe to talk about the weather. That
comment told Jane that it was okay to chat—George was not in so
much of rush.

As for the weather, everyone has something to say—too warm, too
cold, too rainy, too dry. It is a no-risk opener that is sure to get a
response. Jane's reply disclosed some information about leisure activities that she likes. She knew from previous conversations that George
enjoys fishing. But she hooked on to this bit of mutual interest—boating. Notice how from there they went on to discuss what was happening with George's work life. Was George complaining? It seems like it,
but it served to sustain the conversation.

The greeting in the conversation between Jane and George was
merely the tip of the iceberg. It takes something more to get the conversation going. Weather was the opener, but regardless, going beyond
the greeting opened many possible topics for schmoozing.

Researcher Miriam Eisenstein and her colleagues[1] found eight purposes for greeting in a study conducted in New York City. Data collected on buses, for example, showed many complaints as greetings
(e.g., "Gee, this bus is really crowded"). Greetings can be on the run or,
time permitting, lead into conversations conveying information (after
the initial reply "fine"). Those greetings that lead to further elabo-
ration in social talk can lead to the exchange of personal disclosures
that have the potential for social bonding. We saw this with Jane and
George's conversation.

Barack Obama may be the consummate schmoozer when it comes to
greetings and partings. Examples abound of his mastery of this important part of the art. At his first formal address to Congress, he was seen
entering the hall doing the good schmooze greeting all the way from
door to podium, and on the way out as well as partings. As he entered
(and exited) to applause, he made sure to stop many times along the
way to not only shake hands but offer a word of acknowledgement
to the many colleagues lining the red carpet. He was seen and heard
uttering short greetings accompanied by pats on the back with kisses

on the cheek for some of the female attendees and even hugs for some male colleagues close to him.

Obama's schmoozing examples abound. Pats on the back are common, as seen in the following short sequence from Obama's interview with Steve Kroft of *60 Minutes* on Super Tuesday, February 5, 2008:

Obama: How ya doin'? [pats on shoulder as they walk]
Kroft: I'm doin' good.
Obama: Good! It's been a year, huh?
Kroft: Exactly a year.

The informality of the interaction helped to set the tone for what surely was a glimpse into Obama as not only capable of being president of the United States but also a "good guy." His dropping of the final consonant of "doin'" was mirrored by Kroft, setting the informal tone.

Of course, Obama has appeared on many talk shows, some even less politically focused and more informal than *60 Minutes*. On October 22, 2008, this is how he entered the stage of the *Ellen DeGeneres Show*:

[Obama comes out dancing and DeGeneres gets up and dances with him]

Obama: [laughing] Alright, you got a little moves.
DeGeneres: Alright, alright.
Obama: Hey!

[they continue dancing]

DeGeneres: You got some moves!
Obama: [laughing] For a presidential candidate.

[they hug and stop dancing]

DeGeneres: Hi! How are you?
Obama: How are you?

[they go to sit down]

Obama: It's so nice to see you.

[they shake hands]

DeGeneres: You, too.
Obama: Thank you so much.
DeGeneres: OK, you're the best dancer so far—the presidential
           candidates.
Obama: It's a low bar. [they laugh]
Obama: It is a low bar. But I'm pretty sure I've got better
           moves than Giuliani.

Whether or not Obama was a regular viewer of this show, he knew
that DeGeneres often made her entrance by dancing to the music. His
own dancing therefore mirrored her normal behavior and thereby led
to a lighthearted banter. In that brief exchange, Obama used one of the
quintessential verbal moves of schmoozing: joking self-denigration, as
in "it's a low bar." And he went even further by quipping about Giu-
liani. This schmoozing opener led to a friendly interaction that cast
him in a favorable light.

Clearly, when we participate in greeting rituals, we set a tone and
give and receive signals about our mutual availability for further talk.
These signals are both nonverbal and verbal. A greeting on the run,
for example, will have nonverbal cues (e.g., continuing movement in
the opposite direction, away from us) that make it obvious that a conversation will not ensue. However, when the greeting coincides with
a lingering to talk, we must know the appropriate next step. A more
specific question than "How are you?"—something focusing on some
aspect of the other's life—is more likely to open an extended conversation. Finding a next topic of mutual interest is the key in proceeding
from greetings to schmoozing.

"SEE YOU AROUND": PARTING

In good schmoozing, even a greeting on the run necessitates an
appropriate parting. People who are already acquainted do partings
as a way to indicate, "I realize you're in a hurry and we'll talk more
later." Consider the following, in which two female students passed
each other on the way to class on campus:

A: Hey, how are you doing?
B: Fine, how about you? Going to class?

A: Calculus, I hate it! [continues moving]
B: Ugh! Well, catch you later at the council meeting.
A: Yeah, see ya.

This is clearly an example of a greeting on the run. However, even in such situations, partings, like greetings, can function to bring inter-locutors closer to each other when carried out with finesse. It is part of the good schmooze even when schmoozing cannot ensue.

We have here a complaint/commiseration sequence in which a momentary solidarity was established regarding dislike of calculus. The greeting on the run led naturally into a brief exchange where the participants engaged and parted with a promise to participate in a later meeting at which they both are expected to be present. The parting affirms their relationship as part of a group that is scheduled to meet. Despite being a greeting on the run, it does important interactional work for these students.

The fact that greetings often lead to the development of relation-ships is not surprising; that partings may also fall into this category is less obvious. But, as we have seen, almost anything that we do in social talk has the potential to function positively. President Obama apparently knew this instinctively, as was shown by the parting words, pats on the back, and hugs and kisses in his exit after his first speech to Congress. No doubt the subtle features of the good schmooze helped to get him elected.

"YOU'RE SO THIN!": SCHMOOZING THROUGH COMPLIMENTING

A brilliant sociologist, Erving Goffman, once said, "The gestures which we sometimes call empty are perhaps in fact the fullest things of all."[2] Schmoozing is widely considered empty—most folks feel that it carries no real content or information. However, as evident in the pre-ceding examples, it is through schmoozing that we establish the kind of warm feelings that make us want to engage with someone further in conversation. Here is where we use certain speech acts like compli-menting, and yes, even complaining.

Some speech acts and their responses, such as complimenting, tell people that they are approved of. Saying something such as "I like your shirt" is therefore often more than just a compliment—it is a solidarity marker. In many Western cultures, a widely heard compliment is "You're so thin." Saying something like this is a part of schmoozing that functions as an important social lubricant. Typically, it does not end with a mere "thank you." This kind of schmoozing usually leads to mutual disclosures where people learn something about each other that they did not already know. For example, a conversation containing a "thin" compliment went like this:

Nan and Maggie, two adult women, meeting in the supermarket:

Nan: Hey, Maggie. I almost didn't recognize you. You're so thin! You look great!
Maggie: Oh, thanks. I've been trying.
Nan: How much have you lost? Looks like 10 pounds, at least.
Maggie: Yeah, twelve up to now. *Weight Watchers.*
Nan: You must be the fifth person I know who's recently done that on *Weight Watchers.* I'm going to try it. I've had no success with some of the other ones.
Maggie: It's made for dummies like me. Just eat what they tell you and no more. Easy.
Nan: Well, you look fantastic. See you at the kids' recital?
Maggie: I'll be there. See you.

Nan and Maggie were acquaintances who had just one thing in common, as far as they knew at that point—their children took dance lessons with the same teacher. Now, having done more schmoozing, they know something else about each other—they are both struggling with losing weight.

This exchange probably resonates with most women's experience. It is a central part of women's ways of interacting. Through this kind of talk we typically divulge some personal information upon which we can build more of a relationship. As native speakers, it is part of what sociolinguists refer to as *communicative competence*: knowing how to do appropriate talk. Some of us are better at it than others.

We can take a closer look at the kinds of information contained in the short compliment exchange. First, Nan made sure to stop and chat—she did not try to avoid Maggie by going to another aisle. This may sound familiar. Whether out of shyness or just being in a rush, some avoid conversation when they know it can only be long enough to do small talk. But by participating and not avoiding, one never knows where the conversation will lead. A few of these exchanges with the same person might lead to a potential relationship—perhaps, in fact, a new friendship.

The compliment about weight loss was the opener. The response was not just an expression of gratitude—it provided bits and pieces of further information. Maggie disclosed how she was able to achieve her weight loss, but beyond that she also told more. She put herself down, calling herself a "dummy." We saw how President Obama did self-denigration in his greeting sequence with Ellen DeGeneres. This is a very common conversational strategy among women that levels the playing field. By denigrating herself in this way, she told Nan that she is not to be given so much credit for the weight loss. This no doubt gave Nan the feeling of being on equal footing. Nan then put herself down by saying she has had no luck with other diets. Here Maggie implied that if she herself could do it, any dummy can. Nan and Maggie now know just a bit more about each other. The next time they see each other, probably at the recital, they may go on to further mutual disclosures that can lead to furthering their acquaintance.

Norms of interaction vary with genders, regions, and even ethnic or racial groups. The fact remains, however, that within the groups where we interact, we know the rules—even if they happen to be below the level of consciousness. This is part of the concept of communicative competence just mentioned. For example, we know that in our society, a weight compliment usually is appropriate, if not greatly appreciated. This is not to say it is within the norms of other societies. In some developing countries, it would be more of a compliment to say, "How fat you've gotten!" It all depends on what the society values. If food is scarce, being thin and losing weight is not a good thing.

What we can say for sure is that the opener requires further conversation that typically includes some disclosure of information. To say a mere "thank you" and walk away stops the conversation in its tracks.

"OH, DON'T ASK": THE COMPLAINT CULTURE

We Americans are such a bunch of complainers! We might as well call ourselves "the complaint culture." So much complaining swirls around—gas prices, education, taxes. Complaints can be about important issues or not so important—the weather, a bad hair day—just about anything does it.

In English, the term *complain* actually refers to two distinct speech patterns. One kind of complaint is like when in a restaurant, you say, "This steak is well done and I ordered it medium rare." You expect the server to fix it. We hesitate to do this sort of complaining.

We do the second kind all the time. You get on an elevator and there is just one other person on it. You feel like you need to fill up the empty conversational space, so you say, "Uh, oh. It's going to stop on every floor." The other person says, "I know, it's the local." You do not expect anyone to fix the situation. It is just a way of making small talk—even with a total stranger. As we have seen, compliments make small talk, too. In the same conversation between George, the mail delivery person, and Jane just analyzed, the schmoozing could have started with a compliment from George to Jane like "Nice tank top." But that would have sounded like a come-on—making Jane feel like, "Get me out of here!" So, who would have thought? Complimenting can be negative; complaining can be positive.

From the weather to politics—call it griping, grumbling, or just plain bellyaching—the bonding is through the empathetic response. It is part of American culture in some places, especially in urban areas and on either coast. But it does not hold true everywhere, and this can lead to trouble.

We are not trying to be negative—on the contrary. We just want to build a relationship. The griping *bonds*. It is not meant to bite.

Obama's conversations with DeGeneres and George's conversation with Jane eventually led to small, innocuous gripes (about oneself in Obama's case and the workday getting longer in George's case) that sustained the conversation and helped to build a momentary bond. In the case of George and Jane, the next time they bump into each other, they have something else to build on—George's long workday. What started with a formulaic greeting ended with complaining and commiserating. We do it all the time without realizing it. The bonding derives from the empathetic response.

"LET'S DO LUNCH": INVITING

Research on inviting in our culture is scant, but does highlight a very interesting cultural phenomenon—fear of rejection. The late Nessa Wolfson[3] and her students studied how Americans extend these ambiguous invitations that are sometimes, but not always, followed through. She discovered that "Let's get together some time" or "Let's do lunch" are gambits that are usually *sincere* and show something important about how we interact. They found that it was merely self-protection against the risk of rejection at work. Average speakers—of American English at least—are so anxious to avoid rejection that we offer these "leads" in order to ascertain interest in getting together.

Wolfson and her colleagues concluded that it is not lack of desire to get to know the other better, but quite the opposite: by offering a lead that is nonspecific with regard to time and place, a speaker is attempting to assure that both parties save face. In other words, we tend not to be specific because we fear rejection, or refusal. So, these researchers concluded that in order to successfully negotiate an invitation, mutual cooperation is needed. The following is a typical example of how leads occur:

Two business colleagues, John and Jim, meet in the lobby of their office building as they are leaving work for the day:

Jim: Hey, John. Heading home?
John: Yeah, but taking a bunch of paperwork to do later.

[They walk together in the same direction out of the building.]

Jim: I know what you mean. Not enough hours in the day.
John: Hey, looks like that merger is on track. That'll be nice.
Jim: Yes, but still a few possible snags. So, how's the family?
John: Oh, just fine. Scouts camping trip this weekend. Are you taking Andy?
Jim: No, we're skipping this one—soccer meet. Hey, how about we have lunch one of these days, catch up on things.
John: Sounds good. Give me a call or send an e-mail, or I'll get in touch.

Will either man follow up on the lead put out by Jim? It all depends on how eager they are to touch base with each other on a social level. Clearly, they have something in common other than their work—their young sons do scouting together. The question at this point is, do the two men share enough commonality to take up the tentative invitation? To do so involves some risk, however slight. Either one can take the invitation to another step in the negotiation. If John does not take the next step, it is up to Jim—but Jim put out the initial lead. Therefore, it becomes a situation of possible face loss for Jim if he e-mails John to reiterate the invitation and negotiate a firmer one.

With this kind of tentative invitation it all depends on how much we are willing to risk. However, without proceeding to the next step, the loss may be greater than face loss. It may, indeed, be a missed opportunity for relationship building outside the domain of work.

"HEY, COULD YOU DO ME A FAVOR?"

Jeff calls his neighbor Ann in the late afternoon. Both are the parents of young children:

Jeff: Hi, Ann, how are you?
Ann: Fine.
Jeff: How was your Christmas holiday? Is everyone well?
Ann: The holiday was nice and quiet, and we're all healthy now, but the kids were sick at the beginning of the break.
Jeff: Well, I'm glad you had a good holiday. Listen, I wonder if you could do me a favor. I have a bit of an emergency. Sue [his wife] seems to be AWOL. No one knows where she is, and the babysitter was supposed to be here five minutes ago, and I don't have the car seat in my car. Could you possibly come over and watch Emily until she gets here? It should be about ten minutes.
Ann: I'd be glad to. I'll be right over.

The sequence starts out with the requisite schmoozing, but Jeff is in a pinch, so he cuts to the quick. The simple favor sequence reinforces solidarity between these neighbors. Just by asking Ann to do the favor, Jeff is showing trust in someone he knows will be able to handle his baby. One favor like this deserves some reciprocity. Surely that will come. The relationship is reinforced in small increments. Perhaps Ann is flattered to be so trusted.

Since asking favors may lead to refusals, it is really fraught with the potential danger of conflict. That is why in the good schmooze one knows when favor asking is appropriate or inappropriate. Having said that, as social conversations build relationships—as friendships are solidified—schmoozing may go on to include the exchange of "goods and services," the capital on which social life is built.

The previous example is taken from data collected by sociolinguist Myra Goldschmidt.[4] She found that 85 percent of responses to favor asking received positive responses. In other words, among native speakers across situations, she had only a 15 percent refusal rate to favor asking in social situations. Goldschmidt posits that this is a direct result of the fact that we tend not to ask favors of those we know to be either unwilling or unable to comply. Because doing a favor usually requires some time and/or effort, how (and when) to ask a favor is an important part of communicative competence and good schmoozing.

"SORRY I CAN'T NOW, BUT PLEASE ASK ME AGAIN": REFUSING WITH FINESSE

Clearly, not all speech acts are rapport inspiring. When we need to decline an invitation, for example, the good schmooze comes in handy. This is nowhere truer than with what is commonly known as the "refusal."

Sociolinguist Leslie Beebe and her colleagues[5] found that it is among potential friends that refusals are most elaborated. Elaborated refusals frequently led to long conversational exchanges that were intended to build rapport while at the same time saying "no." The researchers found that airtight excuses serve to diffuse bad feelings. These tend to be detailed enough to make the asker understand and forgive. Even as native speakers, we may not always know how to refuse in a way that defuses potential conflict or hurt feelings.

Beebe and her colleagues discovered that the norm for refusing in American English seems to be elaborated refusals with many details and hedges—to soften the negative force of the speech act. This is hard work, to be sure, but it is usually worth the effort in social situations. If we want the relationship but must refuse an offer, invitation, or suggestion, the best way to do it is to soften the blow. Schmoozers would say any combination of the following softeners, for example: (1) "Oh, I'm so sorry"; (2) "I really wish I had known so that I could have fit that in"; (3) "I would have loved to"; and (4) "Please let me know again."

Unelaborated or vague refusals do not work in the good schmooze. They can lead to conflict talk. On the other hand, detailed information in the refusal actually serves to bond. Despite the general perception that refusals are negative, good schmoozers can turn refusing into something positive in social conversation.

REQUESTS AND REFUSALS: AN EXAMPLE OF CONFLICT TALK

Pam and Gary are getting a new neighbor in their neck of the woods—a small community literally in the "boonies." They choose to live here because they are people who thrive on their privacy and seclusion. They find out that Kate is the new owner—a real estate investor from a sprawling city six hours away by car. They meet after the sale is finalized.

Gary and Pam both welcome Kate warmly, bringing her the requisite house-warming gifts. Kate shows her appreciation by inviting her neighbors over to dinner. During dinner, Kate divulges she would like to use the property as a rental site for retreats. Her invitation is an attempt to "schmooze"—in the negative sense of the word. She is trying to get her neighbors to agree to this use, even though it is not zoned for such. Pam and Gary chat with Kate about it, but they begin worrying about what it will mean to have their next-door neighbor rent out her house and property to large groups at a time. They don't object initially. They merely listen and absorb.

The neighbors have a driveway in common—a meandering country road that first passes Kate's house and then ends at Pam and Gary's. The couple has a legal easement down the driveway to their house. Given Kate's intention, they worry about the effect that increased traffic will have on the already worn stones and soil. An additional concern is that many strangers will have access to the code for the new automatic gate. But, as good neighbors, they agree to share the cost of new lime for the driveway and a new gate. However, their concerns persist.

About a week later, Kate tells her neighbors that she will be allowing friends to hunt on her property. Since she is rarely there anyway, this is no problem for Kate. But for Pam and Gary this is the clincher. Now they become really upset. In the past they have had stray bullets hit one of their vehicles from other hunters nearby. This just won't do.

The context is set for a conflict. Kate obviously is not going to live on the property. For her it is a real estate investment. Pam and Gary have lived there for almost 10 years. They do not want to see their own little slice of heaven changed. They envision, rightly or wrongly, suburban-type subdivisions coming in, with the crowds and traffic that go along with this scene. They decide to voice their suggestions to

Kate about how to manage her property according to the unwritten code of the area—peace and serenity.

They call her at her home some distance away. What follows is a summary of the gist of the phone exchange, as it was related to me by Pam. The conversation was not recorded; therefore, it represents a synopsis rather than a verbatim transcript. It also is seen from Pam's perspective.

Over the phone, Gary begins by telling Kate that he is upset about her giving a worker permission to hunt. Kate is taken aback, but says, "I hear you. I'll tell him not to hunt, then." Gary is mollified. He then voices another suggestion about work Kate is having done on the property, suggesting that she might want to arrange for the debris to be removed from sight. Kate says she will do that. Pam and Gary now suggest to Kate that she might want to be careful with invitations to people to use her pool, as one of them left the gate open when it should have been locked behind him. In a huff now, Kate tells them that she really cannot stay on the phone now, and will think about all of the suggestions. Clearly, from her tone, she is getting angry. Here is part of an e-mail that she subsequently sent to Gary and Pam:

> Truly, on the phone I felt ganged up on. It didn't matter to you that I said repeatedly that I needed to get off the phone, as I was in the middle of my workday. You guys were fired up and just wanted to get it off your chest then and there, regardless of what I was saying. You had your list and you were going to release it when you wanted to, period.
>
> As for the hunting, if I were a hunter, or had a partner who was one, like my former husband, I might be hunting. I wonder how you would like that. I figured, since I wasn't hunting, what's wrong with letting one person do it? I wasn't asked to not let people hunt there, I was told by you not to let them. Nothing was ever explained to me why, other than I figured the obvious, which was not to have people crawling all over our property. You should know, based on my desire and expression of it, to secure the property as much as possible that I don't want people crawling all over my property either. I don't feel heard. I just feel pre-judged and judged right now.

Gary responded in an e-mail:

> I'm sorry to see that our conversation was so upsetting to you. I was afraid it might be. But I think it's probably better for all of us

to get this out in the open. Pam and I have been very upset today as well. So on that issue, we are all in the same boat.

So, let's see if we can't just take a couple steps back and a few deep breaths and see what issues we *can* agree on. It probably is reasonable to assume we won't agree on everything. And you're right in saying you can do whatever you want on your property. So can we. But we both stand to benefit if we can come up with some agreed-upon principles.

It would be a horrible shame for things to escalate, like I have seen happen to other neighbors out here. We all depend on each other much more than people in the city do. We do, however, harbor some anxiety that because you do not live here, we are very vulnerable to being manipulated into a situation which is far different from the one we have been living in. That may be progress. But it is human nature to fear rapid change.

Voicing my displeasure about some things coming up is not an attempt to control every thing you do. You have the right to ignore my complaints. But that doesn't mean I have to stop complaining. I don't much like to complain though. As far as renting, that's an issue that is completely out of our hands. The property is not zoned for that use. I'm sure that you as a realtor know much more about these matters than I do.

I'm not here to be the policeman of the block. If I see something peculiar, I can make a note of it, or ignore it if you'd rather.

Hopefully, this will alleviate any feeling you have that I am trying to control you. But if I don't like something, I'm going to tell you. I expect you to do the same. I would like to suggest one covenant for our neighborhood association. No feuds allowed.

Please, when you get a chance, let me know how you stand on these issues and we will either agree or not. But at least there will be fewer surprises for all of us. We all stand to benefit by cooperating with each other's wishes.

At this point, the e-mail exchange went on for several days, becoming increasingly acrimonious. Kate:

If things don't work out, I may sell the property. Hopefully, it won't be to a family with a lot of kids, hunters, extended family and party animals, or loud, rowdy people. But, if I can't make it work, I'll sell it and I can't help who buys it. I'm trying very hard to get the house and farm together in a timely fashion. I have the utmost of regard for your privacy and consideration of your well-being in all ways. I don't know if who I would sell it to would have the same.

I think I'm just growing tired with all the aggravation. . . . It isn't seeming worth it right now, but, I'm not going to make any snap decisions. I certainly could take the money I have tied up in it and make more money somewhere else and that's a motivating idea, if I'm not going to derive the peace and satisfaction I had hoped for by owning this property. I'm saddened and disappointed with many things, which is taking the joy out of it. I came in open, fresh, and positive and I'm now feeling more closed down and worn out with it. What good is that?

What a pity for all the parties involved that things went so awry! We can see it from both points of view. For Kate, she thought she would have a place with good energy that she could use as income producing, at least to pay her expenses of taxes and maintenance. However, she did not understand the unwritten norms of the community and had not researched the written codes for the area. She did not do her homework. Even sadder is that she assumed a shared set of beliefs—that the place was a little gold mine for real estate investment (this was prior to the recent real estate bust).

Gary and Pam were so worried that they consciously or unconsciously were preparing a litany of direct complaints about what they saw were things to come. They reached the point of regurgitating them all at once, promptly angering Kate. What could have been done to avoid this situation?

Pam and Gary might have taken each suggestion one at a time. This tactic probably would have given Kate the time to think about and digest what was a completely different value system about the property. Had they done this, Kate might have complied, as she did with the initial request of no hunting. Taken all together as a barrage of requests/complaints—unrealistic requests as perceived by Kate—it was too much to bear. A fuse blew. Despite the couple's attempt to assuage the hurt, it was to no avail. The hoped-for neighborliness, on both parts, was irrevocably torn apart.

Direct requests such as Pam and Gary's have multiple meanings. They are at once requests, suggestions, and complaints. As we have seen in this situation, such speech acts can be very face-threatening.

When carrying them out, good schmoozers know how to lesson the potential blow. They not only take one at a time, but they soften the impact with hedges and compromises. It seems that Gary and Pam were braced for a fight, and they got one. The damage was done, and there was no going back. Schmoozing turned sour.

Pam and Gary felt bad about the situation. So Pam apologized in an e-mail:

> Kate—Pam here. I can understand why you're upset—this is not a comfortable situation. We were faced with either voicing our displeasure about others hunting while you're not here, or bite our tongues. You're free to do as you wish with your property, but I want you to know that we'd never allow that here if we knew you'd be coming through [ours]. We like you a lot and want to continue on a harmonious path—no wish to control for sure. I do apologize for saying anything about changing the feel of the area by certain modifications. No harm intended, and I'd like to retract that. Don't want a gated community, but sure do like the gate, and your fence is fine. We like the improvements you've made and hope we can be good neighbors for a long time. Glad to watch over things while you're not here and to party together when you are—hope it's more often.

This was to no avail. Kate was not mollified. Here is how she responded:

> I'm now stepping back and looking at myself and realizing that because I'm open, sharing, and giving, that possibly people think they can just step in and tell me what to do or take advantage, which has been the case with some others. I think it's time I not be so open about my life and sharing and just take more time for myself while out there. I have been way too allowing of people just telling me what to do and saying *okay*. It's probably because I'm in a new territory and involved in things that are new to me. But, perhaps I'm too trusting sometimes. I certainly have been duped a bit here and there. I'll be sure to share with you about important things and certainly think it's important to keep the lines of communications open. Right now, I have nothing new to discuss. I think the subjects are worn out. I haven't made any decisions about anything. I don't have any new input on any of the subjects

you've brought up. I'm still recovering from the phone conversation, as the energy was so strong and pointed. I hear you, in what you wrote, but, I'm still needing time to let it go and regroup. My enthusiasm for the place right now isn't the same.

Schmoozing turned into conflict stemming from the lack of a shared view regarding the unwritten code of conduct in the region. The norms of behavior differed even from one part of the state to another. The goals of Kate versus Pam and Gary could hardly have been more divergent. Coming to a commonality here was difficult, but perhaps would not have been impossible if they had all understood this at the outset.

Unfortunately, learning the norms and goals of the "other" is not an easy task, and this is where schmoozing can backfire. By the time the couple apologized, there was no easy resolution. Here is Kate's response:

I'm sorry for the harsh words I sent your way. I feel I went overboard, but, was so triggered in that moment. I am not sorry for defending my position and not allowing people to speak to me so harshly and unjustly in regard to some things. I am not a rug and am responsible to myself to not allow others to treat me like one. I am going to rent my house out monthly instead of doing retreats, or else sell it, or both. I stand corrected on the rental policy and understand the limitations of the zoning. I still don't get that it would have so much impact on the easement road, etc., or cause any harm to your privacy, etc. . . . but, I got it, loud and clear. So, you have little to complain about at this point and hope you find so much to focus on in your life that you choose to stop thinking of things about me. Again, I'm sorry for where I went overboard with my words. However, at least they were based on truth, but, would have been better left unsaid.

Kate's apology was one that said, "I'm sorry, but ..." In other words, it was qualified with a statement that to a large extent undid the force of the apology. At that point, the conversation ceased. When the neighbors came face to face on the road following this conflict, they merely nodded and proceeded along, with no conversation. An icy relationship had been forged. The apologies could not mend the metaphorical fences.

"I DO APOLOGIZE": REMEDIAL EXCHANGES

Apologies, in sociolinguistics, are considered "remedial exchanges." They serve to transform a possible offense into something acceptable. We are all familiar with the typical scene of a woman and man, total strangers, bumping into each other clumsily as they enter or exit a door, or some such scenario. We know that an apology will usually follow. As the formula goes, the story proceeds from there to a full-blossomed romance. Clearly, this is a quite different scenario than the one for the neighbors. The difference is in the damage: one is a mere physical intrusion, while the other is psychological.

Sociolinguist Bruce Fraser[6] found that the most elaborate apologies occur when the situation is a formal one. Fraser's data, much like my own data on other speech acts, indicate that we are more likely to offer a more elaborate apology to strangers or acquaintances. Among intimates, apologies are either less likely to occur or are simpler and shorter in form.

In the neighbor conflict, the apologies were rather elaborated but perceived, at least in part, as insincere or at least incapable of remedying the offense. In situations of heightened seriousness such as that one, the apologies need to be elaborated as well as sincere. Kate's apology, couched in the form "I apologize for my harsh words, but what I said what based on truth," did nothing to assuage the bad feelings that Pam and Gary were now feeling. It backfired precisely because of the second part, the "but" clause. It was a half-hearted apology that merely asked forgiveness for the wording used rather than the content of the conflict discourse.

Apologies must be perceived as sincere if they are to serve as remedial exchanges. We all know that someone saying, "I'm sorry," in the wrong tone will not do. The words must be backed by sincere feelings of regret. If this does not come through, no amount of words will work.

"HERE'S WHAT YOU OUGHT TO DO": GIVING ADVICE

As we have seen, Gary had tried to give Kate suggestions. But they were couched as strong requests, or even complaints. He was advising her on how to run her farm and property. Gary was caught in a quandary: give advice to protect his peace, or remain silent and risk intrusion. His advice was elaborated, despite the fact that he had not known

Kate for long. In fact, he probably was not sufficiently acquainted with her to have given advice at all. It did not work in his favor. Advice giving is a good example of a high-risk form of talk. Indeed, advice is delicate work that can turn schmoozing into conflict.

One major factor that must be taken into account is the difference between solicited and unsolicited advice. Advice that is solicited is more likely to be accepted. A problem is that we often misperceive whether advice is sought. Gary had assumed that Kate wanted advice, since from the very beginning of their relationship, Kate had been asking him how to do things on her property. She also asked both Gary and Pam favors regarding workmen, deliveries, and checking on things. Probably due to this situation, Gary felt it was appropriate to make suggestions to Kate. Because of this, he was stunned when she took offense.

My work on complaining and commiserating[7] yielded a good deal of advice as a response to troubles talk. Advice was a common response by males to female complaints. Not surprisingly, the female recipients of the advice were often irritated by this response. They felt that they were not asking for advice—they were just venting!

The advice in that study occurred most often in family interactions among spouses—husbands advising their wives. But the wives, for the most part, were dissatisfied with receiving advice when all they were seeking was commiseration or empathy. It seems that there were several inherent dangers in Gary's advice to Kate. First, Kate may not have thought it appropriate for Gary to be advising her at this point. True, she had frequently asked Gary for help. But from her perspective, his advice on the telephone came out of nowhere. Second, it also seems clear that Gary's advice to Kate was perceived as overstepping a boundary—their relationship was just not close enough. The offering of advice in a "social" encounter has more potential to be face-threatening than in a family encounter. A further look at other advice encounters in the social domain seems warranted.

"OH, I DON'T WANT TO GO": ADVICE AS RESPONSE TO COMPLAINTS

Alan and Chris are close male friends. During a lunch conversation, they had a short complaint/advice exchange:

Alan: Oh, I don't feel like going to Boston tomorrow!
Chris: You go for one day, you come back, and that's it. What's the big deal?

Recall that complainers do not always seek advice when telling of troubles. Much griping is carried out for the sole purpose of venting. When people gripe to vent, they are often simply seeking supportive listeners. Most complainers in my study on that subject did not want to solve the particular problem under discussion. So when the interlocutor offered advice, it frequently caused friction.

While Chris meant his advice to be encouraging to Alan, it might have worked to irritate his partner. A commiserative reply might have gone something like this:

Yeah, I know it's a pain. But think of the payoff. It'll be worth it.

This sort of reply would have encouraged Alan rather than minimized the importance of Alan's complaint.

When advice is offered, it needs to be done with sensitivity. The trick is to make sure it is not presented as imposing authority. A very informative study on just this issue was carried out by researcher Deana Goldsmith.[8] Her study concluded that one can give advice that highlights complainers' distress, underscores a weakness, or suggests that the problem is under their control. Goldsmith found that this latter type of advice is preferred by tellers of troubles.

Alan's response to Chris's complaint was advice that underscored a weakness. By saying, "What's the big deal?" Alan indicated that Chris shouldn't be whining about the trip to Boston. If he had been more sympathetic, he might have given the clear message that the problem was under Chris's control and that the trip to Boston would have an appropriate payoff.

As these sequences illustrate, we have to be careful when giving advice. First, we need to consider the closeness of the relationship. With those who are acquaintances and not yet good friends, advice should be handled with kid gloves, even when it is solicited. When people are griping to vent, advice is not usually what is sought.

GENDERED SCHMOOZING

We have seen that both the context and the relationship between speakers affect and constrain face-to-face social interaction. Who we are talking to, what we are talking about, and where we are talking determines what we say and how we say it. Good schmoozing takes all of these into account seamlessly. Overstepping boundaries turns the good schmooze into conflict.

Nowhere is this truer, perhaps, than the difference in the way women schmooze and men schmooze. It has been shown repeatedly that women's talk tends to be supportive and symmetrical, beginning in childhood. Men and boys interact in a much more hierarchical structure. The consequence is often miscommunication and misunderstanding between the sexes. Indeed, it often seems like women and men come from two different cultures. Whether it is nature or nurture, the fact is that the interactional space of inter-gender encounters is fraught with potential misunderstandings.

Some examples will illustrate the general shape of women's and men's schmoozing styles.

"HAVE YOU HEARD THE LATEST?": WOMEN'S SCHMOOZING, MEN'S SCHMOOZING

Marge and Penny were having a casual conversation over lunch. The topic naturally began with their daily lives. In focusing on how things were going, they touched on their children and families and their work. Penny started to talk about her boss, for whom she has worked many years:

Penny: He takes such bad care of himself. He eats such crap!
Marge: That's because he doesn't have a wife.
Penny: You'd think by now he'd have found someone.
Marge: If he were looking he would have. He just doesn't care, obviously.

The topic of Penny's boss is of great interest to these women, who are married and for whom nurturing is of primary importance. Discussing this man is an intriguing topic. Marge knows him well, since he works with her husband. Given this, the two women have a springboard for speculation. What good does this kind of schmoozing do? What purpose could it possibly serve?

The genre of gossip has been so generally attributed to female interaction as to be denigrated. But several studies in sociolinguistics have shown that gossip is often anything but negative. It can be a positive schmoozing strategy, and this is true for these women in the preceding dialogue. Sociolinguist Lynne D'Amico-Reisner[9] found female gossip to serve several positive functions. It avoids direct conflict with the person under scrutiny. It also provides a stage for detailed, privileged information sharing. The privilege in the sharing enables people to guide their relationships with one another.

Penny has inside information about her boss that sets the stage for a conversation exploring his status as a bachelor. Marge's contribution solidifies Penny's thoughts that her boss would eat better if he had a wife to look after him. Now, some readers of this exchange might say that the women just want to make sure nobody is left out there to be a bachelor. They would say that the two women are focusing on the negative while not taking into account the freedoms of bachelorhood. Putting that aside, the two women use the topic to solidify a characteristic that they have in common: the importance they place on family. Moreover, discussion of Penny's boss's personal habits is beyond the scope of her professional relationship with him. If she were to confront him directly about his eating habits, it would no doubt be inappropriate. Indirect information sharing about it with Marge *is* appropriate. The two women are friends. Really, the topic is innocuous. The importance is in the function of the gossip.

Gossip about an absent other allows us to vent frustrations. It sets the stage for the listener to provide support. It also enables us to jointly make sense out of a situation. This short exchange enhances solidarity and intimacy in close female friendships.

On the other side of the ocean in Britain, sociolinguist Jennifer Coates[10] also came to similar conclusions about the functions of gossip in schmoozing among British women. Coates's primary finding was that everyday talk among women tends to be eminently supportive. Talk among the women she studied revolved around topics having to do with people and the women's own lived experiences. The exchange of stories, with mutual self-disclosures, was shown to create and sustain an intense level of sharing through collaborative talk.

Men's talk tends to focus about situations rather than other people. This keeps the relationship on a more distant plane. Here is a quintessential example from my own data in the United States. Larry and Mark, like Penny and Marge, were friends having a lunch conversation. The topic was cold fusion.

Larry: That's the problem with the media, you know? They're just looking for these issues to make big stories.

Mark: If you take the logistic curve of technological change that we're in right now, with cold fusion, we're probably on the right point.

Larry: They may still be right, who knows? The phenomenon may not produce exactly what these guys claim, but they're producing something strange.

Mark: And it may produce another theory. To get closer, legitimately.

Larry: I have a funny feeling that there's something in it, I don't know.

The men's conversation could not be more different from that of Penny and Marge. The women were sharing their ideas about an absent other. The men were sharing their ideas about a possible new scientific discovery. For both pairs, this is schmoozing. But for the women, the schmoozing is in talking about another person for the purpose of solidifying their feelings about what is important in their lives. For the men, the schmoozing solidifies their feelings about an impersonal situation.

The topics certainly are divergent, but they serve the purposes of the good schmooze in both cases. Precisely why they are so different for women and men has been a cause for study. Women tend toward the sharing of secrets and personal disclosures more than men. Little girls do this from early on—it is a part of their play as children. Men's talk is much more based on a hierarchical order. This is seen early on in boys' play, and has been documented by many sociolinguists studying children's talk.[11]

Can gossip backfire as a schmoozing strategy? Certainly. Talk about other people in the absence of these others has the danger of getting back to them. When it gets back to them, the words and sense may be twisted. This very thing occurred with Pam and Kate in the neighbor conflict described before. In an effort to get to know Pam when she first purchased the property, Kate invited Pam to join her on a shopping excursion to a city about an hour's drive away. While in the car, the women were chatting about all sorts of things—mostly schmoozing in which they did the usual mutual disclosures that displayed their identity to each other.

Kate asked Pam if she thought Gary might help her out with irrigation of her crops while she was away. Recall that Kate was not present most of the time. She was back at her main residence hundreds of miles away doing her real estate job. Pam tried not to commit her husband, knowing that Gary would not want the extra responsibility. Pam said such things as, "You probably don't want to depend on having Gary do this for you. It's not that he won't do it; it's just that he's not quick at getting things done. You might not have it taken care of when you need to." Pam kept using these kinds of reasons to get Gary off the hook every time Kate asked if Gary might pinch hit for her. Kate did not usually ask Gary directly, probably for fear of refusal.

Kate interpreted Pam's "disclosures" as a wife's complaints about a husband. Kate later used this information in an attempt to drive a wedge between Gary and Pam. In an e-mail to Gary during their conflict, when things were getting heated, Kate said the following:

> Again, congratulations for supporting your wife and being the messenger for her dislike of the retreat idea. Previously you said you didn't have an issue with it, so I can assume you are trying to please her. This is good. Maybe she won't complain so much about you in the future, because of your recent good deeds for her. It got to the point I was uncomfortable being around you guys, as every time she got me alone, she was complaining about you. I have so many wonderful couple friends and this is one thing I find intolerable and choose not to be around. I guess I was already thinking about distancing myself for this reason and you've created a reason to do so. Guess you can't call your attorney for slander from a wife. Maybe it will stop now. You two have a mission together now, in going after me.

Clearly, gossip (or perceived gossip) has its dangers, and should be done cautiously. It can turn schmoozing into conflict, particularly when dealing with a hearer with whom one is not well acquainted. Pam was trying to let Kate in on some personal details in an attempt to establish rapport or solidarity. The disclosures did the opposite and more. It posed a direct danger to the couple's relationship. When Gary confronted Pam with Kate's assertions, Pam was put in the position of having to explain what she had actually said to Kate. It was a mess! This case clearly shows that the attempt at schmoozing not only backfired for Pam, it put her in an extremely awkward position with her husband. Sometimes instead of "don't schmooze, you lose" it's "schmooze, you lose."

SOCIAL SCHMOOZING HIGHLIGHTED

In schmoozing, we do a lot of identity display, as we have seen in the examples thus far in this chapter. In social talk, we choose to present selected aspects of who we are as we negotiate social relationships. An important and highly successful part of positive social schmoozing is the appropriate use of conversational humor. Humor tells our interlocutors that we are individuals who are enjoyable company. Here we take an in-depth look at humor in social conversation.

CONVERSATIONAL JOKING AND "JOKE TELLING"

Conversational joking is commonly referred to as "wit." It is not the same as joke telling—that is a different genre entirely. Linguist Neal Norrick has explained the fine distinctions between the two forms of humor.[12] Like wit, joke telling is a verbal art. But they are subject to different rules. Joke telling is highly formalized and socially marked. The cue is often an introductory statement such as "Listen to this funny one," or "I've got a good one." In conversational joking, however, the humor emerges in the situation itself and from the appropriate cues that make it a laughing matter. One does not have to be a good joke teller to be good at conversational joking. All that one needs to know is how to display a quick wit that is rapport inspiring. That is the essence of the good schmooze.

JOKING THAT BONDS, JOKING THAT BITES

Conversational joking can serve to bond, nip, or bite. Joking that bonds is a widely used strategy by good schmoozers. It often takes the form of uniting people against the foibles of an absent other or situation. Bonding through humor allows us to become a unit without having to define what we are for each other. What makes us part of an in-group is having in common an out-group. The commonality is often established through poking fun. In this, there is identity display through reducing the others to some laughable characterization that makes them different from us.

One way to do this is through word play. This can display wit and build a relationship without the inherent dangers. Linguist Irene Moyna[13] studied word play among a small, expatriate Uruguayan community in Gainesville, Florida. Her examples were quite clever, as we see in the following:

"Vengo de la *Infiernary*" (I'm coming from the infirmary).

The play on words is from *infierno*, meaning "hell" in Spanish. The equation of the university infirmary with hell is a comment on the U.S. health care system. The fact that this word was created by a small group of people gives them a shared sense of humor. The word play creates a special in-group terminology that bonds the participants and unites them against the others. While other speakers of Spanish within the larger community would have an understanding of the terminology, the special meaning created by the in-group could only be appreciated by those who created it. It solidifies the relationship. It is consummate schmoozing.

CONVERSATIONAL JOKING AND THE ABSENT OTHER: GOSSIP OR WIT?

Bonnie and Cheryl are two close female friends who have gotten together on a Saturday morning. They have both had busy weeks with their work and families. As they regularly do, the women have set aside a time during their weekend to bring each other up to date on what is going on in each other's lives. Bonnie has suffered some lower back pain and relates this to Cheryl. The exchange takes on a humorous tone:

Bonnie: Back problems are the scourge of modern man [sic].
Cheryl: The spine is just ill designed.
Bonnie: Exactly. We're not supposed to …
Cheryl: I. M. Pei must have designed it.

Cheryl is using conversational joking in this last remark. She lives in a house designed by the famous architect I. M. Pei, and the women have had many conversations in which they've discussed the plusses and minuses of his architecture. Thus, they have this topic as a shared commonality. It allows them to use the architect's designs as the brunt of the joke. Cheryl is attempting to commiserate with Bonnie's back complaint, but in a light-hearted way.

In aiming the humor at Pei, the women unite in a clear bond. It is a sort of gossip, but is safer, since the joke is on a famous person—one in the public domain. Like joking against a mutually known third party, we tend to do this kind of joking with friends, for it is rapport inspiring.

Conversational joking of this sort is sometimes viewed as a highly developed verbal art. But it is really not always so difficult. Seizing upon a commonality that one has with a co-conversationalist and turning it around into something funny can be a key to good schmoozing. Imagine its usefulness in defusing conflict. It does so precisely by making light of potentially charged topics. If Cheryl had minimized Bonnie's back pain complaint, it would not have functioned so positively. Let's imagine Cheryl's reply to have been something like the following:

Oh, we all have that once in a while. We just have to learn to live with it.

While this kind of response might not have led to conflict, it does not serve to commiserate. It does not bond, as good schmoozing does. Conversational joking that commiserates not only shows empathy, it also enables the display of wit—a verbal art that makes us want to be with the witty one. It is simply fun—a clear way to display and develop relational identity.[14]

The women's joking about the architect established their commonality of having criticized the architecture. They can now apply this prior criticism to the architecture of the human body. When they agree that the spine is just ill designed, much like some of Pei's buildings, they make light of pain. But they also do much more. They show each other their bond and build a stronger bond.

"MY THIGHS ARE BEYOND HOPE": BONDING THROUGH SELF-DENIGRATING HUMOR

Two female strangers were doing laps in a swimming pool. I overheard their conversation as I was sitting at the edge and as they came up for air at the end of the lap lane. We'll call them Ann and Barb:

Ann: What is this supposed to work on, your legs, stomach?
Barb: Your legs mostly. I don't think it does much for the stomach.

Ann: Oh, I'm not interested in the thighs. *They're beyond hope.*
Barb: I've gained five pounds since I started swimming five years
           ago!

As I eavesdropped on the conversation, I realized that the women
were unacquainted. I later asked them in order to verify, and they indicated that this was their first conversational exchange. The dialogue
shows that each woman used verbal self-denigration to put herself on
equal footing with the other.

We saw self-denigration in a previous example of Barack Obama's
dancing with Ellen DeGeneres. This kind of conversational joking
consists of any play activity that makes the speaker herself or himself the center of the verbal playing. By complaining about one's
own physical, emotional, or intellectual shortcomings, speakers
show themselves to be self-effacing and therefore approachable.
This is exactly what Obama accomplished when he referred to his
"moves" as part of the low bar that the other candidates set for
dancing.

In this example, Barb tells Ann that since she started swimming laps
five years ago, she has gained weight. It's an anecdote that displays
some humor, albeit indirect. The humor is in the self put-down. It tells
Ann she understands the struggle.

Humorous personal anecdotes are an important part of the good
schmooze, but one has to be careful not to be boastful. If Barb had said
she's lost five pounds since she began swimming, it would not have
worked in exactly the same way as the self-denigration. Just like Ann's
assertion of "my thighs are beyond hope," self-denigration actually
presents a positive self-image rather than a negative one. This works
better than boastfulness because it conveys a sense of humor. People
skilled at humorous disclosures and anecdotes present themselves as
having an ability to laugh at problems—an admirable character trait
and an important part of schmoozing.

"LISTEN TO THIS": HUMOROUS ANECDOTES

Bonnie and Cheryl, the same women as in the "spine architecture" sequence, are the participants in the following exchange.

Bonnie is telling Cheryl about a women's clothing store that she recently visited:

Bonnie: I found even a funnier store than Harry's. It's called Larry's. She [the saleswoman] said, she starts in with me that I should have been there a few weeks ago 'cause "there was gorgeous" [merchandise]

Cheryl: That's a typical line!

Bonnie: Typical.

Cheryl: They had gorgeous. [laughs]

Bonnie: "We had gorgeous. We had gorgeous." She sits down and crosses her legs and I'm getting undressed. Well, I'm not an extremely modest person among my friends, this strange lady is sitting there, so I tell myself, "Bonnie, don't be silly," she sees ladies in various stages of undress.

This humorous anecdote is expressed through exaggeration and voicing. The fact that they are close friends allows for much freedom in the exaggeration, causing humor. Part of the humorous effect is the common knowledge of the typical line "we had gorgeous." Here the mimicking of the saleswoman's New York accent is important. Imagine the expression "we had gorgeous" said with a New York accent. The "r" is not pronounced. Apart from the pronunciation, the grammar itself has a regional aspect to it—"we had gorgeous" instead of "we had some gorgeous merchandise." Bonnie uses this dialect mimicking to unite them against the "other." The uniting is against the regional dialect displayed by the saleswoman.

TEASING: BONDING OR BITING?

Joking differs from teasing in important ways. The differences can lead to differing outcomes in conversation. Teasing can bite or nip, since it requires that the conversational joking be directed at someone present. This person becomes the center of an interaction in which a humorous frame has been set up. As with all talk, much depends on the context.

Often with teasing the exact message cannot be interpreted through the words alone. We need to use additional cues like exaggerated intonation, laughs, or winks. If the teasing is not accompanied by appropriate cues, it can actually bite. There are clear cases of teasing that bond without a nip or bite; clear cases of teasing that bite and that therefore do not bond; and less clear cases where a bite can actually serve to bond. This latter case is most common among intimates.

An example illustrates the possible nip. Bob is a middle-aged man who has been ill for some time with a potentially life-threatening disease. Denise is Bob's wife, and Molly is Denise's friend who is visiting at their home.

Bob: I walk at the edge of the envelope, every day. I wake up, "Am I still here?" And then I continue on, I push myself out of bed. I thank God. You become religious.

Molly: Well, I'll tell you, you've gotta change your perspective on things a little bit.

Bob: Of course you do. I was telling Denise my perspective is deeply changed. Now I have to help others who have the disease.

Denise: You don't have enough energy to help anybody right now.

Denise and Bob use teasing in the place of quarreling as a regular part of their verbal interaction. Because Bob has had a long illness, he has not been able to do much in terms of household activities. The nip is in Denise's statement that Bob cannot help others if he does not have the energy to help his wife. The play frame helps to diffuse a potential conflict.

Because of Molly's presence, this is social talk. The fact that it is social and not family talk transforms the tease from a bite into a nip. Teasing gives speakers the possibility of reconciling attempts to change behavior while maintaining existing bonds. We can imagine how the nip could be a bite without Molly's presence. The fact that the couple is talking to their guest turns the teasing into part of schmoozing. This teasing avoids direct conflict.

TEASING THAT BONDS

As we just saw, the nip can denote the bite without actually biting.[15] But the play frame is not always easy to interpret. A misfire can easily occur. In fact, because the nip can become a bite, it is a very useful tool for social control. Teasing often disguises the bite, or makes it tolerable.

Teasing can hide aggression, as we have seen. But there is a certain type of teasing with no possible bite in it, and it can only have the function of bonding. This is the teasing that is found in the good schmooze. Let's look at an example of how this works. Carol and Jane are two close female friends are on a weekend ski retreat:

> Carol: Ooh, my feet got cold. I don't know why my feet got cold all of a sudden.
> Jane: You need a hot drink. You're drinking cold soda.
> Carol: I know. I can't drink hot drinks.
> Jane: You don't drink hot drinks—it's not part of your religion.
> Carol: Right [laughs].

Jane teases Carol about not drinking hot drinks. It bonds them by showing that she knows this about her friend. This knowledge displays a past history. It demonstrates insider knowledge, despite the fact that they had not seen each other in some two years. The teasing reaffirms closeness as one of the major goals of the conversation.

Conversational teasing always displays and develops a relationship (whether positive or negative), since the teased and the teaser are present and participate actively in the play. The bonding potential in teasing is high risk with certain interlocutors. It can go too far and bite, turning schmoozing into conflict.

WE DON'T TEASE STRANGERS

Joking is a way of schmoozing with total strangers, whereas teasing is not. Unless we are unusually inept, we usually do not tease people we do not know. This is because of the potential of the bite. We cannot possibly know what will not bite because we do not have shared background information.

Among friends, teasing that bonds derives from a need for affirming or reaffirming friendship. With strangers, however, the bonding is through joking and word play, not through teasing. Strangers can establish a momentary bond through joking and word play, as illustrated in this example:

Two female strangers at a pharmacy in the footcare aisle. The topic is Dr. Scholl's corn pads:

A: They used to make these smaller, but now this is all I can find.
B: Maybe corns are coming in different shapes these days.
A: This is the third place I've looked and this is all I can find. And there are only a few in here, where there used to be about 20.
B: Inflation. They don't want to charge more, so they just give you less.
A: Maybe they're thicker or something.
B: Technology of foot pads is improving.

Strangers can present themselves in a certain way by joking to show their highly developed sense of irony. It tells the hearer that the speaker has a sense of wit, so it has the potential to create a momentary bond. Despite the fact the two women are strangers and know that this interaction is a limited and temporary one, the attempt at humor serves to make light of a situation and establish a momentary good will.

Teasing that nips occurs mostly with intimates, not with strangers. We saw this in the previous dialogue between Denise and her sick husband, Bob. Here is another example:

Gail and Rose are sisters-in-law. Dave is Gail's husband:

Gail: I have a fungus infection in my ear.
Rose: What kind?
Gail: It's from an infection I had many years ago and it never left my ears.
Rose: You can't do anything about it?
Gail: No. Once you have it, you can't get rid of it. It's like athlete's foot in my ears.
Gail and Rose: [both laugh]
Dave: She crawls through the locker room [all laugh hysterically].

| Gail: | I get crusty, and when I get up in the morning, I can't hear because there's fluid in my ears. |
| Dave: | In her sleep sometimes, the whole bed shakes cause she's got her fingers in her ears … it wakes me up when I'm sound asleep! |

First, the joke is a self put-down using a humorous analogy. Second, Dave teases Gail by carrying the analogy further, displaying his own humor. His teasing nips.

Where joking with friendly strangers establishes a momentary bond, it is with intimates that we tend to see the teasing that nips or even bites. With strangers, where no past history has been created, we need to display our identity, to show them we are good people, not dangerous, but witty and safe to be around.

WOMEN, MEN, AND CONVERSATIONAL JOKING

Women and men use different strategies of injecting humor into a conversation. Where women try to establish symmetry through humor, the male propensity is to use verbal challenges and put-downs.[16] For example, the topic of bodies/figures/physique takes on a different form for women and men. Women frequently employ verbal self-denigration through irony about their own physical shortcomings. We saw this in the example where two women were swimming and complaining about their thighs. The goal might be to establish some common bond by telling the addressee that we are not full of conceit.

Males appear to feel freer to tease *others* about bodies. This is seen in the following example, where adult men are playing basketball at a local gym:

A: Man, you've got a big butt. How can you lumber down the court?

B: [No response]

This could be interpreted as a real bite, but if the interlocutors are close enough, it is merely a nip. This type of nip was interpreted by the male participants as typical speech behavior of male bonding during athletic competition. When I asked about their teasing, the men offered that in sports competition, men will pick out the physical weakness of the opponent and use it as a tease. The teasing serves to establish and/or reinforce hierarchy.

For women, on the other hand, to tease about bodies is to touch something that we have been trained to take seriously. After all, if we don't care about our bodies, we are not doing our job (I say this with irony, of course). If women's work is to look good, teasing about this is to touch a place of real insecurity; so it will only happen in self-denigration. Verbal self-denigration about appearance seems to be more a female activity than male, and constitutes an important component of female schmoozing.

CONVERSATIONAL JOKING AND THE GOOD SCHMOOZE

Good schmoozers understand how far they can reasonably go with joking or teasing on certain topics and with certain people. They have developed an insight into what bonds and what bites. Some of us overstep the boundaries. When we do, we enter the dangerous territory of biting that can easily turn into hurt feelings, and even conflict.

We have seen that conversational joking can function to display identity among strangers; we have seen that self-teasing can bond participants; and we have seen that teasing among intimates can nip or even bite. While there is room for the nip or bite among some intimates, this is not necessarily true with friends, acquaintances, and strangers. Certainly, what makes for a good laugh differs from individual to individual. The bottom line is, we all enjoy a good laugh.

An understanding of how conversational humor functions as a verbal activity ought to contribute to our knowledge of how be successful in social talk. It is, indeed, the good schmooze.

CONCLUSION: SCHMOOZING IN SOCIAL CONVERSATION

The bulk of schmoozing in social conversation is done for the sake of getting to know others, for creating new relationships and friendships, and also for affirming and reaffirming existing relationships.

Examining how schmoozing functions in social talk enables us to learn just what is appropriate or inappropriate, what is collaborative and what is rude, what makes us sought-after interlocutors, and what about our talk has the potential to alienate others. This all has to do with being and becoming competent members of our social communities. People who know how to choose topics of interest to their interlocutors draw people into their circle. People who know how to make relevant and humorous contributions to a conversation are people with whom others want to spend time. People who know how to be supportive when support is sought have a wider social network than those who do not know these things. How to greet, how to give advice with content sensitivity, how to commiserate, how to signal solidarity and identity, how to ask the right kinds of questions, and how to be a friend are all skills of social conversation that distinguish the conversationally inept from the conversationally skilled. Studying schmoozing in social talk can indeed give us deep insights into how to be happier social beings.

NOTES

1. Miriam Eisenstein and Jean Bodman, "'I Very Appreciate': Expressions of Gratitude by Native and Non-Native Speakers of American English," *Applied Linguistics* 7 (1986): 167–185.

2. Erving Goffman, *Interaction Ritual: Essays on Face-to-Face Behavior* (Garden City, NY: Doubleday, 1967), 91.

3. Nessa Wolfson, Lynne D'Amico-Reisner, and Lisa Huber, "How to Arrange for Social Commitments in American English: The Invitation," in *Sociolinguistics and Language Acquisition*, eds. Nessa Wolfson and Elliott Judd (Rowley, MA: Newbury, 1983), 116–128.

4. Myra Goldschmidt, "For the Favor of Asking," *Working Papers in Educational Linguistics* 5 (1993): 35–49.

5. Leslie Beebe, Tomoko Takahashi, and Robin Uliss-Welz, "Pragmatic Transfer in ESL Refusals," in *On the Development of Communicative Competence*, eds. Robin Scarcella, Elaine Andersen, and Stephen Krashen (Rowley, MA: Newbury, 1985), 55–73.

6. Bruce Fraser, "Insulting Problems in a Second Language," *TESOL Quarterly* 15 (1981): 435–441.

7. Diana Boxer, *Complaining and Commiserating: A Speech Act View of Solidarity in Spoken American English* (New York: Peter Lang, 1993).

8. Daena J. Goldsmith, "Content-Based Resources for Giving Face Sensitive Advice in Troubles Talk Episodes," *Research on Language and Social Interaction* 32 (1999): 303–336.

9. Lynne D'Amico-Reisner, "Avoiding Direct Conflict through the Co-Construction of Narratives about Absent Others: Gossip as a Positive Speech Activity in the Talk of Close Female Friends" (paper presented at American Association of Applied Linguistics conference, Stamford, CT, March, 1999).

10. Jennifer Coates, *Women Talk* (Oxford: Blackwell Publishers, 1996).

11. Marjorie H. Goodwin, "Tactical Uses of Stories: Participation Frameworks within Boys' and Girls' Disputes," in *Gender and Conversational Interaction*, ed. Deborah Tannen (New York: Oxford University Press, 1993), 110–143.

12. Neal Norrick, *Conversational Joking: Humor in Everyday Talk* (Bloomington: Indiana University Press, 1994).

13. M. Irene Moyna, "'Nosotros los Americanos': Humorous Code-Switching and Borrowing as a Means to Defuse Culture Shock" (unpublished manuscript, University of Florida, 1994).

14. Diana Boxer and Florencia Cortes-Conde, "From Bonding to Biting: Conversational Joking and Identity Display," *Journal of Pragmatics* 27 (1997): 275–294.

15. Gregory Bateson, *Steps to an Ecology of Mind* (Northvale, NJ: Jason Aronson, 1987).

16. Daniel N. Maltz and Ruth Borker, "A Cultural Approach to Male/Female Miscommunication," in *Language and Social Identity*, ed. John Gumperz (New York: Cambridge University Press, 1983), 195–217.

CHAPTER 2

Schmoozing in the Family

In every dispute between parent and child, both cannot be right, but they may be, and usually are, both wrong. It is this situation which gives family life its peculiar hysterical charm.

Isaac Rosenfeld

INTRODUCTION

Guilting, nagging, teasing, scolding, contradicting, whining, bickering, giving unsolicited advice—these are the typical speech behaviors that characterize interactions in families. Family talk may be charming at times, as the above quote asserts, but by and large, the good schmooze does not prevail among intimates. Typical family talk is the contrary of what is found in schmoozing with potential friends. With people who are friendship candidates, we do a delicate dance of negotiation in "talking nice." We want them to like us. We do a lot of schmoozing, not just the networking type, but the "shooting the breeze" kind that builds the relationship. With family members, we no longer need to talk nice—we somehow come to feel that we need not work as hard.

In fact, a recent *New York Times* article republished in my local newspaper[1] reported on a large-scale study of families that highlighted exactly this point. Sociolinguist Elinor Ochs of the University of California at Los Angeles was the principal investigator for the West Coast aspect of the $9 million study that captured thousands of hours of real family interaction on videotape. The article states: "Life in these trenches is exactly what it looks like: a fire shower of stress, multitasking, and mutual nitpicking." In fact, postdoctoral researcher Anthony P. Graesch had this to say about the family discourse captured on tape: "The very purest form of birth control ever devised. Ever."

If schmoozing is a lost art, we might justifiably assert that it is most lost in family talk. It happens logically. We feel that we have nothing to lose. These are the only people in the world who will accept us no matter what. Of course, this is truer with children than with partners and spouses, but we really cannot count on unconditional acceptance. If schmoozing now means sucking up, then why bother sucking up to family members? We already have them in our clutches. We work so hard with others (in the workplace, at school, and with friends) that when we get home, we "let it all hang out."

Good schmoozing leads to more harmonious relationships in all domains, and this is perhaps most important in families. Because bad schmoozing behavior prevails in family interactions, it is difficult to gather data on good family schmoozing. This is true in spontaneous family talk and in family talk that is exemplified in literature and the media. There are numerous television shows and films that center on family interactions. Many are comedies precisely because they highlight the way family members talk—all of the bad schmooze moves are made humorous, even nagging and whining. As a result, much of the data presented in this chapter highlights these negative speech behaviors in an attempt to hypothetically reconstruct how the good schmooze could be carried out. The chapter is organized around the typical talk of families, with examples from parent-child interaction and couples talk. The chapter culminates with an in-depth analysis of nagging, the quintessential conflict arena in families.

"I STUB MY TOE ON THAT BIG BAG": TEASING AND WHINING

The opening line of Tolstoy's Anna Karenina is: "Happy families are all alike; every unhappy family is unhappy in its own way." Indeed, happy families have common ingredients that go into the mix of making for happiness. Likewise, dysfunctional families have similarities in prevailing types of talk. The ingredients are all about habits of everyday talk.

The happy aspects are loving, supportive moves; nurturing moves; and moves that indicate tolerance of personal differences. The bad habits of talk also fall into several categories of negative schmoozing, as mentioned (e.g., teasing, whining, guilting, nagging, scolding, bickering, and contradicting). Teasing can be a positive or a negative verbal move—a double-edged sword that has the potential to bond or to bite. So it is with whining. Indirect complaining, or whining, can bond people through a common complaint. On the other hand, while teasing has the potential to show closeness, it may also serve to indirectly scold and alienate.

Recall that in past research on conversational joking and teasing[2] we discovered that teasing is done only with intimates or near-intimates. People do not tease others who are merely acquaintances, for it would be what sociolinguists term a *face-threatening act*. In other words, we only tease people when we either trust that they will take it the right way (good schmooze), or when we just want to criticize (bad schmooze). This is why teasing is so prevalent in families.

Consider the following interview of the Obama family. They sat down with a reporter for the TV show *Access Hollywood* when they were on the campaign trail in Butte, Montana. It was July 4 and Malia's birthday:

Barack:	Malia is much better talking on the phone to me [on the campaign trail] than Sasha: S gets bored talking to me—"Bye, love you."
Malia:	Sometimes I kinda feel bad for you.
Barack:	You do?
Malia:	I'm like, "C'mon Sasha. He hasn't seen you in like three days" . . . I usually try to have a conversation.
Barack:	You make an effort.
Interviewer:	What could you guys do that's wrong and daddy would get really mad at?
Malia and Sasha together:	Whining.
Interviewer:	Yeah, whining is a bad thing . . .
Malia:	And arguing. They sit us down and say, "You guys are the best thing that you have in your life and we're never gonna get something as good as each other."

[Later in the interview]:

Malia:	This is what you do, daddy.
Barack:	Uh, oh.
Malia:	It's not that bad . . .
Barack:	Okay.
Malia:	But when you come home you know, you have your big, gigantic bag and you leave it in the mud room and sometimes I trip over it.
Michelle:	Yeah, you leave your bag.
Sasha:	Right there.
Michelle:	And it's heavy, and it's right at the front door.
Barack:	[overlapping with above] 'cause I'm so eager to see you guys.
Michelle to Malia:	That's a good one, that's one [high five to Malia] I stub my toe on that big bag.
Sasha:	And you put them right on my shoes.

This is a good example of whining as good-natured teasing—the kind of teasing that has the potential to bond. However, we can in no way presume that the interaction is exactly the same as it would be within the privacy of this family. In other words, would they do exactly the same kind of banter if they were not displaying this for the world to hear and see? Probably not. What the interaction does show is the good-natured quality of how whining and teasing have the *potential* to be realized as good family schmoozing.

Suppose that the Obama women were negatively displaying their displeasure about the big bag in a private family interaction. They might voice their complaint in a raised voice and with a negative accusing and blaming intonation. But the very nature of displaying their family identity to the U.S. public is to show how functional a family they really are. They do this through normal tones indicating loving warmth. When Malia begins by saying, "This is what you do . . .," the future president jokes by saying something to the effect that he knows he is in trouble. At this point, his daughter quells his fears, "It's not that bad." The Obama women then pounce. They join together in their solidarity in the complaint. Mom and daughter display this through the nonverbal high five. But the complaint is all about teasing—positive teasing.

The Obamas come off as a normal family that has its quibbles. But the arguments are all about keeping things functional. The girls simultaneously answer the interviewer's question, "What could you guys do that's wrong and daddy would get really mad at?" They say, at the same moment, that it would be whining. All can then agree that whining is not a good thing. Then they assert that another speech behavior daddy does not like is arguing. This is followed by a display of family moralizing when Malia says, "They sit us down and say 'you guys are the best thing that you have in your life and we're never gonna get something as good as each other.'"

Moralizing about positive values is a part of good family schmoozing that is a useful and important component of socializing children. The Obamas display this, and Malia gets specific by quoting something her parents had ostensibly said. It is not scolding. Scolding would be saying something negative at the moment of arguing like, "You girls stop that arguing. I can't stand it." It might also take on an accusation such as "You sound like a couple of chickens squabbling" followed by some sort of threat—"If you don't cut it out right now. . . ." This is, of course, hypothetical. Perhaps this is what it is really like in the privacy of the Obama family. However, one gets the impression that this is not the case. The parents' moralizing demonstrates family values of being loving and supportive rather than argumentative.

MORALIZING: THE GOOD, THE BAD, AND THE UGLY

Native speakers of any language know that moralizing is not necessarily positive. It is often akin to lecturing. Nobody likes to be lectured, unless it is a formal lecture or church sermon, for example. In family interaction, lecturing has negative consequences. But there is also a good kind of moralizing that is done to instill values, as seen in the Obama family conversation. The distinction between good schmooze moralizing and its opposite can be subtle.

Both sorts of moralizing are exemplified in *Little Miss Sunshine*, a 2007 film about an extremely dysfunctional family. The dysfunctional talk is what makes the story such a superb comedy. Many TV shows and films in the comedy category are funny precisely because they focus closely on the foibles of familial talk. Bad schmoozing in the lives of others, while sad, can be humorous to witness. It is not so much fun when it is one's own reality.

A contrast between the two types of moralizing is highlighted in the film. The family is composed of two parents, Cheryl and Richard, a teenage son, Dwayne, and a seven-year-old daughter, Olive. Dwayne has taken a vow of silence until he can learn to be a pilot. Add to this typical family mix suicidal Uncle Frank and heroin-snorting Grandpa, and you have all the comical ingredients of failed schmoozing.

Good schmoozing, on the other hand, appears out of the mouths of those least expected to have mastered it—Grandpa and little Olive. Grandpa has been evicted from his assisted living facility due to his drug habit. As a result, he is living with his son's family and has taken on Olive's quest to win the Little Miss Sunshine beauty pageant.

The bad schmoozing exchanges are usually sparked by Richard, the father. He is a failed inspirational writer and speaker whose program is all about winners versus losers in life. He constantly lectures the other family members. For example, at the dinner table, when the subject of Frank's suicide comes up at Olive's repeated queries, Richard moralizes, in Frank's presence, "Uncle Frank gave up on himself." On another topic, when Olive voices worry about the contest, Frank lectures that it is not about luck: "Losers worry about luck. Winners have the right attitude." As dad, husband, son, and brother-in-law, Richard is always ready with unsolicited advice for the other family members, which he readily conveys at inappropriate times and in inappropriate ways. It is not surprising that he cannot use his own advice to succeed. His schmoozing is all about empty platitudes that have no substantiation through his own example.

In contrast, Grandpa is the last person one would expect to know how to schmooze. Throughout the film he is characterized as a crusty, curmudgeonly character with a critical tongue and foul mouth. But he rises to the occasion when it is most needed. When his son receives bad news that his inspirational scheme has not sold, father soothes his grown son:

Grandpa: Richard.
Richard: Yeah?
Grandpa: Whatever happens, you tried to do something on your own, which is more than most people ever do. And I include myself in that category. You took a big chance. It took guts. And I'm proud of you.

.

This kind of encouragement is good child socialization. That Richard is no longer a child matters not the least. It is one of the few good schmoozing examples among a litany of failed schmoozing attempts in the film.

Another example also has grandpa doing the unlikely good schmooze with Olive. As a seven-year-old child, Olive is overweight and ungainly. But she nevertheless strives to win a little girls' beauty contest:

Olive: Grandpa, am I pretty?
Grandpa: Olive, you are the most beautiful girl in the whole world.
Olive: Aw, you're just saying that.
Grandpa: No, I'm madly in love with you and it's not about your brains or your personality. It's because you're beautiful. Inside and out.
Olive: I don't want to be a loser [weeps].
Grandpa: You're not a loser. Where'd you get the idea that you're a loser?
Olive: Because dad hates losers.
Grandpa: Whoa, whoa . . . back up a minute. Do you know what a loser is? A real loser is someone that's so afraid of winning they don't even try. Now you're trying, right?
Olive: Yeah.
Grandpa: You're not a loser. We're going to have fun tomorrow [at the contest] right?
Olive: Yeah.
Grandpa: We can tell them all to go to hell [Olive's weeping ceases and she smiles]. Good night, sweetie.

Grandpa's good schmoozing with both his son and his granddaughter highlights the distinction between good schmooze moralizing and the sort of moralizing done by Richard. One leads to positive feelings and the other to bad feelings. Richard's talk about losers has made Olive worry about being a loser. In contrast, Grandpa's moralizing about trying encourages and builds self-esteem. The difference is subtle, but the effects are long lasting.

Sometimes no schmoozing is the best schmoozing. Olive knows this instinctively. When her brother, Dwayne, discovers that he is color blind and will never realize his dream of being a pilot, nobody can comfort him until Olive takes it upon herself. She slowly approaches him, looks him in the eye, puts her arm around him, and gives him a big hug. Only then is Dwayne willing to reenter the family's activities. Good schmoozing is occasionally about just knowing when to say nothing at all—merely showing nonverbal support. Even a child can know this instinctively. Indeed, the film makes it out to be child's play.

DOUBLE-EDGED SWORDS

Moralizing, teasing, and whining are all a common part of family talk. All three speech behaviors can be done as good schmoozing or not. Moralizing focuses on generalizations that teach life's lessons. It is directed at family members by another member who has inherent power to moralize. Parents moralize with children, as seen in the previous examples. Teasing, on the other hand, has another family member as a target; whining does not necessarily have a person as target.

Like whining, teasing differs for female and male interaction; it also is very different in social talk and family talk. Linguistic analyses of boy talk (including adult men) versus girl talk (including adult women), has consistently found that teasing tends to be gentler among females. This is doubtless a product of socialization. Recall that the literature in sociolinguistics abounds with evidence of male hierarchical social structure that contrasts with women's affiliative, symmetrical structure. In other words, if we are to make an overarching generalization about gendered talk, we might say that boys and men use teasing talk more directly and forcefully than do girls and women. However, in families, the differences are not as marked as in social relationships. Let us examine teasing and whining in families more closely, looking at real data collected by ordinary people in their family interactions.

"DOES HE LIKE ME?": TEASING AS GIRL TALK

Girls can certainly be as cruel in their teasing as boys, and this is nowhere truer than in sister talk. However, there is more likely to be a smoother edge to the teasing in families that have mastered good schmoozing. There will be teasing regardless; but the teasing will be more supportive and bonding than critical and alienating. The following sequence of real interaction took place among two grown sisters, in

their early twenties, with their mother.[3] The topic is a familiar one—
"Does he like me?" Linda and Laurie are the sisters.

Laurie:	See, I don't know, I just feel, I feel like he's interested, but I don't know how interested. You know what I mean?
Linda:	Yeah . . .
Laurie:	Well he keeps IMing [instant messaging] me . . . like . . . like . . .
Linda:	*That's* a sign!
Laurie:	And he keeps messaging me and he texts me like every couple days or every other day.
Linda:	I'd say that's a sign, but if he's texting you I'd say that's . . . ah . . . more than just a sign . . .
Laurie:	I don't know. I'm not gonna get my hopes up.
Linda:	What do you think, Mom?
Mom:	I'd say he does . . . he's interested.
Laurie:	Well he came over, right. I'd count that as interested—
Linda:	—aaaat the crack of dawn.
Laurie:	And stayed five hours. That's kind of interested. . . . he offered to help me with calculus, too.
Linda and Mom:	OOOOOOOOOO!!!!
Laurie:	Right!?!
Mom:	Well I expect you to *ace* that test! [laughing]

Laurie wants confirmation that he likes her. Her sister, Linda, willingly and supportively offers that confirmation and wants their mom to
add her two cents. Mom complies, "I'd say he does." But the sequence
must have some teasing, and we see it appear about the calculus help.
Linda and Mom affiliate in their simultaneous exclamatory response
"OOOO. . . .!!!" The sarcasm teases in a bonding manner. It bonds
Linda and Mom and bonds them both with Laurie. But in the end,
Mom must take the mother role in all this. She finally uses a lighthearted teasing about expectations of Laurie's acing the calculus test.
This last statement demonstrates a mother's desire to control the posi-
tive outcomes of her children's lives. Once again, we see the tension
between the desire for control versus the need for connection.[4]

This may be considered by some as typical of female talk. It resembles
the kind of "girl talk" that is widespread in social interactions among

close friends. When we consider the mild teasing, we see this sort of speech behavior in close relationships, not in relationships of acquaintances and certainly not among strangers. It is not surprising, then, to also see mild good-natured teasing in family "girl talk." What is uplifting is the positive nature of teasing that bonds.

Examples are ubiquitous in ordinary female family talk. In the following, Rebecca, Nancy's sister, is a new mother, and their mother is of course a new grandmother:[5]

Mom: How's Taylor [the baby] doing?
Rebecca: She's good. She woke me up at five this morning.
Mom: I remember when you and your sister used to do that to me.
Rebecca: Yeah, and I went to bed at seven last night.
Mom: I remember doing that, too.
Nancy: You still do.

Is it shameful for an adult woman to go to bed at seven? Nancy teases her mom about still doing this—it is not only for new mothers. It is the tease that nips. This one hardly bites. The small tease shows how mother and daughter Rebecca, who is now a mother herself, are growing in similarity. Nancy can tease with a nip because she is not yet a mother. Rebecca can no doubt sympathize. She may be going to sleep early for a long time to come.

Teasing examples of this sort can be found in literature and the media. The following conversation is taken from the 2005 film adaptation of Jane Austen's *Pride and Prejudice*. Two sisters, Elizabeth and Jane Bennett, are chatting at a ball about the male prospects attending:[6]

Elizabeth: Now if every man in the room does not end the evening in love with you, then I am no judge of beauty.
Jane: [giggles] Or men.
Elizabeth: [laughs brightly] No, they are far too easy to judge.
Jane: They're not all bad.
Elizabeth: Humorless poppy cocks, in my limited experience.
Jane: One of these days, Lizzie, someone will catch your eye and then you'll have to watch your tongue.

Since this is a literary (film) example, the sequence embodies wit. Elizabeth compliments her sister, but her sister comes back with a scolding nip. At this point, the sisters do a brief back-and-forth sparring in which they express mild but innocuous contradictions of each other's assertions. Jane's last statement embodies a warning within a compliment. It is all done in the spirit of sisterly teasing.

Boyfriends, babies, and beyond—these are the topics of girl talk teasing. It is all quite different for boys.

"Boys Will Be Boys" Teasing

Male teasing is frequently intertwined with grandstanding. It serves the purpose of establishing a pecking order. This is true in all spheres of interaction—even in workplaces. It is especially salient in families.[7]

Sally, the lone sister in a family of four children, is a college student who arrives home for Thanksgiving break. Sally's three half brothers are Joe (13), Frank (11), and Nick (9). Because she has not seen her family for several months, this initial conversation was meant for catching up. It took place around the kitchen table. Sally reported that this schmooze, like many she has had with her brothers, ended with all three of them chasing and wrestling each other around the house. As Sally herself indicated, "boys will be boys."

Dad: What do you think of this guy? [points to Joe] He's grown up! Look at his muscles.

Joe: I have a line here. [flexes bicep]

Dad: Frank won the Class Clown Award at school.

Frank: Yeah, cuz of all my dirty blonde jo–

Sally: *–dumb* blonde jokes.

Frank: Ye-yeah, that's what I meant. And, um, I was like, "keep it real people" when they gave me a round of applause. A- and I walked off the stage like this. [waves to a fake audience]

Dad: He's funny guy! So sweet, man.

Joe: Yeah, cuz they laugh *at* him not *with* him.

Frank: Hey, keep it real people.

Sally: I can't believe how big you guys are.

Nick: You're my favorite sister. [pats Sally on the back]

Sally: I'm your *only* sister.

Nick: Still my favorite.

Frank: A- and Sally, watch this. I was like, hi-yaw! [pretends to punch somebody]

Sally: Why are you so serious, Joe?

Dad: He's a teenager now. He's grown up!
Joe: Dad, stop. Just stop saying that. She knows how old I am.
Sally: Yeah, but you're just so serious all of a sudden. Wouldn't
       even give me a hug . . .
Joe: So?
Frank: Sally, watch this! [pretends to wrestle somebody to the
       ground]
Nick: Frank is so stupid!
Sally: He just has a big imagination. [whispers to Nick] Go beat
       him up.
Nick: Ok! [chases Frank around the house, followed by Joe]

Mocking is a part of teasing, and we see this clearly here. The teasing is all in good spirit. The boys are displaying their new muscles,
growth, and general good humor to their lone female sibling. Sally
plays along. After all, it has been awhile since she has interacted in
such a way. It is all a part of this family's typical schmoozing. Indeed,
boys will be boys.

"ALL IN THE FAMILY": TEASING, BICKERING, AND SARCASM

Teasing may be a double-edged sword, but bickering is a family
speech behavior that can rarely if ever be part of good schmoozing. We tend to think about elderly, long-married couples when the
term *bickering* is conjured up. No linguist has taken on an analysis
of what constitutes this type of talk; however, it is clear that bickering is a kind of arguing that is done without raised voices but
with a good dose of rancor. It occurs in response to what a speaker
considers repeated unpalatable actions on the part of another family member. Partners and spouses bicker with each other. So do
siblings.
    The 2008 film *Smart People* highlights bickering in family interac-
tions. It centers on the ordinary goings-on of a family in which Mom
recently died. Dad is the quintessential curmudgeonly professor who
has taken grieving to the ultimate. His teenage daughter, Vanessa, takes
on the domestic duties while still in high school. Her brother, James,
is a student at the college. The fourth family member, recently arrived
in the household, is Dad's loser middle-aged stepbrother. Like in *Little*

Miss Sunshine, this dysfunctional relative provides much comic relief. However, at times he is the sole voice of reason.

As in all families, the locus of a great deal of schmoozing takes place around the dinner table. This family is no exception. A critical scene takes place over a sad Christmas dinner with this grieving family. It highlights sarcastic bickering. When James pours himself a glass of wine, Dad says that teenage children are not old enough to drink wine:

James: I need something to wash down this rubber ham.
Vanessa: I downloaded the recipe from the Internet. I translated it from Old French. [goes on to explain the history of food philosophy in those times]
James: Maybe you messed up the translation and that's why it tastes like burnt tires.
Vanessa: I could jam it up your ass for you.
Dad: That's enough. [gets up from the table and walks away]
Vanessa: Well, this is cheerful.
James: Shut up.

[Doorbell rings. Uncle goes to answer it. It is the father's girlfriend, a physician, who shows up unexpectedly with a cake that she swiped from the break room of the hospital. The cake bears the logo of an antivenom cure. Uncle quips sarcastically]:

Uncle: Welcome. We could use a little antivenom in this snake pit.

The family needs the presence of an outsider to diffuse the bad schmooze atmosphere. When they all reconvene at the table, Vanessa serves the guest a hefty plateful of food. They display their identities for the newcomer, who has not previously met the family:

James: Vanessa here is the perfect little housewife . . . I mean daughter.
Vanessa: If by perfect you mean not retarded slash suffering from insurmountable credit card debt, then yes, I am indeed perfect.
Dad: You two, please stop the bickering.
Uncle: These children haven't been properly parented in many years. That's why I was brought in, to ensure that they don't kill each other. Merry Christmas.

The family has fallen into a pattern of bickering. The film's ingredient for a transformation is to bring in a new interlocutor. It is bad form to bicker in front a stranger. After all, they are children, but grown children who know better. Bickering is a family thing—no strangers allowed.

Clearly, negative patterns of family schmoozing are difficult to break. Parents are the role models, and children will follow suit. Bickering and unhappy talk model the same for children, both young and grown. Family members perpetuate persistent habits of talk for each other. When the bad schmooze reigns, the good schmooze is hard to do.

"YOU CAN SAY THAT AGAIN": WHINING AS SCHMOOZING

Bickering, teasing, and whining share many characteristics. The overlap is what makes them sometimes difficult to disambiguate from each other. Couples typically do a lot of all three, and contrary to folk perceptions, at least the latter two have the potential to function positively in good family schmoozing just as in social schmoozing. In the case of whining or complaining, the outcome all depends on the response. In my own research, I have found that spouses and partners, especially when they have been together for a long time, tend to offer negative schmoozing replies to complaints. These include contradicting and giving unsolicited advice or lecturing. These examples were recorded from dinner talk between a long-married wife and husband:

Wife: What a horrible nose his wife has!
Husband: Listen, in some societies, that may be beautiful.

In another conversation between the same spouses:

Wife: He's such a complainer!
Husband: Well, if you were a [???], you'd be a complainer, too.
Wife: Not necessarily.

These gripes about other people are part of the genre of interaction commonly known as "gossip." It is more difficult to imagine such complaints among acquaintances who are not very close. Here, the husband contradicts each of his wife's gossipy gripes. In the latter sequence, each contradicts the other. It sounds like the beginning of bickering. Perhaps the husband does not want to encourage whining with a personal focus. This has been noted to be a hallmark of women's talk as opposed to men's talk. Recall that men's whining tends to focus more on impersonal situations rather than about other people. Consider this example, from another middle-aged couple, but more recently wed:

Husband: The media is making such a big deal about Tiger Woods. It's crazy. Can you believe they're spending so much time on this story?

Wife: I know. Like there aren't more important issues to cover!

The complaint's focus is different from the other two, and perhaps it is the reason for the more supportive sort of response. The fact is, the issue brought up by the husband is one that focuses on a news story and on which both can easily agree. Perhaps in the first two sequences, the husband was not going to get involved in whining about another person, be it a physical characteristic or that fact that the other person is a complainer! To complain about a complainer is somewhat ironic.

In the large corpus of griping/whining data that I collected among intimates (97 conversational sequences), contradiction was the most frequent response. Taken together with advice, these two types of responses accounted for almost half of the data. Of course, it depended on the topic of the gripe. The important finding is that in complaining that forms part of family schmoozing, contradiction and advice abound as responses. This is much less the case with friends, potential friends, and strangers. With those interlocutors, we tend to respond with agreement, reassurance, or commiseration.

"HERE'S WHAT YOU NEED TO DO": SOLICITED AND UNSOLICITED ADVICE IN FAMILIES

As seen in some of the previous examples, contradiction as a response to ordinary gripes leads to bad feelings. It is rarely part of good schmoozing. Recall that advice is also a response that sometimes falls into the same category, but it is largely dependent on whether the advice is solicited or unsolicited. It overlaps to a large extent with moralizing, and like moralizing, it can be both positive and negative.

That unsolicited advice in response to griping is not what is usually sought by the griper is true in family as well as social interactions. When the griping or whining is just to vent or let off steam, most people are seeking a more supportive response that shows empathy. Unsolicited advice typically backfires.

SOLICITED ADVICE: GOOD SCHMOOZING

Advice that is sought can set the stage for good schmoozing among couples and particularly with children. The 2007 film *Juno* has as its central theme the unexpected pregnancy of a 16-year-old girl. While the topic seems somewhat hackneyed, the film unfolds with clever dialogue and novel twists. Juno has been raised by her father and stepmother. There is a particularly poignant scene where a very pregnant Juno and her father have a good schmooze about an important life issue—finding true and lasting love:

Dad: You're looking a little morose, honey. What's eating you?
Juno: Ah, I'm just, like, losing my faith in humanity.
Dad: Can you narrow that down for me?
Juno: I just wonder if, like, two people can stay together for good.
Dad: Like couples?
Juno: Yeah, like people in love.
Dad: Are you having boy trouble? 'Cause I don't believe in people dating in your condition. That's kinda messed up.
Juno: No, dad.
Dad: I mean, that's kinda skanky . . .
Juno: Please stop. That's not what it's about. I just need to know that it's possible that two people can stay happy together forever.
Dad: Well, it's not easy, that's for sure. And I don't have the best track record in the world, I know. But I've been with your stepmother for 10 years now and I'm proud to say we're very happy.
Juno: Yeah?
Dad: Look, in my opinion, the best thing you can do is find a person that loves you for exactly what you are. Good mood, bad mood, ugly, pretty, handsome, whatever. The right

person's still gonna think the sun shines on your ass. That's the kind of person worth staying with.

Juno: Yeah, I think I've found that person.

Dad: Yeah, sure you have—your old D-A-D. You know I'll always love you and support you no matter what kind of pickle you're in—obviously!

Juno: Well, I think I'll go out for a while. I won't be back too late.

Dad: You did mean me, didn't you?

Whether or not Juno was whining, griping is in the ear of the listener. To be sure, her statement, "I'm just losing my faith in humanity," sets the stage for fatherly advice and a good schmooze conversation.

Unsolicited Advice: The Failed Schmooze

In the sequence from the film, Juno asks for her father's advice. As in real-life child-parent interactions, parents want to give advice so that their offspring can benefit from their wisdom. Parents want the best for their children—young or grown. Sometimes we try too hard. In the following exchange, Karen, a college student, has the exact same dialogue with her father every time she goes home for the weekend:[8]

Dad: So how's school?

Kelli: Pretty good, just a lot of work. My classes are going to be a lot more intense than I thought, but, I guess it's time.

Dad: Well, you really should start kicking it into gear. I mean, graduating early, and doing really well in your classes as it is, you really need to work harder. [smile]

Kelli: [laughing] Thanks, Dad.

Dad: But really, Kel, I'm really proud of you for sticking with it. It'll be tough, but I know you can do it.

Kelli: [smile] Thanks, Dad.

Dad: How's work going?

Kelli: Good. Tough but good. I'm only doing one day a week now, and even that might be too much with my classes, but we'll see. I need to make some money, but if it gets in the way, . . . we'll see.

Dad: Well, school does come first. Don't stress yourself out about it too much. Did you look for shoes?

Kelli: Yeah, I guess, but they're just expensive and seeing as I'm not sure how much longer I'm going to be staying there, I don't know if I really want to get any.

Dad: [smiling] Well, you know I gave you some money. You really should get some new ones; the ones you have are really going to mess you up later.

Kelli: I know I know, I'll work on it.

Good schmooze or failed schmooze? Encouraging advice or same old song and dance? He just wants her to succeed. Given the repeated nature of the conversation, she probably gets the idea. Nonetheless, judging from the laughing and smiling, we get the feeling that it is the good schmooze gone out of control.

"DON'T BOTHER. I'LL JUST SIT IN THE DARK": GUILTING

Family schmoozing is often about indirect ways to get others to do things or behave in certain ways. Guilting is one of these ways. The old joke about Jewish guilt goes something like this:

Q. How many Jewish mothers does it take the change a light bulb?

A. [sigh] Don't bother, I'll sit in the dark. I don't want to be a nuisance to anybody.

Of course, Jews have no monopoly on instilling guilt. But it is part of the stereotype of language used with children, especially adult children. My graduate student Rachel Organes did in-depth research on this very topic.[9] She found that people believed guilting is rarely a speaker's intent. Rather, guilting talk is the talk of control without being directly controlling. It is an attempt to get people to do what they want without having to be so forward as to issue a direct request.

In the previous joke, the mother really wants her children to do the task for her, but does not wish to ask. By saying she will sit in the dark, she implies that they should know better. The example is similar to a television commercial several years ago for Rice Krispy Treats. In the ad, the batch of treats is gone so quickly that it makes the mother's head spin. But does she complain? Heavens no! She merely says, "Don't worry. Your mother can make another batch." The wit is in the hidden reality that making another batch is so effortless. However, the opportunity for guilting is too tempting to pass up.

Columbia University doctoral student Rebekah Johnson has carried out a large-scale study that centers on adult child identity and guilting in family talk.[10] One of her important findings is that guilting persists beyond the time that children have passed into adulthood. Among her many examples from real family talk is the following. This time, the meal is Christmas brunch in Iowa (neither Jewish nor Catholic, traditionally thought of as guilting cultures) and the adult children, Ramona and Kenny, are home for the holidays:

Ramona: Well, I recall I was in bed the other day, and dad came in—I was actually reading, I had already been awake—and he [dad] came and said we have to get up now and drive. And I was like, "I want to eat breakfast first, I'm hungry, yesterday we shoveled for three hours and I didn't eat." And he's like, "Okay, eat quick, let's go." And I said, "Well, I'd like to shower, too." An' his sense of timing was different than my sense of timing in the morning anyway.

Mom: [to dad] And what was your reasoning?

Dad: 'Cause I just came home from taking you to work . . .

Kenny: Get it done. Do it while the roads are still junk so you can see what it's like.

Dad: And it was icy on the road so that we could actually drive on icy roads, by the time we went driving, most of the ice was gone so there was no way to replicate what, what I was trying to do.

Mom: And did you communicate that to her?

Dad: Sure. [ironic voice] I just said let's go whenever you're ready.

Ramona: Well, you didn't, I—I didn't realize the importance of leaving immediately for ice. And I also f-for some reason got this impression that we were gonna be out for an hour or two driving by the way were talking about it. So I was like, well I need to get completely ready first. Had I felt like it was going to be 20 minutes out and

	come back, I, maybe I could have been like, let's just go now and come back. I didn't get that sense, I felt like it was going to be a long thing. And I wanted to get all ready for the . . .
Mom:	So there was a definite lack of communication.
Dad:	But-but our common, but-but . . .
Mom:	Everybody knew what they were talking about, but the other person didn't.
Ramona:	Yeah.
Dad:	But we were able to actually replicate what we needed to get, so we got the right snow conditions.

Dad was eager to provide Ramona with practice driving in snowy and icy conditions. Ramona did not completely understand this. The fact that the family was able to discuss the miscommunication is a testament to good family schmoozing. The conversation is an example of the need for families to recognize grown children's adult needs when they become adults. But habits die hard.

Guilting can be done with humor and teasing. In the following situation, a young woman is home for the holidays and at a family gathering with relatives including Tio Jose and Tio Eddie, her uncles and her dad's brothers. As they go to sit in the garden (this is Florida, after all), they discover a paucity of seating. Tio Jose goes inside and grabs a chair; however, he grabs if for himself. The conversation is translated from Spanish:[11]

Mom:	Rudy [the dad], go inside and grab a chair for your daughters.
Dad:	Ay, no. Tell them to go get it.

[Tio Jose grabs a chair from inside]

Dad: Ay! What a gentleman! Grabbing a chair for the girls!

[Tio Jose brings the chair outside and sits in it. Everyone laughs.]

Dad:	Oh my God! I thought you were being a gentleman by bringing the girls a chair.
Mom:	We thought too much of him. [laughing]
Tio Eddie:	Of course he would only bring himself a seat.
Tio Jose:	What! I am a gentleman. Look. Jessie come sit here and Maria sit there. See! Now they are sitting.

Mom: After we told you!
Dad: Trust that from my brother. [laughing]

Some sorts of schmoozing may be universal across cultures. Here the adult brothers do mock scolding of each other, all in the form of teasing that is part of good schmoozing.

FAMILY SCHMOOZING HIGHLIGHTED: NAGGING

"I ASKED YOU TO PICK UP THOSE TOWELS"

Nagging occurs primarily in families. It is a type of talk that is relevant to both parent-child and couples communication. To be sure, it is widely agreed that nagging is unpalatable. It is certainly not good schmoozing. The question that arises, then, is why is nagging so ubiquitous in the domestic context?

The goal of nagging among family members is typically an attempt to accomplish the everyday necessary tasks of domesticity. One family member takes on the role of "cleaning boss" and attempts to assign household tasks. Why is it that this family member must nag while another with the same given power need only issue a request without nagging? The analysis of nagging data reveals clues to this mystery. The fact is it all has to do with power in family dynamics.

Nagging is related to griping, complaining, and scolding. But while it shares qualities with these speech behaviors, it is distinct in several ways. Complaining, at least the griping kind, occurs over a wide range of relationships among people and in many spheres of interaction. Recall how griping unfolds in social schmoozing:

Two male colleagues schmoozing over lunch:

A: Boy, the service here is so slow.
B: I know. By the time the burger arrives I won't even want it.

Small gripes are even heard between total strangers in an effort to establish a momentary solidarity based on a shared negative evaluation.[12] Direct complaining rarely occurs among interlocutors of great social distance, since it is a *face-threatening act*. When a person complains in order to obtain a remedy for an offense, it is the antithesis of rapport inspiring. Such is the case with nagging as well. It is a documented linguistic fact that neither direct complaining nor nagging prevail in ordinary social talk. This is because both are alienating rather than rapport-inspiring speech behaviors.

Nagging occurs most where the relationship has already been established and where it has less chance of hindering the relationship. One individual perceives an inherent right to nag or disapprove. Often we find nagging from parent to child as part of the socialization process. Consider this example, taken from an old Cosby show:

Season 2: Episode 7, "Rudy Suits Up"

Cliff (Cosby) walks into the living room and sits on the couch next to his teenage son, Theo, who is watching TV. Sondra, Cliff's oldest daughter, walks into the room, greets them, and sits on the couch on the other side of Theo. Cliff suddenly turns off the TV, and as he does this, Theo protests. At this point, Theo asks what they will do if they cannot watch TV. Cliff suggests they talk, and he proceeds to try to engage the children in talk about school with the typical question, "How's school?" Theo starts complaining that his math teacher had called him up to the chalkboard to do a math problem and made him stay there until he did it:

Theo: She had the nerve to turn her back on me and start teaching the class. . . . I was up there the whole period.
. . .

Sondra: Theo, I think I know why you're not performing well in class. . . . it sounds to me as if you're suffering from performance anxiety . . . you have trouble performing before an authority figure because you're intimidated. . . . Here's what you do. You create a picture in your mind. You visualize yourself standing in front of the chalkboard, working the problem correctly. And then you visualize Miss Westlake standing there smiling with her arms open, ready to embrace you.

[Theo's face turns to disgust.]
. . .

Cliff: Visualizing Miss Westlake is not your problem. I think that when you're standing up at the board, your problem

is that you don't know what you're doing. . . . What Theo
needs to do is visualize himself up in his bedroom, doing
his homework . . . So I think you ought to come along
with me because I want you to *visualize* yourself doing
your homework and *visualize* the fact that you are really
doing it and then visualize your father driving you to a college campus. I want you to visualize good-looking women
who want to date boys who *visualize* themselves with good
grades . . .

Theo: And I could also visualize myself in a nice sports car to
drive 'em around in.

Cliff: Good. And I also want you to visualize yourself paying for it.

[Theo gives him an amused but defeated look and continues up
the stairs.]

Because this is TV and not real life, the nagging is carried out
in humorous terms. Nonetheless, it is nagging, but with a clever
twist.

Real-life nagging is rarely humorous. If it were, it would not have
the negative connotation commonly associated with it. As seen in this
example from Cosby, nagging is tinged with the speech act of criticizing is found mostly in family talk. We rarely criticize strangers or
acquaintances. To do so would be tantamount to picking a fight. Family face-to-face interaction too often has nagging and criticizing as a
focus. To be sure, it is a turnoff—for children and spouses.

Nagging is never good family schmoozing. Let us take a look at
some conversational exchanges taken from real familial interactions.

"FOR THE UMPTEENTH TIME, WILL YOU PLEASE TAKE THE CLOTHES OUT OF THE DRYER?"

The excerpts of conversation in this section vary in context. These
situations range from interactions with roommates and parents to
interactions with spouses, partners, and children. The data represent
a variety of contexts and relationships with a considerable age span
of participants, from late teens to early middle age. I also conducted
five open-ended interviews, with three women and two men, in order
to delve more deeply into folk perceptions of nagging in families.

Interviews took place over the course of several months. Since from the spontaneous data it began to appear that occurrences and perceptions of nagging differed for women and men, the insights of individuals of both sexes lend insight in the interviews. The consultants' ages spanned some 30 years, from mid-thirties to mid-sixties, in order to uncover any generational differences in perceptions of nagging.

Nagging talk incorporates several moves. The first move is a request. When the request is repeated it becomes a reminder. When a reminder is repeated, it becomes nagging. Thus, it is not nagging until it follows a prior request and reminder. This is what accounts for the perception of nagging as a repeated behavior.

The initiating move, the request, is typically in the form of a command or a hedged request—with intimates, it is often very direct, as in "make sure you take the clothes out of the dryer as soon as it buzzes" (from wife to husband). With those who are less intimate (or more careful of politeness), it may be couched in the form of an interrogative, as in, "Why don't you change your shirt?" (from a girlfriend to her boyfriend in a relatively new relationship).

The second move by the nagger usually follows (sometimes after a lapse of time) noncompliance (or at least suspected noncompliance) with the request. It typically takes the form of a question. Examples would be: "Did you hear me?" or "Did you do as I asked you to do?" This second move is the reminder. It takes the interrogative form in order to ascertain compliance or noncompliance.

The third or subsequent move by the nagger is often an exclamation of some sort that expresses exasperation:

Look at this. It's all wrinkled!
I give up. I'm not asking you anymore!
Never mind. I'll do it myself!

A final, culminating move in nagging can either be a scolding or a threat, depending on the relationship (e.g., parent/child). None of these aspects of talk could reasonably be part of good family schmoozing.

To summarize, then, nagging is more than one move in an interaction—it comprises three or four turns. First is the request, typically followed by a question to ascertain compliance. The question serves as a reminder. Continued noncompliance often results in an expression of exasperation. Nagging, then, requires repetition. One request does not constitute nagging.

WHAT DO WE NAG ABOUT?

Nagging focuses on a variety of topics that revolve around domestic issues. The focus of nagging is typically something important to the nagger but not important to the person being nagged. Themes of nagging are diverse. They frequently focus on getting a family member to do a chore (e.g., take the clothes out of the dryer; clean the garage; take out the trash; start dinner). This theme accounted for almost half of the data. A quarter of the data focused on asking a family member to *stop* doing something. Most of the remainder of the sequences involved attempts by the nagger to get another person to call someone, either to find out information or to call them to stay in touch. Miscellaneous exchanges focused on such nagging as telling a grandchild to eat more and sermonizing to grown children about the need to teach their young children more about religion.

One of the female consultants, a middle-aged professional with a husband and two grown sons, talked about topics of nagging with a retrospective insight into how it occurred with her own family:

> In my experience, nagging has to do with matters of control and order in the environment or with schedules—matters that in the total scheme of things are relatively minor, but the person doing the nagging wants control of the environment or of schedules, that is, someone who's chronically late or whatever. . . . In other words, the wet towels lying around . . . are a threat to how I want my environment to be.
>
> I think I also take it more personally—all those little annoyances drive me crazy, while in the grand scheme of things, they are very unimportant. Of all the kinds of things I've nagged about, if something were to happen to the person who I love but nag to death, I would say I'd give anything to have them back; they could leave all the wet towels they want.

While the focus of nagging seems at the time to be important to the nagger, it may be understandable why it is unimportant to the recipient of the nagging.

Nagging of children was typically on themes that would do the child some good, such topics as taking medicine or doing homework. The following is an insight from one of the female consultants on nagging about homework:

As for homework, you want them to be successful in their own right. You have the perspective that they lack, that these grades and learning matter for the future, and as a reflection of you, I think it's a really pretty rare parent who is so detached from their children that they don't see them in some sense as a reflection.

Parents do not wish to see the natural consequences of having their children ignore such important requests. To not take medicine, for example, might result in continued symptoms. Parents try to control such aspects of life for children, and often resort to nagging to do so. Natural consequences for the child necessarily mean natural consequences for the parents. Parents understand these consequences better than their children. But is nagging necessary? Is it possible to gain compliance through other verbal means? If we want to transform nagging into good schmoozing, this puzzle needs to be solved.

DOES IT REALLY DO ANY GOOD?

Clearly, nagging is irritating and frustrating to both naggers and recipients. It is not surprising that topics of nagging tended to focus predominately on getting household chores done. The person who takes on the role of cleaning boss perceives an inherent obligation to assign chores. The question that arises is, does this role of "boss" really have power? Most of us know that this kind of boss must deal with frequent reneging on duties within the family unit. Perhaps children can get away with this in families, where unconditional parental love reigns. With couples, however, the case is somewhat different. The sort of power possessed by the nagger is distinct from true power typically found in social and professional relationships.

People with this latter type of inherent power seem never to need to issue a request more than once. In the following two sequences, the first is a request by a mother to her teenage son and the second to her teenage daughter:

A: Mother, to B: son, just before a party when trying to clean up:

A: What are you doing now?
B: Cleaning my aquarium.

A: I need for you to help clean up, not make new messes. Please do the carport!
B: Okay.

One half hour later:

A: Son, I need the carport cleaned.
B: Okay.
A: Have you started it yet?
B: No, not yet.
A: Fine. I give up. I'm not nagging you any more. I'm really angry now.

The same mother with her daughter:

A: Mother; B: daughter, age 19, at home from college on vacation:

A: B, Would you please empty the dishwasher?
B: Okay, in a minute.

Twenty minutes later:

A: B, I need the dishwasher done right now.
B: Yeah, I heard you.

One hour passes (A is angry now):

A: B, get down here right now and do what I've asked you to do!
B: Chill, mom. I said I'd do it.

Contrast these sequences with the following exchange, in which the father issues a directive to his son (the same boy as in the first sequence):

Father, A, to teenage son, B:

A: B, would you come downstairs please and put away those tools.
B: Okay. [immediately obeys]

The father in this sequence had no need to nag. Indeed, as the individual who gathered this data indicated, his children immediately comply with his requests.

The first two exchanges stand in sharp contrast to the third, where the father issued one directive and only one. His request is reminiscent of what occurs in workplace interactions where jobs need to get done. Nagging is rare in the workplace precisely because the rights and obligations of roles are strictly circumscribed. The consequences of not carrying out one's assigned tasks are clear-cut. Aside from systems of tenure, the majority of jobs have assigned duties, and if a worker does not carry these out, the natural consequence is likely to be loss of one's job. So, bosses ought never to have to nag employees, for if a request becomes a reminder and the task is not accomplished, the result is firing. As a result, workplace nagging is rare; family nagging is ubiquitous because we do not fire family members—at least not normally.

In the interview data, only one consultant talked of a coworker, a status inferior, who nags. She describes her secretary's nagging:

> I have a secretary that nags. She nags about formalities in the office. The office deals with clients, and there has to be a little spontaneity because not everyone is on time. Sometimes everybody comes at once. So you just have to get them in without the paper work. So she nags, and she nags until . . . even though you say you understand, she still nags. She gets so mad. She has to keep things in order. If we take the patients before the paperwork is done, it has to be put in order later, and it's confusing for her. I see it as nagging and I think she has to lighten up a bit.
>
> *She won't get fired if she keeps nagging?*
>
> No, because she keeps our office together.
>
> *So she has some sort of power. More than most secretaries do.*
>
> Oh yeah, she does. Nobody is organized enough. I guess we allow her to do it because we need it, we have to have it.

The issue of power/status/authority here is analogous to the familial situation. While the secretary is indeed a status inferior in some respects, she takes on a very important role in this workplace. Without her efforts, the office would fall apart. In some manner, then, this worker is responsible for running things smoothly, just as is the "cleaning boss" in a household. Given that the place could not function properly without her efforts, she has the right to nag and, indeed, on some level, this nagging, while not exactly appreciated, is considered justifiable by the counselors. She does not have to worry about losing her job. They need her. In contrast, she does not have the power of being a status superior to the counselors; therefore, she must resort to nagging at times. If indeed she had such power, she would need only to issue a request.

Since we do not typically fire our family members (though we do more with partners and spouses than with children), nagging, or causing someone to nag, has dire consequences in families. It is among the worst kinds of failed family schmoozing. While it has been known to lead to divorce, it rarely leads to disowning children. This may explain why nagging is a persistent speech behavior in the domestic arena between parents and offspring. Just why some parents nag while others need not do so must lie in family members' perceptions of power of the person issuing the request.

GENDER AND NAGGING

We have seen power (or lack of power) clearly demonstrated in the examples of nagging. A person who has inherent family power is able to have requests carried out quickly and immediately without having to resort to nagging. This appears to be the key to why it is that women are so frequently the naggers. In her 1990 best-selling book *You Just Don't Understand: Women and Men in Conversation*, sociolinguist Deborah Tannen[13] had the following to say about the gender stereotype of women as naggers:

> That women have been labeled "nags" may result from the interplay of men's and women's styles, whereby many women are inclined to do what is asked of them and many men are inclined to resist even the slightest hint that anyone, especially a woman, is telling them what to do. A woman will be inclined to repeat a request that doesn't get a response because she is convinced that she *really* wants him to do it. But a man who wants to avoid feeling that he is following orders may instinctively wait before doing what she asked, in order to imagine that he is doing it of his own free will. Nagging is the result, because each time she repeats the request, he again puts off fulfilling it. (p. 31)

Tannen hints of power play in this tug-of-war between the sexes when it comes to nagging. Power emanates from style differences, in her view. We must wonder which comes first—the style or the power. One male consultant reflected on this issue in talking about his former partner's nagging:

> She nagged me because she was weak. The person who's nagged starts to grow until there's an eventual satisfaction. . . . The nagger starts out with power and she gets half way through it and she's probably at your weakest point.

The term *nag* points to negative connotations of words terms typically associated with women. In linguistics, this phenomenon is referred to as *semantic derogation*. Such terms, while once having been neutral, have, over a period of time, taken on negative meanings. The noun *nag*, as defined by one dictionary consulted, is "a small light horse." This over time became derogated to mean an inferior or aged or unsound horse. This source even gives one old definition as "prostitute." Indeed, the examples offered by that dictionary all have female subjects as naggers: "She's a good wife but she does nag so"; "She nagged her husband at every opportunity." It seems clear that nagging has come to be known as female activity, despite the fact that the original definition made no specific reference to "female" horse.

One of the male consultants offered that we tend to refer to male nagging as hounding. Pursuing the connotations of *nagging* versus *hounding*, we immediately sense a difference. To the native English speaker, nagging is a negatively tinged behavior, and, indeed, so is hounding. Going back to the nouns from which the two terms are derived, however, we notice clear distinctions. While a nag is an inferior or unsound horse, a hound is a useful hunting dog.

Only a small number of the sequences in the data involved men nagging women: four in which a husband nagged his wife and two with a boyfriend nagging his girlfriend. In one, the husband asks his wife, every time she is about to get into the car, not to slam the door. This falls into the nagging category of speech because it has been requested repeatedly for several years, every time the couple gets into the car. It follows a single incident early in the relationship in which she slammed the car door so hard that it hurt the husband's ears.

In another sequence, the boyfriend and girlfriend are living together, and he deems it time to begin dinner preparations:

A is female graduate student in linguistics, age 25; B is a male graduate student in MBA program, age 29.

Situation: Both studying. They talked about preparing dinner. B asked A to cook rice.

B: Did you cook rice?
A: No, not yet. Isn't it too early?
B: Could you cook right now?
A: Okay.
B: No! We just have to warm up curry! It will take five minutes and rice takes 30 minutes.
A: Yeah, but that means we have to eat dinner at 5:30.
B: Okay, but don't be too late.

[Both studying again after 30 minutes, he hounds her again]

A: In a minute.

[after a minute]

B: Can you . . . Never mind!
A: Okay, okay.

[A walked into the kitchen and cooked the rice]

He wanted her to cook the rice but was ready to give up trying. Eventually, he succeeded. Perhaps in this particular relationship, such activity was perceived as her role, and either he would not do it, could not do it, or she knew how to make it better. He was obviously hungry and she was not. How could he have done this via good schmoozing? Perhaps he could have hinted about being hungry. He certainly could have "sweet-talked" her into cooking. The strategies are numerous.

In contrast to this example, in two-thirds of the data, women were the naggers. There were mothers nagging sons and wives nagging husbands. While my female undergraduates collected data on their mothers nagging their brothers, the male students collected data on their mothers nagging them. Perhaps mothers find the need to nag male offspring more than female offspring. If so, it lends credence to Tannen's observation about men's refusal to carry out women's domestic requests. An example follows:

Billy has many points on his driver's license and is in danger of losing his car insurance. He has gotten a ticket for an expired registration in the past and it is now time to renew his registration. On the phone with his mom:

Mom: Have you renewed your registration yet?
Billy: No, not yet.
Mom: You know you won't have insurance if you get any more points on your license. You got a ticket for that last year.

At the end of the conversation:

Mom: You're going to send your registration in this week?
Billy: No, but I got the form and I'll send it when I finish my exams.

Perhaps young men, as in this exchange, are rehearsing their resistance to being nagged when they refuse to comply with their mothers' requests. Likely they will go on to be the partners and spouses that Tannen described. The fact that mothers nag sons more than daughters hints at the socialization aspect of "boys will be boys." When the boys become husbands, they continue the power struggle. Their wives now take on the role of nagger.

The next sequence is a typical example of wife nagging husband. The mom, a young mother (age 25), wants to take a shower after giving the kids a bath. Their daughter Mary (age four) wants to draw, and mom asks dad (husband, late twenties) to play with their daughter:

Mom: B, Mary wants to draw and color. I have to shower. Can you play with her? All the crayons and papers are on the table already.
Dad: Okay.

While mom is coming out of the bathroom, she hears Mary complain to her father:

Mary: But dad, you too have to paint!
Mom: I asked you to play with her.
Dad: [who was reading the newspaper] Ah! I have to draw, too?

As mom gets dressed, she hears Mary again asking her father to draw with her.

Mom: [to her husband] You can't read the paper now! We have
      two kids. One plays with one and the other one plays with
      the other.
Dad: [No response. He goes to play with their young son].

A year later, this marriage dissolved. Clearly, nagging behavior was
one of the culprits in the bad schmoozing habits that led to constant
conflict.

How do we remedy such a situation? This is tough. If nagging is
failed schmoozing, women will have to figure out another way to sat-
isfy their requests. One logical way, of course, is to give up the role of
boss in matters domestic.

One of the female consultants had the following insight into gender
and nagging:

> If most nagging is domestic and women are responsible for the
> domestic part of life, then these issues are going to resonate more
> with them than with the men. Even women in their twenties who
> are married or partnered are more responsible for that sphere of
> life even if they're working.

One of the male consultants gave his insight:

> Well, don't take offense, but it's only been since the beginning
> of this century that women have begun to have authority. When
> women are coming from the other end, they feel that they're not as
> authoritative as men, so they have to keep asking and keep asking:
> "Honey, take the garbage out." And the man says to himself . . .
> "I'll take it out when I get around to it."

Clearly, gender, power, and authority enter into conditioning for all
speech behavior. We speak in a certain way due to our socialization. If
girls are socialized into cooperative styles emphasizing symmetry and
boys into hierarchical styles emphasizing status,[14] it is no wonder that
women nag the boys and men in their lives. In a world of cooperation, women may expect compliance with reasonable requests; nevertheless, when confronted with the hierarchical style of boys and men,
it just does not work. Requests need to become repeated reminders
that turn into nagging. If our styles constrain how we request and the
responses to requests, then by nagging we lose power. Without power,

we are forced into nagging. Failed schmoozing is the result. The cycle is vicious.

NAGGING: THE FAMILIAL CONFLICT ARENA

With the exception of sporadic incidents in other spheres of interaction, nagging as the failed schmooze is found principally in families. It is a speech behavior that is not typically encountered except among intimates or near intimates. One rarely hears of nagging among friends and acquaintances, for it is within this arena that interlocutors find themselves doing a delicate dance of negotiating relationships. Consider the following insight from a female consultant:

> Nagging is repetitive action, asking someone to do something repetitively. It's mostly in the family. I don't nag my friends.
> *Why not?*
> Because I want them to stay my friends. So, I guess I take for granted the family.

When friends and acquaintances develop a closer relationship, they may begin to develop speech behavior that approaches that of the domestic scene. Certainly, there will be an increase in teasing. The teasing, as indicated earlier, can stay positive and be part of good schmoozing. Nagging is rarely if ever a part of the good family schmooze.

CONCLUSION

Unfortunately, family interaction is all too often bad schmoozing. Negative talk (including nagging, contradicting, guilting, and so on) is the source of a good deal of family conflict. These are face-threatening acts. Family members are the most precious people in our lives. That negativity abounds in familial interactions is a result of close bonds and attempts to make sure things go well in the lives of our loved ones. Too often, it backfires.

Certainly, how we talk with members of our families affects the most important people in our lives. What can we learn from the analysis of ubiquitous bad schmoozing in families? This question is timely and important. The heightened awareness of how we talk and the repercussions of the talk is a first step toward family harmony with partners, children, and extended family.

The understanding of how family talk affects child socialization and relationships between couples and other family members is critical to the creation of a more egalitarian society. The transmission of societal norms and values begins in interaction with family members from early on in childhood. The creation of more democratic interactions in the larger world must begin in the family domain.

It is true that parents have the important job of teaching children the norms of appropriate talk. These norms take years to be fully inculcated. However, more than just appropriateness and politeness are taught in family interaction, as we have seen. The good schmooze with children provides a model for adult relationships with loved ones. The seeds of harmonious relationships are sown at home.

NOTES

1. Benedict Carey, "Video Project Holds up Mirror to Families," *Gainesville Sun*, May 23, 2010.

2. Diana Boxer and Florencia Cortes-Conde, "From Bonding to Biting: Conversational Joking and Identity Display," *Journal of Pragmatics* 27 (1997): 275–294.

3. Data collected by Lindsay Walters, 2010.

4. Deborah Tannen, *I Only Say This Because I Love You* (New York: Random House, 2002).

5. Data collected by Nicole Brabec, 2010.

6. Data collected by Amanda Garcia, 2009.

7. Data collected by Sara Hashem, 2010.

8. Data collected by Kelli Crowthers, 2009.

9. Rachel Organes, "'If You Do That I'm Going to Be Heartbroken': The Language of Jewish American Guilting" (MA thesis, University of Florida, 2009).

10. Rebekah Johnson, "Discursive Practices in the Family Context: Negotiating Identity, Guilt and Acknowledgment in Family Discourse" (paper presented at the American Association of Applied Linguistics conference, Atlanta, March 6, 2010).

11. Data collected by Maria Castillo, 2009.

12. Diana Boxer, *Complaining and Commiserating: A Speech Act View of Solidarity in Spoken American English* (New York: Peter Lang, 1993).

13. Deborah Tannen, *You Just Don't Understand: Women and Men in Conversation* (New York: William Morrow, 1990).

14. Daniel N. Maltz and Ruth Borker, "A Cultural Approach to Male/Female Miscommunication," in *Language and Social Identity*, ed. John J. Gumperz (New York: Cambridge University Press, 1983), 195–217.

CHAPTER 3

Schmoozing at Work in the Workplace

You think that the heads of state only have serious conversations, [but] they actually often begin really with the weather or, "I really like your tie."

Madeline Albright

INTRODUCTION

President Bill Clinton's secretary of state, Madeline Albright, was the first woman in this important role. In her interactions with world leaders, she used what many people, particularly women, know intuitively about the good schmooze. Certainly, Albright's world of work was as important as any could possibly be. Nonetheless, as the above quote shows, she invariably found good schmoozing to be the prelude to serious diplomatic negotiations.

In an interview on National Public Radio (NPR)[1] about her new book, *Read My Pins*, Albright went on to tell how she took what I refer to as good schmoozing to a new level through costume jewelry pins. In fact, pins helped her tremendously in making small talk with heads of state. She used pins as symbols to convey a mood about what she wanted to accomplish in her diplomatic dealings on any particular day. So, there always was an immediate conversational opener and topic in addition to the weather. After all, "I like your tie" is analogous to the compliment "Interesting pin." As we have seen, compliments are conversational openers in some contexts. In the context of diplomatic negotiations, however, one seldom thinks about this particular speech act as the schmooze that is the preamble to more serious talk.

Various societies other than ours know that small talk, or schmoozing, is a must-do before getting down to business. It lubricates the social setting that leads effortlessly into work interaction. For example, the Japanese never start right into business talk, even in the most serious of discussions in business meetings. They consider it rude to dive right into work talk without some prior schmoozing about the family and other "small talk" topics. Madeline Albright used this same tactic to her advantage. Her pins were not only topics of small talk, they also signaled important information to her interlocutors. Albright goes on: "This all started when I was ambassador at the U.N. and Saddam Hussein called me a serpent. I had this wonderful antique snake pin. So when we were dealing with Iraq, I wore the snake pin." After that incident, Albright decided that it might be fun to speak through her pins. She used them strategically, as conversational schmoozer openers leading to diplomatic talks: "As it turned out, there were just a lot of occasions to either commemorate a particular event or to signal how I felt. There were balloons, butterflies, and flowers to signify optimism and, when diplomatic talks were going slowly, crabs and turtles to indicate frustration."[2]

We tend to think of workplace schmoozing as conflated with the concept of networking. There is even the joke, "Work is the curse of the drinking classes." This is a reversal of the real adage, "Drink is the curse of the working classes." To say that work interferes with drinking alcoholic beverages is tantamount to saying that work unfortunately impinges on social life. Perhaps if there were more talk that brings with it the warm feelings of pure interaction, the world of work would not be so dreaded by so many.

In fact, much schmoozing in the sphere of work is exactly the same as it occurs in the social sphere. That is, it is the kind of talk that people do when they *chat*, as opposed to *chat up*. For Madeline Albright, the chat included concrete symbols of her mood. They served as conversational openers—the small talk that preceded important diplomatic transactions. In the mundane world of work, chatting can entail verbal techniques for sending the message, "I'm interested in you and I am a person you want to talk to."

CHATTING OR CHATTING UP?

The novel *Snowed In* by Christina Bartolomeo tells the story of Sophie, a young woman searching for a heightened sense of self-assurance. A good deal of schmoozing between close female friends is highlighted in the book. For example, in a phone conversation with her best friend, Marta, Sophie encourages Marta to attend her work-place holiday office party. This is pure social schmoozing. Each friend takes a turn commiserating and encouraging the other to take positive steps in her life:

Sophie: Hey, how are you doing with your date for the office party?

Marta: I'm thinking of not going . . . to tell the truth, I'm getting tired of all this . . . I work like a dog. I go out at night and then I'm working too, **schmoozing** half the time.

This exchange illustrates how the concept of schmoozing at work has devolved into an unpleasant chore—never a fun way to pass the workday. Recall that this sort of devolution is termed *semantic deroga-tion*. That is, a term that was once positive has taken on a negative connotation. The good schmooze should not be construed work. It used to be enjoyable. This lost art ought to be reclaimed, even in the workplace.

Julia Child was an excellent example. She was not afraid of the good schmooze; in fact, it helped to make her career. A cursory reading of her biography or viewing of the 2009 film *Julie and Julia* clearly illus-trates. Soon after her marriage to a diplomat in 1949, Julia moved to live with her husband in Paris. She did not yet speak French. Julia was not daunted by the fact that, back in those days, the French disdained anyone who could not speak good French.[3] Despite this shortcoming, she had enough self-confidence to make friends with the baker, the butcher, and all with whom she came into contact on a daily basis. No doubt her schmoozing skills—even across language barriers—helped launch her fame as the consummate food personality of her age.

One evening while in the women's restroom of a restaurant or theater powdering her nose, Julia struck up a conversation with two French women doing the same. She complained to them that she was studying at the Cordon Bleu, but that the headmistress of the school did not think highly of her skills and would not allow her to take the test to certify her as a Cordon Bleu graduate. As coincidence would have it, the other two women just happened to be working on a cookbook project at the time. The restroom conversation was the opening of a relationship of friendship. It later became the most important work relationship of Julia's life and career. That brief schmoozing encounter eventually landed Julia the task of writing their book to appeal to the American audience. The rest is history.

The good schmooze was the door into a social relationship. The social relationship became a working partnership. The benefits of chatting were indirect. They derived from the warm feelings of interaction. It was not chatting-up.

WORKPLACE SCHMOOZING IN THE MEDIA

Undoubtedly, there is a fine line between just chatting and chatting-up. Consider the following conversation, taken from the film *Two Weeks' Notice*.[4]

June Carver is applying to be George Wade's assistant to replace Lucy Kelson, George's current assistant. Lucy is conducting the impromptu interview with June. Due to its length, the lines in this sequence are numbered consecutively.

1. Lucy and June [simultaneously]: Hi. [they shake hands]

2. June: It's a pleasure to meet you.

3. Lucy: You too.

4. June: I know I don't have an appointment, so feel free to throw me out at any point.

5. Lucy: Well, I have security on standby. [they each chuckle]

6. Lucy: Uhh, have a seat, please.

7. June: Thanks.

8. June: Oh my God, I'm still shaking.

9. Lucy: Yeah.

10. June: But I have to tell you, Ms. Kelson, you're a legend here.

11. Lucy: Me?

12. June: Editor of the *Law Review*, those letters you wrote on the Richmond case; you're an inspiration to a lot of us.

13. Lucy: Well, yeah, I . . .

14. June: I know I don't have a strong background in property, but neither did you when you graduated, and look what you've accomplished.

15. Lucy: Oh, well, you know, not—not that much, really. I just . . .

16. June: And, there's this. Obviously, I've never met Mr. Wade, but in an issue of *Public Policy* magazine, he was being interviewed about the challenges of urban development, and he said that, um . . .

17. June: Is it ridiculous that I'm quoting this?

18. Lucy: No. Not—not yet.

19. June: [quoting the article] "When I think about how architecture can shape a community and turn strangers into neighbors, how the right design for a park makes people feel secure, how our school building can be functional and beautiful, so our kids feel engaged instead of imprisoned . . ." When I read that it made me feel like I'd be working for a cause, not just a company.

[George Wade walks in while she is quoting him and Lucy is smiling throughout the reading of the quote]

20. George: Mmm . . . okay. You're hired. [June stands up and turns around to face him]

21. June: You're Mr. Wade. [they shake hands]

22. George: Yeah, someone has to be. Although, I didn't write that; Lucy did.

23. Lucy: No, you did. I remember being shocked.

24. George: See? We've been working together so long it's hard to remember who did what.

25. June: Sounds like an amazing team.

26. Lucy: George, do you mind . . .

27. June: [speaking to George] I was just saying how incredibly presumptuous it was of me to come waltzing in here, but Ms. Kelson was nice enough to see me, so . . .

28. Worker: They're calling from the zoning commission, Lucy.

29. Lucy: Oh, right. Okay. June, why don't we set up a proper interview for tomorrow.

30. George: No, that's all right. It's all right. I could finish up with June.

The fact that June gets through an impromptu interview and even gets noticed by the boss demonstrates the success of her schmoozing. This sequence aptly demonstrates the fine line between schmoozing that is good chatting and chatting-up, or "sucking up."

The ability to use humor and wit is as effective in the workplace as anywhere else, as seen in the previous interaction. In line 4, June quips that Lucy should feel free to "throw her out." Lucy comes back with a quick sarcastic retort, "We have security on standby." Obviously, each is able to demonstrate a lighthearted goodwill that serves to set the stage for the interview as a more casual conversation. June employs several schmoozing techniques. First, in line 8, she confesses that she is nervous when she says, "I'm still shaking." This admission of vulnerability shows her to be humble—a quality most admire. However, in line 10, June quickly recovers when, in almost the same breath as admitting her nervousness, she offers a compliment to Lucy about her being a "legend." This might be chatting-up rather than just chatting. However, June's ability to convey the compliment smoothly makes it part of displaying positive interactional feelings.

The interview proceeds in this manner. When June starts quoting something George wrote, she manages to interject a question in line 17 asking if it is ridiculous to be quoting it. Her question is somewhat of a self-denigration, again showing her to be a person of humility rather than a braggart. Of course, when George walks in and happens to overhear June's quoting him, he jokes "You're hired" in line 20—a typical line from a script. Nonetheless, scripted scenes such as this one often give us glimpses of how things can be done in talk.

Because there is such a blurred distinction between good schmoozing (the original sense of the term) and its opposite, schmoozing-up (the current sense of schmoozing), interactions such as this one run the risk of being interpreted as the bad schmooze. It is a short distance between perceiving it as chatting or chatting-up.

CHATTING-UP BACKFIRES

An episode from the popular TV comedy *The Office* aptly illustrates the fine line.

These snippets of conversation are from the show season 5, episode 20, titled "Dream Team":

The Dunder Mifflin office just got a new boss, Charles Miner. Charles walks by Andy's desk. Andy is leaning back and looking at his computer desktop happily, which has a picture of two guys playing soccer.

Charles: You a soccer fan?
Andy: Oh. Oh my God. I'm so embarrassed. You weren't sup-
         posed to see this. This is like, my secret obsession.
Charles: Well, that makes two of us.
Andy: No way!
Charles: Yeah.

The show then cuts to Andy alone, where he admits, "I hate soccer. But guess who doesn't hate soccer? Charles Miner." When Charles walks away, Andy looks over at fellow coworker Jim Halpert. The show cuts to Jim alone, who states, "I've never been a kiss up. It's just not how I operate."

Later in the show, Jim finds himself talking to the new boss and trying to get the new boss to like him. As Jim listens in on Andy and Charles discussing a soccer game, the following dialogue ensues:

Charles: What about you, Jim? You a fan of the game?
Jim: Uh, no. Nope. Not really.
Charles: Well, it's not for everybody I suppose.
Jim: Ah, it's cause I'm more of a player.
Charles: Oh yeah?
Jim: You bet.

Dwight, another coworker, senses Jim trying to schmooze and jumps into the conversation in order to test him.

Dwight: Really, Jim. I had no idea you played soccer. 'Cause you
        never ever talk about it.
Jim: Well, I do. I play.

Dwight: You can be so modest sometimes.

Jim: Well, maybe we should get back to work.

Dwight: Maybe you and Charles should kick the soccer ball around.

Jim: Maybe we will someday.

Dwight: Maybe you will tonight after work, whaddaya say?

Charles: It's a great idea, Dwight!

Dwight: Oh ideas are just part of what I bring to the table. I don't try to be anything that I'm not.

Charles: Whaddaya say, Jim? Huh, you wanna play some soccer? Hey, anybody else?

Dwight: Game on!

Charles: See you on the field there, bro. Can't wait!

Obviously, Jim's attempt at sucking up with Charles did not go over well. He made himself out to be something that he was not—a soccer player. In truth, he could not play the game, but he was merely trying to find a commonality with Charles. This attempt went overboard. Bad schmooze. It usually backfires in that it does not bring the participants in the interaction closer—on the contrary!

The previous example from *The Office* is quite different from the example from the film *Two Weeks' Notice*. Both Jim, in the TV show, and June, in the film, were trying to get ahead in the world of work. However, they went about the talk-in-interaction differently. June showed both humility and a sense of humor—good schmoozing. Jim was simply portraying himself as something that he was not.

TALK SHOWS AND WORKPLACE SCHMOOZING

Schmoozing as ordinary small talk has become all but reified in the modern media. Talk shows, both on radio and TV, epitomize this phenomenon. The talk show genre has seen a phenomenal increase in popularity over the past decade. I posit that this is due to our need to participate in schmoozing, albeit as audience if not as direct interlocutors.

The popular TV talk show *The View* is an excellent example of schmoozing for a viewing audience. While the talk that goes on in the show is workplace talk for the panelists and guests, it closely resembles ordinary social schmoozing. The schmoozing that occurs on *The View*, among all women, is tantamount to gossip. A sampling of any single episode is illustrative. In one 2009 show, the topics of the talk were the following:

1. David Letterman's situation of being blackmailed over affairs that he had with women.
2. Cohost Lucy Ling's sister's ordeal on being held prisoner in North Korea.
3. Should Lucy Ling have a baby?
4. Bernie Madoff's life depicted in a book by Brian Ross, who was interviewed for this show.

This episode of *The View* thus focused on scandals and stories that highlighted sex, money, children, and everything in between. This media workplace is, of course, a public one; nonetheless, schmoozing abounds and folks at home tune in to listen as if they themselves are part of the good schmooze. Schmoozing is the ingredient that captures a loyal following.

Perhaps the quintessential success story of master of television interview schmoozing is Oprah Winfrey. She has been called "The Mistress of Daytime Television." A better characterization of this popular figure might be "The Queen of Schmooze."

Winfrey interviewed former vice presidential candidate Sarah Palin on November 16, 2009. Here is an excerpt from that interview (W is Winfrey; P is Palin):

W: One final question—should I be worried because I've heard that you are going to get your own talk show?
P: [laughter] Um.
W: Yeah, come on. [sing song]

[pause]

P: Oprah, you are the queen of talk shows [O: no] there's nothing to ever [O: no, no] to worry about.
W: Should I be worried?
P: And you are and you can't shut off my mike so let me say this too, Oprah, about the [pause] or maybe you can you're the boss,
W: No, I won't, go ahead.

P: The in-inspiration that you have provided, I got to talk to
     Oprah just a little bit backstage beforehand and I talked about
     um in the nineties, those were the years where I was a stay-
     at-home mom got to watch you more than I watch you now
     but got to watch you back then and being quite inspired by
     some of the challenges that you were facing and you overcame
     those too just seeming too as a normal American woman with
     a lot on your plate being able to handle it all you provided
     a lot of inspiration and I appreciate what you've done all of
     these years.
W: Thank you for saying that.
P: Thank *you*.
W: Thank you for saying that.

The tone is set as an informal one, unlike the serious interviews to
which Palin was subjected during the presidential campaign. Here
Winfrey and Palin are having a warm chat in which Palin compliments Winfrey in a lengthy monologue where she highlights her
own identity. This looks like Palin is just shooting the breeze with
the famous talk show host. Palin avoids Oprah's question. Instead,
she goes on to talk about how she derived inspiration from watching
Oprah's show when she was a stay-at-home mom. In so doing, Palin
displays her identity as similar to many in the viewing audience—
just ordinary women with Oprah to look forward to as part of their
humdrum daily life.

Whether or not Palin succeeded at schmoozing is a matter of one's
perspective. No doubt for many she succeeded. She did avoid Winfrey's question, but who noticed? In the avoidance, she shifted the
focus from being portrayed in an identity of media personality to one
of ordinary folk. It attempted to project a certain image with which
the women of the audience could identify—the typical housewife
taking care of ordinary but important tasks of home and hearth. She
cast herself as "one of us" rather than someone important like Oprah
Winfrey.

These schmoozing tactics are subtle. Is this the good schmooze? If
the benefits are indirect, it is. It would benefit Palin to come across
as a person who is likable. The direct benefit would be to get viewers
to see her as someone they would like to have in office. This kind of
schmoozing, for direct benefit, is the way the concept of schmooze has
devolved to mean "working the room."

Clearly, interviews on talk shows are never exactly the same as ordinary social talk. This is workplace talk that is aimed to simulate ordinary social conversation but that displays the identities of interviewees (and also interviewers) as certain kinds of people. We all display aspects of our multiple identities whenever we schmooze. Media talk shows are no different.

"Man, Have We Got a Program for You Today": Comedy Talk Shows and Schmoozing

The comedy news programs currently popular on TV, for example, *The Daily Show* and *The Colbert Report*, are parodies of serious news programs. They function to highlight both how schmoozing is done in interviews of celebrities and authors as well as, in Colbert's case, to give an ironic twist to such schmoozing. At the end of his show on October 12, 2009, Jon Stewart, as he often does, set up Colbert's show, which comes on the air immediately after his. In this sequence, the two put a sarcastic spin on schmoozing:

Stewart: Let's check in with our good friend Stephen Colbert at *The Colbert Report*, Stephen?
Colbert: Nice to see you, Jon, how's the family?
Stewart: My wife is good, yours?
Colbert: Great. Anyway, tonight on *The Report*, which basic cable news host's family is just doing good, and whose is doing great? We'll give you the scoop.
Stewart: Stephen, you can't do that. You can't ask me how they're doin' and then . . .
Colbert: [interrupts] Chilly today, huh?
Stewart: Yeah, I guess it's chilly, I mean, I didn't really go outside . . .
Colbert: [interrupts] Well, watch the Colbert exclusive, today's weather. We'll report what other shows don't have the balls to investigate, Jon?
Stewart: I was just making small talk.
Colbert: No such thing as small talk, Jon. Only small shows.

The humorous focus on "small talk" is parodied. Ordinary schmoozing about the family and weather are rendered ridiculous through

Colbert's ostensible competition over these small talk phenomena. This comedic parody illustrates that small talk is the quintessential ingredient of currently popular media shows that focus on talk. These talk shows demonstrate how schmoozing in the public workplace functions to draw people to tune in.

SCHMOOZING AND POLITICS IN TELEVISION AND FILM

As we have seen, lighthearted humor and wit coupled with talk that displays one as a person of humility is a golden combination. Examples come from all kinds of workplaces, even the highest office of our nation. President Obama is perhaps the consummate example of these two qualities. His interview with David Letterman in late September 2009 provides a good example. He was asked by Letterman if race was the issue behind recent Tea Party protests of his health care reform agenda. Obama replied, "You know, I was black before I become president." The statement is humorous in stating the obvious. It was also stated in a spirit of warmth and approachability, with neither hostility nor defensiveness. It sent the message, "I got elected despite my skin color, and folks should not think the objection to my policies has anything to do with that."

Indeed, not having a sense of humor can be hazardous to a president. Richard Nixon was a prime example. He was portrayed precisely in this light in the 2008 film *Frost/Nixon*. It featured the famous 1977 David Frost interviews with the former president. While Frost wished to highlight Nixon's scandalous involvement in Watergate, Nixon's goal was to exonerate himself. He attempted to schmooze with Frost, not to win him over, but to disarm him. Nixon's team had done a background analysis of Frost and discovered that Frost came from a fairly humble background before he went on to study at Cambridge:

Nixon: Did the snobs look down on you? No matter how high I got, they still looked down on us.

Frost: I don't know what you're talking about.

Nixon: Yes, you do. Oh, come on now. No matter how many columns are written about us . . . it's still not enough. We still feel like the little losers they told us we were.

Frost was not going to be charmed by such talk. Perhaps he was disarmed—but the viewer is left to wonder if good schmoozing might have done a better job at disarming.

Near the end of film, Frost comes to visit Nixon to say goodbye before flying back to England:

Nixon: You know all those parties you have they're always talking about?

Frost: Yes.

Nixon: Do you actually enjoy them?

Frost: Of course.

Nixon: You've got no idea how fortunate that makes you—liking people, being liked, having that facility. Your life must be charmed. I don't have it. Never did. It kind of makes you wonder why I chose a life that hinged on being liked. I'm better suited to a life of thought, to intellectual discipline. Maybe we got it wrong. Maybe you should have been a politician and I a rigorous interviewer.

Frost: Maybe.

There is at times a blurred line between social and workplace schmoozing. What works for social life usually also works for workplace relationships. Wit and humor may serve to charm and disarm, but neither is a goal of good schmoozing.

"WANNA GO TO HAPPY HOUR?": SCHMOOZING AT WORK WITH COWORKERS

Kathy (pseudonym) is a competent office manager at my university. I use her as an example of the good schmoozer in the workplace because somehow she is able to have harmonious relationships with all who work with her. This includes staff members who work as her subordinates and superiors, in addition to faculty and administrators. Just as in any other workplace, in academia one is likely to encounter and have to work with a range of personalities—from quiet and introverted, to bombastic and loud-mouthed, with everything in between.

As office manager of a small department, Kathy deals with the department chair and at least a dozen faculty members who are always requesting some of her time for this reason or that. However, Kathy works most directly with one other staff member, Julie. While Kathy has only worked in this office for six months, Julie has been employed there for six years. In fact, Julie wanted Kathy's job. This could have made for a very awkward situation. Because Julie did not get the job, Kathy became Julie's supervisor. This was particularly uncomfortable because Julie was in the position of having to teach Kathy several aspects of her job while being Kathy's subordinate.

At first, Julie was furious when she was not hired for this position that is higher on the employment ladder in the institution. After a few months, however, it became obvious that the bad feelings had abated, and the two women developed a professional and personal rapport. How did this happen?

My observations of the interactions between the two employees were as observer and overhearer. I became curious to know just how Kathy managed to win Julie over; moreover, I was interested in how Julie resolved her bad feelings about being passed over. The good schmooze had to be at the core.

I requested about a half hour of time from both Kathy and Julie to get their thoughts. The following gives insight into how schmoozing skills in the workplace worked for Kathy's relationship with her program assistant and Julie's relationship with her new supervisor.

KATHY: SCHMOOZING TO SMOOTH THINGS OUT

Kathy told me that when she heard there was an inside candidate for the position, she honestly thought it was "wired" to the insider. So, when she got the job offer, she was surprised, but delighted. But she was concerned about the fact that Julie, whose boss she would be, did not get the job. "I wondered how she would feel about having me as her supervisor." The department chair, Kathy's boss, told Kathy that Julie is a very nice person and that she should not be worried. Nonetheless, Kathy was still uneasy.

On Kathy's first day of work, Julie had just received a disciplinary letter. Needless to say, Julie was quite perturbed and was up-front about the situation to Kathy (Julie is a very sharing person—this is one of her charms). The disciplinary action derived from Julie's attendance at work. Here is how Kathy handled the sticky situation:

Kathy to Julie: I don't blame you for feeling this way. Please feel free to always communicate to me any concerns that you may have.

Kathy indicated that by the end of the first day, she felt that they had reached a pretty good understanding and that "we were going to have a good working relationship."

I asked her, "Was it awkward?" She replied:

Not for very long. We hit such a personal note discussing the things we had in common. We did this through chit-chat as we sat here next to each other at our desks. For example, looking at the photos at her desk, I said, "I see you have a daughter—I have a son about the same age." And something like, "What kinds of things do you like to do when you're not in the office?" Questions of getting to know her better. The evolution of the conversation on that day, after discussing our children, was a big part in our good working relationship. It led to "Where have you worked on campus?" By the end of the first week, I felt that she was someone I could be a friend with. The first couple of weeks I felt really comfortable and we shared a lot. Then both of us seemed to get the feeling—maybe I shouldn't divulge so much! But now we have a friendly relationship. Our conversations as we sit at our desks are more like catching up with a friend. I take kind of a big sister role—try to mentor her more in a personal role, not just a work-place role. I try to advise her gently.

Me: Do you get together outside of work?
Kathy: We have intentions but we haven't socialized. We have gone to department happy hour together.
Me: How did that come about?
Kathy: I said to her one Friday as the workday was ending, "I thought I might go—do you want to?"

I then asked Kathy to tell me about her previous work setting and the relationships she had with coworkers. She said:

Kathy: I actually supervised some pretty unpleasant folks.
Me: How did you deal with them?
Kathy: Diplomatically. I tried to stay friendly and cheerful. There was an older woman who was a sweetie pie when we first hired her. Then it changed when her probation period was done. She became difficult and began fighting with coworkers—backstabbing. Things never really resolved

with her. She would be happy for awhile. We devised processes that would keep certain personalities from interacting with each other. It wasn't as efficient as it could have been had she not been difficult.

Julie: The Consummate Schmoozer at Work

I asked Julie about how she felt upon her first day working with Kathy and knowing that she did not get the job. Was she resentful?

Julie: I wasn't angry at her. If your husband's cheating on you you're not mad at the other woman, but at him. No, I wasn't angry at her. It was just—my feelings were hurt—because they didn't choose me. I took it personal—I'm very sensitive.

Me: You wear your heart on your sleeve, as the saying goes.

Julie: . . . but Kathy is very sensitive, too. In that way, we're very much alike. I know that I can be a handful. The flip side is that there's never a question of where I am emotionally. I get over it quickly once I get it off my chest.

Julie is indeed a person who is right up front about sharing her feelings with those around her, and this is true now even with her new supervisor, Kathy. As soon as they established common ground, you could see and hear them sharing stories about their lives. Julie, especially, has no reservations about personal disclosures—something women often do with each other to establish common bonds.[5] Recall that when Kathy found herself disclosing to Julie early on, she had to ask herself if she should stop—was she divulging too much to a coworker—and a recent coworker who was her subordinate? The work relationship is different than the social one. In this domain, there is more to lose. One cannot be too careful; however, one does want to establish rapport, and this is one way to do it—sharing of personal disclosures.

Back to Julie's narrative:

Julie: I said to myself before that first day working together, "I'm not going to train her." I was thinking my supervisors must be crazy. However, the first day she was here, I made sure to be very welcoming. Thank heaven she was so nice and approachable. It made it a reason for me not to have resentment. We became friends very quickly—same interests, similarities . . .

Me: Like what?

Julie: Where we have both lived, for example. We've both been here all our lives and attended this college. We made connections in casual conversation. Kathy is not as vocal [as I am] if she doesn't like things.

Me: You seem to get along with everyone.

Julie: Yeah, but not everyone sees that I'm clever, not just ditsy. I'm absent-minded, but I kind of like to ride that wave— not so much responsibility to take. I make up for it on the flip side. I might forget to do something . . .

Me: You talk to people very well.

Julie: Being able to read people and paying close attention without being obvious—their personality type.

Me: Can you teach it to people?

Julie: First, you can't take yourself too seriously—requires a lot of self-reflection. . . . you have to be able to have lunch with the custodian as well as the president of the college and feel equally comfortable. But it has to be genuine. I have to be optimistic—see the good in whoever it is. It has to be from the heart. You can't just try to be that way. You have to genuinely feel mutual respect and have or want to have some kind of mutual history.

Clearly, I was trying to ascertain if Julie believed good schmoozing could it be taught. She hit on the difference between chatting and chatting-up. The good schmooze has to be authentic, or as Julie put it, "from the heart." Julie continues on:

Julie: We're work friends. There's a difference between coworkers, work friends, and regular friends. If Kathy weren't my supervisor, we'd probably have a closer social relationship.

Me: I consider you a successful schmoozer.

Julie: They would have fired my ass a long time ago [if I weren't]. I get 500 bonus points for doing something worth one point. The idea of talking to strange people in other offices from other areas, blindly, is so scary to them [her supervisors], they're so glad to have me do that job. It's almost like I'm immediately given these bonus points. It makes up for sometimes my not being here on time. It drives them nuts that I'm not here at 8 A.M. sometimes, but it would drive them more nuts to have to make that phone call. I'd like to think they accept my faulty parts because of that.

Julie uses her schmoozing skills to make up for some of her shortcomings at work. In her own assessment, these include being "ditsy," not remembering to get to tasks quickly, and most importantly, not showing up on time for the start of the workday. Julie is simply not a morning person! Because of her schmoozing skills—the good schmooze—she is able to get away with it.

I asked if Julie could provide a concrete example of how she gets these bonus points. Here is what she said:

Julie: I had to call downstairs to talk to someone in the budget office for Kathy [the budget is Kathy's job]. It's been a change for Kathy doing the budget. The woman downstairs got snippy with me when I asked about a tuition waiver for someone. She was short with me on the phone. I said, "I understand that's not what you do, so could you point me in the direction of someone to ask about this." She replied again with a short, non-helpful response. I was taken aback. I said, "Well, I'm just trying to answer your original e-mail to Kathy, so I'm not sure why you have an attitude." She said, "What do you mean?" I said, "Maybe you're having a bad day, but I'm just trying to answer the question—it seems like you're being short with me." She started backpedaling and was probably surprised. Most people think of me as bubbly. I've used humor all my life. If you don't have humor, you're in trouble. So, if I'm confrontational, the other person is thinking one of two things: (1) Something must be really wrong that day and they need to pay close attention, or (2) maybe I'm being a jerk (because it's totally abnormal for me to be like that). You gotta have humor—be able to look at your own faults. It helps you figure out how to communicate with others.

Me: So, your assessments of the good schmooze at work?

Julie: Humor as part of being bubbly, but beyond that, weighing other's values. It's a good combination. So when they treat you unfairly and you cease being bubbly, they step back and reflect on their own behavior.

Kathy and Julie's work relationship was built through a series of good schmooze conversations in the office. This was important, given their close working relationship and background of who got the prize job. Only through schmoozing did they succeed.

Other aspects of workplace schmoozing are more fleeting. One of these spheres of interaction is in service encounters. Schmoozing in these kinds of encounters takes on a different nature.

"SO, HOW ARE WE DOING TODAY?": SERVICE ENCOUNTERS AS WORKPLACE TALK

Depending on the part of the country in which one resides, service encounters more or less abound with schmoozing. These sorts of interactions involve customers with workers, medical personnel with patients, and any kind of workplace where the purpose is to serve the public.

The world of work involving service encounters is particularly fraught with confusion between chatting and chatting-up. Where selling a product is the goal, there is clearly more chatting-up. Nonetheless, the good schmooze can make for a good salesperson. It entails showing an interest in a customer rather than unctuous chatting-up. Schmoozing can also make an otherwise boring job interesting. This section analyzes real examples from workplaces that illustrate how the good schmooze can benefit both the servers and the served in institutional interactions.

"Are We Feeling Better Today?": Schmoozing in Health Care Workplaces

Workers in caretaking encounters often use the inclusive pronoun *we* when asking about *you*. This is an unconscious strategy to blur the line of separation between two people. Some find it belittling; others find it endearing. With medical personnel it takes the *how are you* question to an inclusive new dimension, entailing more than just a greeting.

Hospitals are workplaces where talk between workers and patients can clearly benefit the type of care one receives. It can also make an otherwise unpleasant stay more pleasant for the sick. For hospital workers, it can make the workday (or night) more interesting through meeting new people from all spheres of life. The weather is always a good opener. We see this in a recent conversation overheard between a patient and a medical technician. The patient opened the schmooze with the simple comment, "Hot today, isn't it?" The technician responded: "I'm from here, so I'm used to it."

Patient: From [this town]?
Technician: All my life.
Patient: Where'd you go to school?

[technician tells the name of his high school]

Patient: Oh, my son went there too, but he's a few years
                    younger, I think.
Technician: I'm 30.
Patient: He's 25.
Technician: My brother is 26. He went to [same high school].
Patient: [tells son's name]. He played soccer. Did your brother
                    play soccer?
Technician: Football. But they probably know each other.

This brief innocuous chat was totally unrelated to patient care. It was all about schmoozing while having a test set up—*interactional* rather than *transactional*. Nonetheless, it passed the time for both patient and worker and perhaps created some small connection between the two. There were no direct benefits. But one never knows. Since both lived in the same town, it was possible that they would come into contact with each other again. If not, at the least they created a momentary goodwill.

A more striking example of how important good schmoozing can be in the hospital workplace derives from a nurse making her first contact with a patient upon the shift change:

Nurse to patient: Good morning.
Patient: You must be Lydia.

Lydia: Welcome to the club!
Patient: You mean you had it? [surgery]
Lydia: Two years ago.
Patient: Wow, and look at you now! [and a conversation
            ensued]

Here, nurse Lydia used the good schmooze in introducing herself to
the new patient with her opener, "Welcome to the club." It established
an immediate bond. She indicated that she knew what the patient was
going through because she had undergone the same procedure not so
long before. The patient was heartened. He realized that in a short time,
he would be back on his feet as a normally functioning being, just like
Lydia. This particular nurse chose to work in a place where she could
use her own surgical experience to encourage her patients by chatting
with them about what they were going through. She understood this
experience firsthand. It was not merely clinical, but personal.

"IT WON'T BE AN EVICTION, SO THAT'S GOOD": SCHMOOZING WHEN BREAKING BAD NEWS

The good schmooze serves to bond, as it did with Lydia and her
surgical patient. Recall that it also serves to soften a bite. When conveying bad news, it comes in handy as a conversational tactic that soft-
ens the blow. In the following conversation,[6] the interlocutors are an
apartment complex manager and a man facing possible eviction. The
manager conveys the news to the tenant:

Tenant: So this is gonna be pretty bad?
Manager: It's gonna be a little high, but it won't, um, we could—it
            won't be an eviction. So, that's good.
Tenant: Ok, well . . .
Manager: So she's going to ask you to pay an extra fee for being
            late.
Tenant: It's definitely not your fault, but I mean, [whistles]
            that's kinda steep for a mistake, isn't it? Why didn't you
            call me?
Manager: It is, because it's the last day of the month.
Tenant: Or something and say "Your rent is late?"

[later in the conversation]

Manager: Can I get you a bottle of water?
Tenant: Yeah, I think I'm gonna need that. Do you have any-
          thing stronger? [laughs]
Manager: We have coffee! [laughs]
Tenant: No, just kidding.
Manager: I'll pour you a shot . . . [laughs]
Tenant: There you go, now we're talkin'!

The interaction ended with positive feelings. The manager succeeded in softening the bad news with this talk. Despite the fact that the tenant was a month late with his rent, the manager said he would not be evicted. He would simply have to pay a fine with his late rent. The manager served this up as good news—"it won't be an eviction." This seemed to mollify the tenant somewhat. The manager then showed his sympathy with an offer of a bottle of water.

Offers are typically speech acts of generosity. In making the offer of water, the manager deflected the tenant's question of why he did not call. Then, an attempt at a more lighthearted exchange ensued when they joked about "something stronger" to drink. Bad news was served up with generosity and wit. As the song goes, it "makes the medicine go down." The good schmooze helped to defuse a potentially nega-tively charged interaction.

"MAY I HELP YOU FIND SOMETHING?": SCHMOOZING IN SALES ENCOUNTERS

A young woman finds herself killing time while walking aimlessly around a department store in the mall.[7] She stops at the cosmetics counter, pretending to seriously contemplate a lip gloss purchase. A sales clerk approaches:

Clerk: Looking for anything in particular?
Customer: Just trying to find a new lip gloss . . . how much is this
           one?
Clerk: I believe it's marked . . . $12.

The customer winces, clearly indicating that $12 is outrageous for a tiny tube of lip gloss. The sales clerk notices and replies, "You know, we have our new beauty-to-go station. I mean, the size of the lip gloss is smaller, but it's less expensive!" This customer proceeded to the beauty-to-go section and decided to purchase a $7 lip gloss. At the checkout, as the cashier was scanning the lip gloss, she asked, "Have you checked out our beauty-to-go section today?" When the cashier realized the obvious, she giggled an apology. The first sales associate did a very good job of schmoozing. She succeeded in reading the body language toward the $12 and hence did not push the product. The cashier was bubbly and friendly enough to the customer. On the other hand, she seemed disingenuous when she started blatantly speaking from a script ("Have you checked out our beauty-to-go section today?"). The scripted questions are only effective when they make sense in context and seem believable.

Schmoozing in sales encounters is obviously intended for the purpose of making a profit and/or commission. Nevertheless, even if a purchase is not realized at the time, the good schmooze itself has the potential to build rapport and create positive feelings. One never knows when a customer may come back! The sale may not be immediate, but the interaction itself may be satisfying.

"JUST THE REGULAR TODAY?": SCHMOOZING AND GETTING-TO-KNOW YOU

Getting to Know You was a popular song from the 1950s Broadway musical *The King and I*. The king of Siam had hired a governess/tutor for his children. It was clearly a relationship of boss and employee. However, as the king and the governess got to know each other, the relationship warmed up. This happens often in the workplace, among coworkers and even with customers and sales personnel. An example from a real interaction lends insight.[8] This conversation was overheard at a local coffee shop. It took place between college-aged female server (we'll call her Sarah) and an older man (we'll call him Mr. Johnson) who appeared to be a regular:

Sarah: Hey Mr. Johnson, how's my favorite customer doing today?

Mr. J: I'm doing well, thank you Sarah! I just got back from New York. I was visiting some relatives up there.

Sarah: Really? How was it?

Mr. J: It was great. The weather was really nice up there.

Sarah: Glad to hear that. What can I get for you, regular black coffee, no sugar as always?

Mr. J: You know me—that's what I get. By the way, Sarah, did you get the e-mail that I sent you about this teaching opportunity I found? I thought you might be interested in it.

Sarah: An e-mail? No, I didn't get any e-mail from you. You sure you sent it to the right address?

Mr. J: I'm positive. You should check again, see if you can find it.

Sarah: Okay, will do!

[comes back with coffee]

Sarah: Here you go, Mr. Johnson!

Mr. J: Thank you, sweetheart. Appreciate you putting up with an old fart when y'all are so busy.

Sarah: Oh, are you kidding me?! You know I love you, Mr. Johnson! Take care now!

Mr. J: You too, Sarah!

Sarah's schmoozing ability is striking, and no doubt comes with experience at working there. Obviously, she remembered what Mr. Johnson usually came in for. She was interested in what he had to say and made him feel very comfortable. Their relationship was formed solely at the coffee shop. Despite this, Sarah obviously had such an impact on the Mr. Johnson that he e-mailed her information that he believed she would find of benefit. Because of the rapport that Sarah had formed with this customer (and perhaps many others), customers probably come back again and again. Sarah's schmoozing is pure chatting, as clerks of this sort do not typically make a commission on the number of coffee servings sold. Moreover, this particular customer even went out of his way to do a little job networking for Sarah. That is an excellent example of the indirect benefit of just being a nice person who is willing to chat with her customers while serving them. It makes her day more interesting, but one never knows where things may lead.

In contrast to this exchange is one that I experienced recently at a similar coffee shop. I stopped in to grab a pick-me-up on the way to campus before a four-hour teaching stretch. I ordered my beverage and proceeded to wait at the next counter for the finished product. Instead of making conversation with the customers, the baristas were making conversation with each other, completely ignoring the customers in line while chatting and focusing only on each other. The only exchanges with the customers were inquiries about what they were ordering. The two young women proceeded to complain and commiserate with each other (audible to customers) about their lack of sleep and their long hours of work on top of their studies.

I could not help but think that their chatting interfered with the swift delivery of my coffee! As I stood there waiting patiently (or not so patiently), I listened to them schmoozing. Undoubtedly, they were bonding with each other, but they were doing it with the customers as audience. Perhaps their workplace schmoozing served a positive purpose for them, eventually leading to a social relationship. One cannot tell without more information about perfect strangers. Nevertheless, it seemed in such clear contrast to the good schmooze that is so rare between server and customer seen in the earlier exchange between Mr. Johnson and Sarah.

Workplace schmoozing encompasses both talk with coworkers and, in service encounters, talk with customers. When customers in service encounters are audience to schmoozing among coworkers, the customer can be made to feel invisible. This is never very good for business. Perhaps not making a commission leads naturally into such a situation. But the good schmooze with customers can have indirect benefits, as we saw with Sarah's interaction before with Mr. Johnson.

Being treated as invisible by servers will resonate with many readers. Most of us have been at the grocery checkout queue and overheard cashier and bagger complaining to each other about how many more hours they have to go until they get off. While we can be sympathetic, it makes for bad business. The more successful employees, even cashiers and baggers, eventually reap the indirect benefits of good schmoozing with the customers. The benefits, however, are not immediate. In fact, there may never be benefits at all beyond getting-to-know you. Getting-to-know you may eventually lead to a better work life. At least it will lead to more satisfaction at work. This is no small benefit.

"Aren't You Adorable?": Schmoozing with Children in Service Encounters

Schmoozing in service encounters can be with customers themselves or with accompanying family members. The following sequence took place while a young woman worked as a cashier in a toy store.[9]

I opened the store on Friday morning and my first three customers were a mom holding her toddler daughter, Jenny, and her six-month-old daughter, Maddy, in the cart:

Cashier: Hi! Did you find everything you were looking for?
Mom: Oh, that and more. [laughs while putting her daughter down]
Cashier: [to the toddler daughter with a higher pitch of voice] Hi . . . I'm Brooke. What's your name?
Jenny: [shyly] Jenny . . . I'm three . . .
Cashier: Wow! You're so grown up! [motioning toward the items] Is all of this for you?
Jenny: [nods]
Mom: [higher pitched voice] That's right! Tell Brooke what today is.
Jenny: It's my birfday!!
Cashier: It's your birthday! Happy birthday! [to her mother with normal voice] Is Jenny signed up for Geoffrey's Birthday Club? She'll get a birthday balloon, a crown, an announcement about her birthday over the intercom, and also a $3 coupon . . .
Mom: [laughing] I would love that coupon. [to Jenny] Do you want a birthday balloon?
Jenny: [nods]
Cashier: [to Jenny with higher pitch of voice] Okay Jenny, let's go up to the service desk and get you a balloon and a crown, okay?

[While another employee began filling Jenny's balloon, Maddy started crying.]

Cashier: [higher pitched voice] Oh, what's wrong? Are we sad? Do you want a balloon, too?

[Maddy, hearing the employee talk to her, begins smiling.]

Cashier: You're so pretty when you smile! Aren't you just a pretty girl?

Mom: [higher pitched voice] Can you tell her thank you? Yeh . . . yeh . . . say thank you . . . [tickles her] [normal voice to worker] Thank you SO much for you help. I really appreciate all of this.

Cashier: Oh, it's no problem at all! Your girls are beautiful! If you need any more help, just let me know, okay?

Mom: I definitely will. Say "bye" girls!

Jenny: Bye! Thanks.

Brooke: [higher pitched voice] Happy birthday, Jenny! Come back and see me again, okay?

Jenny: [smiles] Can we mommy?

Mom: Of course, sweetie. Bye, and thanks again . . .

Cashier: You're so welcome. [higher pitched voice] Bye girls!

The cashier did not make a commission on signing children up for Geoffrey's Birthday Club. It is a marketing technique for the toy store. Her interaction with the children was part of the good schmooze with them as well as with the parent. What are the benefits? The mom gets positive feelings and so do the kids. She may very well be inclined to come back for more shopping. The cashier's benefit is not for increased sales. She was just passing the time cheerfully while participating in the world of work. Spreading good cheer is no small accomplishment. After all, she stopped a fellow human from crying!

"ENOUGH OF THIS SCHMOOZING!": TOO MUCH FOR SOME

Not everyone wants to schmooze in service encounters. Indeed, schmoozing norms differ greatly from region to region in a vast country such as the United States. City dwellers often prefer the anonymity that comes with living in an urban environment—that may be why they choose to live in a city. For them, too much schmoozing with strangers is annoying. It becomes particularly problematic when migrating or even traveling to other parts where schmoozing is preferred.

Kim moved here almost two years ago from Denver, and her parents were originally from New York. She was therefore used to a big city mentality. Thus, she was very surprised when she moved to a southern college town and began working at the UPS Store. She related the following anecdote:[10]

> This particular branch was located pretty far enough on the outskirts of the town; so many people come from neighboring small towns and more rural areas. These people tend to expect a lot more small talk than I was (and still am) used to. My boss has even told me I should make more small talk with customers, to a degree that I would find annoying if I were the customer. Many have told me what seem like their life stories while my instinct is to serve them as quickly as possible and move on to the next customer. One woman in particular told me an unsolicited, long, and (I thought) too personal story about her nine-year-old grandson.
>
> She related about how her husband had taken him on a camping trip where they had (as people do when camping) gone to the bathroom outside. Her grandson apparently then attempted to do the same on the playground at school and when questioned, told his teacher, "But my peepaw does it." She went on for quite some time about this incident. Throughout the story she referred to herself as "meemaw" and her husband as "peepaw," terms I had never heard before and only later found out that some people call their grandparents by these names. This is just one incident of many where I felt like way too much small talk for my taste took place.

Schmoozing in service encounters is clearly not for everyone and not for every place. In some locations, however, it is expected. It makes a brief encounter go more smoothly and offers a pleasant way to pass a fleeting interaction.

We turn now to a particular workplace setting where schmoozing took on a unique character.

WORKPLACE SCHMOOZING HIGHLIGHTED

"I Just Made a Sale!": Bragging or Schmoozing?

A few years ago, in collaboration with colleague Andrea De Capua, we conducted a study of talk among stockbrokers in a Washington,

D.C., office.[11] The data were fascinating. The mostly young male brokers schmoozed all day long, but the talk was competitive. In fact, the interactions centered on bragging, boasting, and bravado. While this kind of talk is a certain sort of schmoozing, the language almost exclusively emphasized sexual prowess and athletic abilities. The boastfulness was almost always humorous, and, as such, was like good schmoozing. The competitive nature, however, made the talk something different—a contest of one-upsmanship.

As in most if not all brokerage firms, this was a work setting where compensation was pure commission; brokers received a percentage of their sales of stock, and they had to reach a certain gross production per month in order to remain in the company. Most of us have a vague notion of what a brokerage room looks like. This office consisted of a large room filled with desks—everyone easily visible and audible to everyone else. There was minimal privacy, and the workspace was called "the bullpen," a standard industry metaphor derived from the sport of baseball. As described by one broker: "You're less than three feet away from the guy sitting next to you, so everyone hears everyone's conversation, both business and social."

In this brokerage house, all of the brokers were male and all (except for one Nigerian) were white North Americans between the ages of 24 and 35. They all had college degrees, had played athletics in college, and had been members of fraternities. They came from various parts of the East Coast and had worked together for the prior two to four years. The one African male who did not fit this profile was well liked and respected; nonetheless, he was not a member of the in-group and did not socialize with the other brokers after work. As a Pentecostal Christian, he was very involved in his church and religious activities. He did not drink, dance, or engage in mating rituals. The two women who worked in the office with the stockbrokers also had college degrees but were salaried employees.

Due to the intense pressure to sell stocks, bantering exchanges were attempts by the brokers to display themselves as competent and powerful individuals. Humor functioned as a release valve for the tensions as well as a means of social control. Male bonding was accomplished through the use of metaphors of current events, sports, and sex, contributing to a locker-room atmosphere. The humor in such a context served two functions: first, it helped to establish a pecking order; second, it served to bond the members of the group. The question, then, is: What kind of schmoozing was this? Can it be good schmoozing when there is a constant display of superiority? Let us take a closer look.

The following example was spoken in the context of one of the brokers, Bill, bragging to the rest of the office about being the number one producer in terms of dollar amount of sales. He used a favorite topic, the male sex organ, as a metaphor for success in selling: "Just picture yourself on top of the Empire State Building with your dick hanging out, watching yourself peeing down the street."

Although not usually associated with *human* behavior, the need to mark one's territory among males of certain other species is accomplished by urinating around the perimeters of the claimed area. Bill was clearly drawing on the metaphors of being on top of the world and staking out his position to proclaim his superior status in the brokerage house hierarchy.

Obviously, the most important element in determining prestige in this workplace setting was monetary compensation. Because compensation was completely based upon performance, how much brokers earned determined their rank within the bullpen hierarchy. Given the fluctuations of the stock market and the nature of sales, this hierarchy was always in a constant state of change, and anything that improved a broker's standing was cause for celebration—or at least making it public knowledge.

Personal superiority was expressed by boasting of one's sales ability and with references to physical prowess. The brokers, except for the one anomaly, were all sports fanatics. They spent a great deal of their leisure time both playing and watching sporting events. During their lunch hour, they often gathered in a lounge area to watch sports as they lunched, schmoozing all the while. For these brokers, sports served as bonding and as competition. Consider the following conversation:

Dave: Shit, I got this fucking bruise on my leg from blocking that shot.
Burt: What'd ya want, ya play the game and if ya gotta get physical, ya block the shot with your body. Ya know, you're such a wimp, I'm gonna call you Merlot.
Dave: What the fuck're you talking about?
Burt: That's because you bruise like a grape.

Burt not only ridiculed Dave for complaining about his sports injuries, but in so doing displayed his quick wit with his reference to bruising grapes and wine. The simile was humorous, but competitive. While humor typically works toward the good schmooze, here it worked to perform a certain identity by Burt. That identity was one of superiority—never a good schmooze strategy.

SEXUAL BRAVADO

In our culture, the man in good physical shape is believed to be more likely to attract women. The following excerpt took place in the bullpen:

Dave: You going to the gym today?
Merl: [loud enough for everyone in office to hear] Right now I'm going to get a shirt that says "Under Construction" and in a couple of months I'm gonna get another T-shirt [does flexing pose, everyone is now watching him] "Open for Business."

The purpose of such bravado is to heighten the teller's identity as competitively competent. Even ethical breaches can do the job in this kind of schmoozing. For example, over drinks after work, Rob recounted a story about cheating his way through a college course:

I cheated like a fucking motherfucker in that thing. Every single test I cheated. The final exam comes and I'm like fucking—I have no idea what fucking thing is on there. There's this old, old lady [the professor] and she's mean and she's like this business lady and I'm like, "Fuck it." And I see her look at me and I'm like, "She fucking caught me." And I'm like, "Fuck it, fuck it."
[laughter]
And I go up and hand in my test and she says, "I want to see you in my office tomorrow." I'm like fucking scared shit. The next day I go and she tells me, "Thank you for being such an asset to the course."

The thrust of Rob's story was that not only did he successfully cheat, but that the professor in fact honored him for his class performance. This may meet schmoozing expectations in a particular workplace, but not in most. We have seen in prior examples that people who can "think on their feet," particularly using humor, are admired. While this was certainly true in this brokerage house, the topics and language that were acceptable here went beyond traditional boundaries and transcended ordinary taboos.

Verbal posturing, insults, and put-downs were the norm. While much humor was evident, it is the opposite of self-denigrating humor that goes far in the good schmooze. In fact, the denigration of others was a hallmark among the brokers. He who got the laughs got status. Even verbal dueling was made humorous, as in the next exchange:

> Dave and Jack had just overheard Pete misspell something to a client over the phone. When Pete finished the call, they teased him about his poor spelling.
>
> Dave: Ya can't tell Pete anything—the guy is just beyond it.
> Jack: He's so far gone, he won't ever get it. He's lucky that when he's with women, it's his balls and dick that get to do the talking.
> Dave: They're not doing him much good, either, the way I hear it.
> Pete: Would ya all shut the fuck up? I make big money so who the hell cares how I fucking spell.
> Brad: That's right, women don't care about what ya got up there but what ya got between here. [stands on desk and points to head and crotch]
> Jack: Yeah, but ya gotta have something down there or you're a goner.
> Dave: [to Pete] We're gonna have to start calling you Secretariat cuz you go through life with blinders.
> Pete: What the hell're you talking about?
> Dave: You can't see anything except what's in front of you, Secretariat.

The first quip in the duel was Jack's put-down of Pete, which equated his inability to spell with a lack of verbal ability. This put-down led to sexual innuendo, sexual insult, reference to earning capacity, and more sexual innuendo, culminating in a final put-down incorporating a witty sports allusion, equating Pete with a racehorse wearing blinders. Not only was this a witty sports allusion, but it was also a somewhat obscure one in the scheme of sports knowledge trivia. Consequently, it seemed that Dave won this round in the joust not only by using his wit against Pete, but also by demonstrating his superior sports knowledge. The brokers who participated successfully in the duels bonded into a cohesive group. They learned the rules of what counted as schmoozing in this world of work.

BRAGGING AS SCHMOOZING?

This sort of talk is akin to a fraternity or locker room-like atmosphere. A fraternity is a group of young college men bonded through similar interests and initiated through adversity, for example, rites of passage commonly known as pledging, hazing, and hell night. It is a highly competitive, hierarchical organization; only certain men are chosen as members based primarily on how well or how much they exhibit the qualities or attributes valued by that particular fraternity.

One of the brokers commented on the fraternity atmosphere prevalent in the brokerage house:

> It's like a fraternity atmosphere. It's mostly men and there's no need to worry about social pleasantries; you can just basically do or say what you want and not offend anyone except maybe the women.

It is well known that fraternity and locker room talk is filled with ego grandstanding. Language displays such as sexual prowess and athletic abilities as well as the use of heavy swearing are markers of the social identity of those who belong.

While this sort of schmoozing may have been the norm in this particular workplace, overt grandstanding is inappropriate in most work settings. Clearly, those who do not adhere to the same norms of speaking (either by choice or due to different background knowledge or life experience) will have difficulty becoming members of the in-group. It is only those in the in-group who even possess the ability to compete by virtue of who and what they are.

In some brokerage house cultures, initiates go through rites similar to those of fraternity pledges. In such brokerage firms, an initiate is termed a *geek*: "A person immediately out of the training program and in a disgusting larval state between trainee and man" [sic].[12] One can progress from geek to man only by developing the requisite schmoozing style. This includes both mastering the rules of speaking and being an effective salesman. The rules of speaking include knowing how to sell and how to boast about one's sales ability.

This is precisely the new, negative sense of schmooze. It is the current connotation of networking, making a connection, and seeking direct benefit. The direct benefit demonstrated here is monetary reward. The popular literature on how to succeed in sales urges people to focus on winning and on being number one: "Just be positive and tell yourself that you are the greatest . . . Say it out loud . . . I am the greatest! Say it again . . . make the walls shake."[13] Many readers may remember how the boxer Mohammed Ali rallied himself and his supporters (and rattled his opponent) by reciting a personal poem of encouragement before a bout:

I'm going to knock him down in five,

He's going to take a dive,

I'm going to sting him like a bee

So he won't see.[14]

This is not unlike the bragging, boasting, and bravado in the brokerage house just described. The brokers boasted to psych themselves up for their sales pitches; to generate new business, they had to constantly place cold calls (contact people they did not know in order to sell them stocks). Recall that to remain with the firm, brokers were required to sell a certain minimum dollar amount of stocks. Two months of below-minimum sales and the broker was asked to leave the firm. Low or no sales and the broker was broke.

The brokers in the interactions presented here learned their schmoozing lessons well. Those who did not participate in this highly competitive talk were not as likely to succeed in this stressful environment. Therefore, while it took a certain kind of talk to make it there, this was a far cry from the good schmooze. This example shows us exactly how talk in interaction can be taken to lower and lower levels. As we have seen, the erroneous sense of schmoozing in the workplace has come to be something like *working the room*. The sense of schmoozing in the brokerage house discussed here was something else entirely: one-upsmanship done in a bragging but bantering style. Neither one is representative of what workplace schmoozing should and can be.

CONCLUSION: SCHMOOZING AT WORK IN THE WORKPLACE

The modern U.S. workplace is a diverse one, and it is likely to become increasingly so. Given this state of affairs, schmoozing in the sphere of work must revert to what it used to be. Workplaces cannot afford to alienate people who do not share norms of talk specific to the likes of fraternity houses or male locker rooms, for example. In the first place, it excludes women. As we well know, women make up more than half of the modern U.S. workforce (this is true even in broker-age houses these days). Moreover, it alienates all who hail from other ethnic, racial, and religious groups.

The TV series *Mad Men* highlights what workplace schmoozing used to be like among the all white, college-educated males. Women and foreign or ethnic others were not allowed in. The brokers described in this chapter were no different—even though this was less than a dozen years ago! The past few decades have seen sweeping changes in U.S. society and, in turn, U.S. workplaces. The lost art of the good schmooze needs to prevail at work just as it does at home and in social and educational interactions. We tune into talk shows as audience to schmoozing. It is not possible to just passively watch it on TV or listen to it on talk radio. We can—and indeed we ought to—live the good schmooze at our own places of work.

NOTES

1. NPR interview, September 29, 2009.
2. Madeline Albright, *Read My Pins* (New York: Harper Collins, 2009). This excerpt from *Read My Pins* by Madeleine Albright is used by permission of Harper Collins.
3. French attitudes have changed since that time.
4. Data collected by Laura Hucke, 2009.
5. Diana Boxer and Florencia Cortes-Conde, "Humorous Self Disclo-sures as Resistance to Socially Imposed Gender Roles," *Gender and Language* 4 (2010).
6. Data collected by Shael Millheim, 2009.
7. Data collected by Kelsey Bryant, 2009.
8. Data collected by Horia Ionescu, 2009.
9. Data collected by Becky Bickel, 2009.
10. Data collected by Katherine Schinn, 2009.

11. Diana Boxer and Andrea de Capua, "Bragging, Boasting and Bravado: Male Banter in a Brokerage House," *Women and Language* 22 (1999): 5–22.

12. Michael Lewis, *Liar's Poker* (New York: Norton and Company, 1989), 153.

13. Joe Girard and Robert Casemore, *How to Sell Yourself* (New York: Warner Books, 1988), 21.

14. Ibid.

CHAPTER 4

The Good Schmooze in Education

One attraction of Latin is that you can immerse yourself in the poems of Horace and Catullus without fretting over how to say, "Have a nice day."

Peter Brodie

INTRODUCTION

It is a fact that if we care about other people, we worry about how to say "have a nice day" and other pleasantries of this sort. In the early 20th century, a noted anthropologist, Branislov Malinowski,[1] termed such language *phatic communion*. We fret about how to achieve phatic communion in languages other than our own. But we also need to think about how this and other schmoozing techniques impact our daily lives in our *native language*. You can have the ability to conjugate all the verbs, work out all of the logarithms, troubleshoot all the mechanical problems of your computer, and still not come out ahead if you don't know how to say, "have a nice day" (in other words, schmooze) at the right time and the right place and with the right person. This fact is as true in the educational sphere as anywhere.

Nowadays, you pretty much have to have a higher education to at least have a chance of getting a decent job. Moreover, with the job market the way it is, being a good student alone is no guarantee. As Walker Percy once said, "You can get all As and still flunk life." The art of good schmoozing may in fact be more important than the diploma or the transcript showing good grades. It is frequently *not* the nerds who end up being the most happy and successful. That is, of course, unless the nerds also have good interactional skills. But then, perhaps they would not be nerds. We think of nerds as people who are very skilled at a certain sphere of knowledge, but who do not know how to talk to people. Indeed, "Education begins the man [sic], conversation completes him [sic].[2]

This belief in the intrinsic value of conversation, beyond formal education, may in fact be dying out as higher education becomes increasingly digitized. On June 10, 2010, outgoing governor of Minnesota Tim Pawlenty appeared on Comedy Central's *The Daily Show* to be interviewed by Jon Stewart. He suggested that the future of higher education may lie in what he termed "iCollege" (as in iPhone):

> Pawlenty: Do you really think in 20 years, somebody's gonna put on their backpack, drive half an hour to the University of Minnesota from the suburbs, haul their keister across campus to listen to some boring person drawn out about Econ 101 or Spanish 101? Or do you think . . . is there another way to provide the service other than a one-size-fits-all monopoly provider that says show up at 9 A.M. Wednesday morning for Econ 101? Can't I just pull that down on my iPhone or iPad whenever the heck I feel like it from wherever I feel like it? And instead of paying thousands of dollars, can't I pay $199 for iCollege instead of 99 cents for iTunes?

Here Pawlenty expresses the belief that education can take place in a conversational void. We merely need access to information, whenever we want it and wherever we are, in order to become educated citizens.

We may in fact be able to succeed with online courses, but only if we enable discussion and real-time interaction with the teacher and other students. I assert that the discussion is most effective when it is face-to-face. Perhaps this criticism will be rendered moot as video programs such as *Skype* become more user friendly for entire virtual classrooms. Until then, without that sort of conversation with teachers and fellow students, higher education through an ostensible iCollege would be a lonely endeavor that entails the absorption of information in the form of facts without the encouragement to critically think about that information.

The discussion part of school is what makes for good teaching and learning. In some respects, discussion can be akin to schmoozing. But it can differ greatly from the kinds of social schmoozing discussed in prior chapters in this book. The 1973 film *The Paper Chase* made this point clearly. Professor Kingsfield (played by John Houseman) expounded to the first-year law students at Harvard on the first day of class:

> We use the Socratic method here. I call on you, ask you a question, and you answer it. Why don't I just give you a lecture? Because through my questions, you learn to teach yourselves. Through this method of questioning, answering, questioning, answering, we seek to develop in you the ability to analyze that vast complex of facts that constitute the relationships of members within a given society. Questioning and answering. At times, you may feel that you have found the correct answer. I assure you that this is a total delusion on your part. You will never find the correct, absolute, and final answer. In my classroom, there is always another question, another question to follow your answer. As you're on a treadmill, my little questions spin the tumblers of your mind. You're on an operating table; my little questions are the fingers probing your brain. We do brain surgery here. You teach yourselves the law, but I train your mind. You come in here with a skull full of mush and you leave thinking like a lawyer.

This may have been almost 40 years ago, but a good education remains something beyond just access to the facts. It entails knowing how to weigh the ostensible facts, interpret them, and behave accordingly. Kingsfield's questioning may not be our idea of social schmoozing precisely because the students do not get to do the questioning. Thus, while it is a two-way give-and-take of interaction, the roles are highly circumscribed. Nonetheless, the Socratic method is a large part of education's schmooze, at least in some aspects of classroom discourse. But it is not just about getting the facts. If it were so, iCollege would certainly be a superior idea.

So, until iCollege takes over completely, interaction in the discourse of higher education will continue to take place in various face-to-face contexts. Of course, there is the vast arena of talk in actual classrooms on all levels. This sphere of talk, referred to as *classroom discourse and interaction*, has been extensively studied in sociolinguistics. But there also are other important sorts of interactions in education where the good schmooze can serve to prevent one from "flunking life." These include office hour chats, laboratory and study groups, and advising and mentoring sessions, to name a few. All of these contexts have important implications for individual success or failure in the educational domain. Whether the desired goal is gaining entrance into a needed course, getting a good grade, becoming a ratified member of the specific educational community, or obtaining a stellar reference for a future job, the consequences of knowing how to do the good schmooze in the educational domain are far-reaching.

"I LOVE THAT OUTFIT": GOOD SCHMOOZE, BAD SCHMOOZE IN EDUCATION

Just like social schmoozing, in the sphere of secondary and higher education, the good schmooze typically initiates around a topic relevant to the sphere of interaction. After a relationship has been established, the speech behaviors can progress to more personal ones. It may seem inappropriate to start out with personal talk, such as compliments about clothes rather than about one's work. Such schmoozing can come off as false and obsequious.

Consider this sequence, taken from a TV sitcom. The dean of education is talking to a group of students who are painting a dormitory room. She gets upset, but then discovers the identity of one of the students as the daughter of a benefactor:[3]

From the TV show *Saved by the Bell: The College Years* ("The Rave" episode)
   The dean arrives at the dorm suspicious of the students.

Zach Morris:	Dean McMann, ma'am, I can explain everything. You see, while Michael Rogers is away, we thought we'd surprise him and paint his room.
Dean McMann:	You're going to paint his room . . .
Zach Morris:	Yes, we sure are, and we have an extra paintbrush if you'd like to join us.
Dean McMann:	Oh, you know I'd love to, but my overalls are at the dry cleaner. I spilled cider on them when I was watching *Hee-Haw*.

[phone rings, she answers]

Gerald, yes. I know [looks at wrist] I'm late for my 10 o'clock. Just tell him he's suspended and to have a nice day. [hangs up]

All right, who are you people? Name?

Leslie Burke:	Leslie Burke.
Dean McMann:	Burke? As in Burke Library? Burke Hall? Are you Walter and Edith's daughter?
Leslie Burke:	Yes, I am.
Dean McMann:	Hellooo. Your family has been so generous to this university. I've been meaning to stop by and get to know you. I love that outfit. Don't you dare paint in it.
Leslie Burke:	Oh, I won't.
Dean McMann:	Well, will you excuse me? I've got to go be harsh with someone.

Mr. Morris, I don't believe a word of your story. I've met a million guys like you who don't know what a privilege it is to be at this university. You are on my list. [dials phone]

Gerald, did you suspend that student? Did he cry? Good.

This fictitious conversation aptly illustrates a false attempt at schmoozing. Before Dean McMann discovers the identity of Leslie Burke, she is mean and sarcastic with the group of students. She quips about her overalls getting dirty while watching a TV show, *Hee Haw*, which she surely does not watch—it would be beneath her to stoop to such low humor. But when she discovers who Leslie Burke is, despite her own institutional power, she attempts to schmooze with the student through a false compliment. Of course, because Burke is no ordinary student, Dean McMann's attempt to sweet-talk Burke is so obviously due to the philanthropy of her parents. The clothes compliment is humorous because it is out of place. It is too personal, not related to either the work of the school or the painting going on. It is unctuous—not good schmoozing.

The dean's sudden shift of attitude is the focus of the humor. She is clearly a disciplinarian at heart, willing to display the power of her position at every opportunity. How she ever got to a position of power without knowing how to do the good schmooze is worth contemplating.

"THAT WAS A REALLY GOOD PRESENTATION"

An exchange taken from a real interaction stands in stark contrast to the TV sitcom example. It involved a college teacher, Beth, with a graduate student who was herself a teacher of young children.[4] Because the teacher worked full time in the school district, she was attending evening classes toward her master's degree. She came up to Beth regularly after class to make an observation about how what they were doing in class reflected in her own students' work. After several of these chats after class, the student asked Beth if she would mind reading and commenting on her master's thesis.

Student: That was a really great presentation today. Thanks.
Beth: Absolutely.
Student: I've really been seeing how what you are teaching us shows up in my students' speech and writing.
Beth: I'm so glad!
Student: Yeah. I'm sure it has always been there but I didn't notice it until you pointed it out to us.
Beth: Yeah, it's always like that. You know that there is something different about the speech, but unless you know what in particular is different, it's hard to pinpoint how to teach alternatives.
Student: Right. I was wondering, I'm working on my master's thesis and I'll be finishing up this semester. Your work is similar in some ways to my topic and I was wondering if you would mind reading it before I turn it in?
Beth: Sure—I'd love to.
Student: Thank you! Well, thanks again for your sessions and I'm looking forward to next week.
Beth: Take care. Have a good week!

Beth eagerly responded that she would be glad to do the favor of reading the student's work. She reflects on the relationship, built over a period of time with schmoozing after class:

> I doubt that she had in mind the whole time we were talking that she wanted me to read her thesis, but as our conversations developed, she realized that it was within my specialty area. I think that her coming over after class so many times built the relationship that led her to be able to ask for such a big favor, and from my perspective, I'm extremely busy but I value the relationship and I'm willing to spend some time on it.

The student began with a compliment to Beth relevant to the topic under discussion in class. It seemed perfectly genuine, not at all obsequious. In other words, the student really wanted to have a one-on-one chat with Beth. The compliment was the opener, and it led to further chatting, culminating with the student's earnest request.

Beth is an experienced, and, in fact, an award-winning college teacher.[5] Her teaching in this context was part of an effort to train classroom teachers in a particular aspect of sociolinguistics in education as data for her own PhD dissertation. To do this, she had to develop relationships with the professor responsible for the class in addition to the teachers who were graduate students attending the course. Much of the rapport rested on her ability to build relationships with both groups, students and professors. She was able to do this via schmoozing before and after class. She explains:

> I don't have to stay for the part of the classes that I don't teach, but I stay anyway. I do it so I have an idea of what's going on in class, but mostly to help build the relationships. One of the professors drives me to the subway station after class, and we spend the time talking from the classroom until she drops me off—about how the class went, which students seem to be getting the content, which are annoying, which we like, which we don't like. We also talk for about 20 minutes or so before class and I tell her how things are going with teaching and my dissertation and I generally end up asking for her opinion or advice on something. We talk about general things like the weather or the fact that I've bought and sent back three pairs of boots this winter because even though they were supposed to be waterproof, they weren't. We talk about what's going on in the school she's teaching at and what she thinks will end up happening to the school because it is performing so poorly. We really get along. After our very first meeting before the semester started, I gave her a hug and she seems to really like me, both for my personality and also for what I'm bringing to her classroom. She mentioned several times that she was looking forward to learning from my presentations. I don't have to meet with her before classes—I know she will be in the adjunct office so I go there to find her—and I don't have to stay for class or wait for her after class, but it's good for building our relationship. I think it makes her more likely to confide in me and talk about problems at her school and what she's thinking about career-wise.

One of the students in her class is particularly difficult and we talk about him at the end of every class. When she drives me to

the train station, we talk about what he does and doesn't understand and how his presence affects the climate and culture of the
classroom. We talk about a lot of the other students and I've asked
her for feedback about my teaching, but she hasn't suggested any
changes. She tells me about the quality of their work and how well
they are doing with their assignments. She recently told me that
she is spending the week of spring break looking for a full-time
job—she is an adjunct—and I feel like this is information that
she is trusting that I won't share with others in the department,
and that she only shared because we have a good relationship. I
recently found out that she has a daughter whose birthday was
the other day, and that she has a grandson that is just a few years
younger than me. Finding this out let me know that I only knew
so much about her, but I think that the relationship is growing
based on our conversations every week.

The schmoozing lesson here is that students—novices and experts
alike—who make it a point to get to know the professor in charge
have an opportunity to get an edge. This is not just about networking.
The schmoozing outside of the classroom can be more important than
showing your knowledge in class. But it has to be genuine.

Examining the sequences just offered gives cues about the subtle
difference between "sucking up" (as in the dean with the benefactors'
daughter) and Beth's schmoozing interactions. I always urge my students to visit me in my office hours. Few undergraduates take me up
on this invitation. Those who do stop by give me the chance to get
to know them better. In so doing, they have a better chance of letting
me know who they are, what their lives are like (do they work, live at
home, struggle with life?), and what their goals might be. It usually
gives them the benefit of the doubt in my grading; moreover, when
they ask me for advice or a recommendation, I can help them. Without
the extra schmoozing, I have little to go on.

Emil[6] is one student who really understood this. Despite being a few
years behind in his undergraduate studies due to service in the military
in Iraq, he was an eager participant in class. That, of course, impressed
me. Emil's joint major in political science and linguistics made for
interesting insights into the course, sociolinguistics. He always raised
his hand to offer his firsthand perspective on the discussion.

The problem was that much of the class grade was based on essay
examinations. This was a real issue for Emil, whose family had emigrated

to the United States from Central America when he was 10 years old. Thus, while he had done his secondary education in the United States, he still had problems in English writing. I got to know all of this only because Emil stopped by my office hours frequently to chat about his future. This engaged me in mentoring him. In fact, he ended up doing a senior thesis under my guidance and went off to do a prestigious summer internship in a government agency, with my recommendation.

It all got started before coming to the university, when Emil was a student at the local community college after his military service. Emil gives insight into how he found linguistics through the good schmooze with one of his professors. In his own words:

> This occurred in the middle of the fourth week of my general anthropology class. Before taking the class, I had seriously considered doing anthropology as a major. Having read about what anthropologists do, the field seemed like something that I would want to do as a career. Four weeks into the course, however, I decided that anthropology was not something I wanted to pursue. This made for a sensitive situation because I had already told my professor that I was considering anthropology as a career and as a result, he had offered several pieces of advice on how to pursue that career goal. I didn't want to hurt his feelings by telling him that I had changed my mind, but at the same time, I didn't want him to continue assuming that anthropology was what I wanted. After class was over that day, the professor said to me:

> Professor: Are you going to try to get into UF for the spring semester?
> Emil: No, it's past the deadline already. Besides, I'm not 100 percent sure anthropology is right for me.
> Professor: [a little disappointed] Really?

Emil explains:

> At this point, it was obvious that we were both uncomfortable. Although I'd merely stated that I wasn't completely sure I wanted to do anthropology as a major, it was obvious by my professor's reaction that he knew I was no longer considering anthropology as a major. My attempt to be nice, however, left open an opportunity to expand on the conversation, as opposed to if I flatly stated,

"I don't want to do anthropology." This turned out to be of great benefit later as the conversation proceeded:

Emil:	Yeah, don't get me wrong, I enjoy the class, but I can't see myself doing anthropology as a career. The only part I really have interest in is linguistic anthropology, but I don't want to major in anthropology just because of that.
Professor:	Well, if that's your interest, then you can major solely in linguistics.
Emil:	Linguistics is a separate major?
Professor:	Yeah! You can't major in it here, but you can at the University of Florida. You should look into it.
Emil:	Okay, I'll do that. Thanks professor!

He goes on to explain:

I decided not to do anthropology as a major and eventually switched to political science, but I didn't forget the professor's advice. I looked into the program as he suggested, eventually adding linguistics as a double major. Were it not for that conversation, I wouldn't have even considered linguistics as a major.

Emil's illustration was not all about networking and gaining favor. He distinguished himself from the ordinary student. By schmoozing, he showed himself to be serious and motivated. The good schmooze prevailed over any shortcomings in essay writing. A nice guy, a smart enough fellow, Emil was able to get guidance that is above and beyond the normal by going just a bit farther than most students do in talking to his professors. They got to know him. They gave advice that opened up new worlds. They recommended him. Educational schmoozing led to career opportunities.

Heather's schmoozing is another, similar example.[7] She is bilingual in English and Chinese. In her own words:

It was the beginning of a new semester and I went to visit my professor during her office hours. My intention was to discuss the possibility of being a part of her research study for a gain in personal experience. The professor, on the other hand, was planning on conducting an experiment on some Chinese subjects, and she was looking for someone who could help translate her consent form from English to Mandarin Chinese:

Heather: I am very interested in being a part of your research. Is there anything I can do for you?
Professor: Actually, I am in need of someone who can translate the consent form so the subjects can understand the purpose of the experiment when they come in.
Heather: I'm fluent in Mandarin Chinese. I think I can help.
Professor: Unfortunately, I can't pay you though, but you can get course credit for doing this.

Heather goes on: We finish discussing the details of the research study and finally carry on to a lighter subject:

Professor: So, tell me, what are your plans after you graduate?
Heather: I'm not so sure. I never thought I'd say this, but I think I'd like to go into teaching. I've been teaching English to some Chinese researchers in the pharmacology department here for awhile now. Their professor hired me to help them with their conversational English skills. I've really enjoyed working with them and teaching.
Professor: Oh? We have a visiting scholar from Korea who recently joined us in our department. He is looking for someone to help him with his English. Would you be interested? I can give you his e-mail.

Heather ended up tutoring the Korean visiting scholar for a year, and he later asked her to tutor his children as well. Although the professor wanted to but could not pay her for the work Heather did for her, she gave Heather an alternative job opportunity that paid very well. While Heather admitted that she wanted to make a good impression on the professor by telling her about her teaching experiences, she was not expecting any favors. One thing led to another, and voilà!

Schmoozing with teachers is necessary for getting research experience, as in Heather's case, and recommendations, as with Emil. This kind of schmoozing is difficult, for it is hard to disambiguate sucking up from just getting a teacher to know about you. Emil did this by being a "regular" during office hours. He did not merely stop by once and issue a request. He got to know me over a period of time in which I was able to find out who he was outside of class.

Students who appear once to issue a request are usually not as successful. This is true particularly if the professor does not think of them as superior. From my own experience of this sort of situation over many years, I can say honestly that because writing letters of recommendation is such a time-consuming task, I do not hesitate to turn down requests of this sort when I am not sufficiently acquainted with a student outside of their classroom participation.

Mary is a good example. She had taken two courses with me as an undergraduate. In the first semester, she sat in the back row with a group of her friends and whispered a great deal with them during class discussion. In the second semester, she changed her tack. She sat in the front of the room, always participated, and became a class leader. She was a B+ student in that second class. Like Emil, she had trouble writing a coherent essay. So, while her oral work in the course received an A, her written work brought her average down.

Mary never came to talk to me during my office hours during the academic year except one time—to request a letter of recommendation for a summer internship. I turned down the request. I advised Mary to ask someone who would give her a more glowing letter than I could write. After all, she was not a superior student. I did not know anything about her other than her class behavior (first inappropriate and later better).

In contrast to Mary, Maddie is a more successful example of how to ask for this sort of favor.[8] Maddie knew that she would need a professor's recommendation at the end of the semester and decided she needed to get to know her teachers well enough before asking. She did her homework. She researched her history professor and found that the professor had a doctorate in social work. She figured she was in luck, as she had spent many summers volunteering at a Lighthouse camp and, as such, would have something to discuss with her professor. At the end of a class, she approached her professor:

Maddie: I saw the other day that you have a PhD in social work. I've spent many summers with handicapped children and I have a soft spot for them.

Professor: Yeah, I used to work in the field, but decided to start teaching.

Maddie: Oh, do you still have any opportunities to work with the children?

Professor: Yes, as a matter of fact I do. I founded a club a few years ago that goes to schools and spends an hour each week mentoring handicapped children.

Maddie: Really? Would it be possible for me to get involved with you in the club? I have been trying to get involved with that sort of thing since I moved to Gainesville.

Professor: Yeah, that would be wonderful. We would love all the help we could get. I can forward you the details if you would like.

Maddie: Thanks! I'm really excited about this opportunity and I can't wait to get started helping out you and the club!

Schmoozing with this professor enabled Maddie to become part of something in which her professor was directly involved. This opportunity allowed her to get to know her professor better, and by the end of the semester, Maddie had this professor's recommendation for a paid summer internship. The schmoozing was just Maddie's foot in the door. She showed her worth to the professor, and they got to know each other. Her talent and acumen for working with children was the real proof of her worth in the field. Only then did she request the reference.

Good schmooze or bad schmooze? The line is always fuzzy. The fact is, without doing her homework and extra work, Maddie might not have succeeded. But she was really interested in getting more experience working with handicapped children. Her schmoozing with the professor enabled her to get this training. It ultimately also enabled her to demonstrate her talent, thus landing the recommendation.

THE GOOD SCHMOOZE FOR TEACHERS

Teacher talk is the stuff on which colleges of education are built. The training of teachers has long been one of the primary endeavors of teacher certification programs. However, no matter how well one has mastered the material of what is taught or the methods courses, a teacher can still not have learned the subtleties of what goes into effective teaching. This is something that usually comes with experience.

The first step in being an effective teacher is finding common ground with one's students. As anyone who has taught a class knows, this can be very problematic. Common ground is most important with younger students and those from demographic groups other than one's own. Without shared background, the schmoozing challenges increase. This issue has been widely portrayed in TV and films. Films about classroom discourse have largely focused on depicting the struggles of teachers with problem students in problem schools, which are often high schools.

In films about problematic classroom interaction, almost invariably the teachers/coaches have to deal with overcoming racial and ethnic barriers or delinquency among the students. The dramas focus on the difference one teacher can make in literally saving the lives of these students through their encouraging and mentoring in the classroom and in the athletic arena. This not what we typically think of as good social schmoozing, since it is often monologic rather than dialogic. That is to say, there is an abundance of one-way talk consisting of lecturing and moralizing.

For better or worse, classroom interaction is usually teacher fronted. Rather than face-to-face, it is face-to-faces. The teacher is in front of the class and the students face the teacher, not each other. The conversation of school is therefore not what we typically think of as *conversation*. Even when lecturing is not the norm, the teacher initiates, a student responds, and the teacher provides feedback. The result is that the teacher speaks two-thirds of the time. Can we consider it schmoozing? Perhaps we can consider some ways in which teachers succeed or fail in their talk.

Several recent and older films come to mind: Michelle Pfeiffer as the teacher in *Dangerous Minds*; Samuel Jackson as *Coach Carter*; and Edward James Olmos as the teacher in *Stand and Deliver*. Each of these examples portrays a dedicated teacher facing extraordinary odds against reaching their students, who live in slums, with all the family and societal problems engendered by the situation.

In *Dangerous Minds*, the teacher takes on a high school English class in a slum neighborhood of New York. Just as she is about to give up hope of ever being able to do this difficult job, she stumbles upon a hint of success. When talking to her colleague about having her students read the poetry of Dylan Thomas, he mistakes "Dylan" for Bob Dylan. A light bulb goes on in her head. She decides to have them read the lyrics of Bob Dylan, and has the students relate them to their own lives and struggles. They get interested in the work. It leads to discussions about their personal life narratives. This is classroom schmoozing, but not exactly what we think of as typical "shooting the breeze." The ability to relate the official goings-on (e.g., the teaching) to the students' lives is the essence of good teaching. It is a theme seen through dramas that highlight stories of how education, with the right teacher, can help to lift a person out of poverty and squalor.

Coach Carter deals with a similar struggle. It is based on a true story of the life of Ken Carter, a businessman who had been a high school basketball star. He willingly and enthusiastically takes on coaching the current team of his high school, but the players are a bunch of ne'er-do-well ghetto kids. They cope with drugs, teenage pregnancy, gang fights, and the like. The coach's schmoozing reaches them because he focuses on the positive. Rather than say "You can't. . . .," he says, "If you do. . . . you will. . . ." It is all about being respectful. He shows respect for the student basketball players while demanding respect from them. While he is always in command, Carter displays himself as a positive role model with positive schmoozing (even though the majority of his talk is monologic). Through this example, he engenders discipline and self-respect. This is something they had not previously had. The following example illustrates:

Carter: Okay, young sirs. We're gonna take it to the next level. Everything I know about basketball I learned from women. I have a sister. Her name's Diane. She was always on my case about every little thing. Matter of fact, she still is. "Turn down that radio!" "Did you eat the last piece of cake? "Did you drink all the Kool-Aid?" [laughter] She was always in my face. So when I call Diane, we're going to play straight man-to-man, pressure defense.

. . . .

Now we have Delilah. She was my childhood sweetheart.

Student: Sir, was she hot?
Coach: Ooh, yes sir. She was sssssssssteamin' hot. [laughter] Ah, but she was the devil. That girl was eeevil. I remember once she tricked me into stealing brownies from Christ the King First Baptist Church bake sale. She smiled, and got her way out of it while I damn near had to wear a pillow on my butt for a month before I could sit down. Delilah, gentlemen. She's our trap defense.

The students could easily relate to these examples from the coach's life. They mostly had sisters who tried to socialize them, just as Carter's sister Diane did. In presenting the strategy of Delilah, they could also relate to a "steamin' hot" but evil girl. Carter brought the talk to the relational level. He got their attention. They went on to be a winning team despite their initial low ranking.

Perhaps the consummate example of good teacher schmoozing derives from the now-classic 1988 film *Stand and Deliver*. In fact, the more recent *Dangerous Minds* appears to be a takeoff on the earlier film, but with a different demographic (African Americans). *Stand and Deliver* depicts the real-life story of Jaime Escalante, who quits his job as an industry engineer to take on teaching mathematics in a poor, East Los Angeles high school composed mostly of students of Hispanic origin. Escalante brings math to life with schmoozing about how they can easily grasp the concepts. Like Coach Carter, he does this through examples that relate to their own experience:

Teacher: Whoever heard of negative and positive numbers?
Student 1: Yeah, negative numbers are like unemployment. Ten million people out of work—that's a negative number.

. . .

Teacher: You ever play with the sand?
Students: Yeah.
Teacher: The sand that comes out of the hole that's a positive, the hole, is a negative. That's it. Simple. Anybody can do. Minus two plus two equals . . . Come on a negative two plus two equals, anybody can do it. Fill the hole [whispering] minus two plus two equals, come on just fill the hole, you can do it . . .
Student 2: Zero.
Teacher: Zero, you're right. Simple. That's it! Minus two plus two equals zero. You just fill the hole. Did you know that neither the Greeks nor the Romans were capable of using the concept of zero? It was your ancestors, the Mayans, who first contemplated the zero. The absence of value. True story, you burros have math in your blood.

It is impressive to consider the schmoozing techniques that go into Escalante's superior ability to engage these students. Here the schmoozing is indeed dialogic. Escalante does not merely lecture the students about how to behave, but he truly interacts with them. By this point, he has already developed solidarity with them, first by mirroring their ethnic background and using it to an advantage. He shows himself to be part of their in-group in his own identity. Second, he teases them strategically. He is able to do this because he also uses self-denigrating teasing and joking about his own attributes. The students allow this teacher to tease them. They know that it is all done in a positive spirit.

The students come to really relate to him and start listening to the mathematics goings-on. The material is presented in such a way as to make them talk about math in relation to their experiences. Since this is Los Angeles, the beach is part of the students' everyday lives. Given this, Escalante provides the sand problem to introduce negative and positive numbers. They understand. He culminates this discussion with a real boost to their collective Hispanic heritage. He tells them that their ancestors, the Mayans, were able to master these concepts even though the Greeks and Romans were not. He makes them feel a sort of ethnic self-worth that they had never before experienced.

There is one female student in the class, Anita Delgado, who is already leagues ahead of the rest in math. She is the one with the greatest potential. However, her father, a restaurant owner, has her quit school in order to work in the family business. Escalante and his wife go there, ostensibly to have dinner, but really to talk to Anita's father, Mr. Delgado:

Teacher:	She talks about going to medical school.
Mr. Delgado:	No, I don't think so. . . .
Teacher:	She should make her own choices.
Mr. Delgado:	*Un momento, yo soy el padre de la nina, no usted* [one moment, I'm the girl's father, not you] . . .
Teacher:	She could go to college, come back, and teach you how to run the place.

Escalante goes to bat for Anita with her father, not wanting to waste her great talent. The attempt at good schmoozing with Mr. Delgado initially upset the father, but it ultimately succeeded. Not long after this conversation, Anita showed up again in school. Her father obviously had registered the teacher's assessment of his daughter's talent and eventually relented. It would not have happened but for the teacher's going above and beyond the requirements of his job within the four classroom walls.

How does Escalante do the good schmooze with this parent? First, he gets the father's attention and invites him to sit at the table. Only after complimenting the intelligence of the daughter does the teacher moralize about the fact that Anita should be allowed to make her own decisions about staying in school.

Anita ultimately takes the advanced placement examination in math and gets the highest score possible. She goes on to college on a full scholarship. Escalante succeeds with most of this group. The good schmooze turns their lives around. True story.

The good schmooze for teachers is a nuanced talent. It is essential if a teacher is to transform the lives of students. The films focusing on delinquent high school students differ dramatically from those depicting the education of more privileged students. Two films set at Harvard Law School illustrate. They show just how teacher talk serves not to engage the attention but the contrary: to weed out those who do not have the mettle. Those of us who are baby boomers will recall the now-classic movie *The Paper Chase* (1973; referred to at the start of the chapter), which was so popular as to be made into a TV series. In this scene, Professor Kingsfield called upon one of his students, Hart:

Kingsfield: Mr. Hart—Can you relate the next case to the summary we've been building?
Hart: Thank you, I prefer to pass.
Kingsfield: What did you say?
Hart: Well, I have nothing relevant to say concerning the case. When I have something relevant to say, I shall raise my hand.
Kingsfield: Mr. Hart, will you step down here. [steps down to the podium]
           Mr. Hart, here is a dime. Call your mother. Tell her there's serious doubt about your becoming a lawyer.

Hart: [slowly walks away, then turns around] You are a son of a bitch, Kingsfield.
Kingsfield: Mr. Hart, that is the most intelligent thing you've said today. Now you may take your seat.

[Hart smiles, students chuckle, Hart tosses the dime].

Surely this is dramatic license. One as strict a disciplinarian as Kingsfield would probably not invite Hart back to sit down. It would be a loss of face. Bad schmooze, indeed.

The comedic film *Legally Blonde* borrows from the previous type of bad teacher schmoozing. This occurs when the principal character, Elle Woods, attends her first class at Harvard Law. The professor calls on her randomly to answer a question, but she had no idea that she was to do any reading before the first class. The professor promptly dismisses her and tells her not to return until she is prepared.

Obviously, this is a stereotype that the public has with what transpires in higher education at the more serious institutions (e.g., the Ivy League). This is surely not the case in reality. The fact is that professors make every effort to build rapport with their students. We do this because we want to be more effective teachers. Most of us truly wish the outcome of our teaching to be a great leap in knowledge among our students. Even those who are not inherently good schmoozers try hard in this regard. After all, at the end of each semester, our students get to evaluate us! So, getting on the good side of students can be good schmoozing, for the sake of an interesting class; in contrast, it can be bad schmoozing—only for the direct benefit of getting a good evaluation. Which sort of schmoozing it is usually becomes clear and rather quickly at that. Students tend to lose respect for the unctuously friendly teacher.

At times, teachers resort to using sarcasm in the classroom. Like teasing, it is a double-edged sword. That is, sarcasm and irony can be interpreted by students to either have a negative impact on the class or a positive effect on the relationships between teacher and students.

"YEAH, RIGHT": SARCASM IN TEACHING

A linguistics professor was lecturing his class. "In English," he explained, "a double negative forms a positive. In some languages, such as Russian, a double negative is still a negative. However, there is no language in which a double positive can form a negative."
A voice from the back of the room piped up, "Yeah, right!"

E. T. Thompson

Sarcasm is rarely thought of as positive. Most people believe that it is biting and negative, as in "Yeah, right!" But Jodi Nelms (aka Eisterhold)[9] found that this is not always the case. Sarcasm, and its corollary, irony, can have some very positive functions. Nelms undertook an in-depth study of the functions and uses of sarcasm in college classes at the University of Florida under my mentorship. She videotaped 48 classes with varied course content and professors (male and female; experienced and new). She found 114 sarcastic utterances, most of them uttered by the professors rather than the students.

Nelms found that sarcasm in the classroom was more often than not used positively. She ascertained this through post-sessions with students who were in the class where the professor used sarcasm. In other words, she played back to the students videotaped portions of the classes in which the sarcastic utterances occurred. The most frequent positive use of sarcasm in her data was for humorous intent. These instances functioned to build classroom rapport, lighten the atmosphere of the class, spark interest in the subject matter, and lessen the gap between teacher and student. Sarcasm was also employed positively when professors were trying to make a point, to push students, to respond to minor irritations, and in at least one case, as an indirect reprimand.

As we have seen thus far in this chapter, building rapport in the classroom is always considered a worthwhile investment on the part of the professor. The amount of effort that is put forth will not only benefit the professor in terms of improving course evaluations and decreasing the number of problem students, but it is also an important factor in ensuring that the class functions smoothly. Students appreciate when teachers show themselves as human. Self-denigrating humorous sarcasm can create this effect. One example in Nelms's data derived from a situation in which a professor was about to show a slide but could not get the projector to work. Upon discovering that it was not plugged in, she said, "Well, that would help a little." Clearly, such comments are widely heard and serve to humanize the professor. A student commented on the professor's use of self-denigrating sarcastic remarks: "If you make fun of yourself, it's an easier response than having the kids go, 'oh . . . she's an idiot' or 'whatever.'"

Another sarcastic comment was made by a male professor to a student when the student did not bring in a transparency for a presentation (this was back in the days before computerized classrooms). It illustrates an attempt to lighten the atmosphere. When the student tried to give the excuse that he could not afford to buy a transparency, the professor's reply was to ask him to write it all on the chalkboard. The professor then said, "Did you calculate in the cost per data point of the chalk?" The entire class showed an appreciation of the humorous intent of the remark by their robust laughter. While the student who was the focus did not reply, it was clear from the videotaped interaction that he felt comfortable proceeding with the presentation. The professor's comment served to relieve some tension.

The next example also illustrates a situation where the professor employed sarcasm in order to deflect some type of uncomfortable situation for the student. This was uttered by a male professor to the class as a student had just finished presenting for the first time in his class. The student, Nina, was anxious to sit down, but the professor wanted her to remain at the front of the class to answer questions: "Ok, class, ask away. Nina is *dying* to entertain you."

In the post-viewing interview, Nina reported that the professor was "jokingly harassing her, like, 'ask her questions and make her sweat a little.'" She also reported that the professor laughed when this exchange was taking place, showing that a serious matter such as making a classroom presentation can be handled in a tongue-in-cheek manner. Nina felt much more comfortable beginning her presentation after the professor uttered his comment—the redness in her face began to abate and her body seemed to relax.

This situation also illustrates the notion that humorous sarcasm can be completely serious. The professor was in fact encouraging the students to ask Nina questions, and he did want her to "sweat a little" so that she would be able to learn from the experience and be better able to handle the situation when presenting her work outside of the classroom setting. The professor in this course commented that Nina was "scared stiff" and that he was "just being facetious." The word *just* in his comment implies that he did not intend harm to the student and that he was indeed teasing her. He realized that Nina did not want anyone to ask her any questions. At the same time, he was acknowledging the fact that the rest of the class also realized her wish not to be asked questions. The students knew that they would themselves be presenting soon and that they were all nervous about being challenged by their classmates. So, although the professor was indeed encouraging questions from the audience, he was fully aware that it would not be easy to encourage a lively dialogue.

Sarcasm was also used positively when employed in expressing indirect reprimands. While this function seems counterintuitive, an example should serve to clarify: A professor had a slide up on the projector during a class lecture. She had just changed slides when a frustrated student asked if the professor could leave the last one on a little longer. The professor had been reviewing the material from the previous class, so had gone over the slide quickly. The professor reacted to the student's request by saying, "Start writing fast" in a joking tone.

In the follow-up interview, the teacher said that she was upset at having to waste class time for this student, who had been absent the period before. The professor stated in the interview, "I was chiding them, but yet I'm doing it in kind of a laughable way cuz I don't want to humiliate them."

This sort of indirect reprimand, in the form of sarcasm, can serve as a face-saving strategy. Sarcasm often serves to soften negative feelings toward a speaker or situation. It also serves to makes the professor seem fairer and more concerned for the students. A more direct/literal comment (e.g., "You missed the previous class so I shouldn't give you more time to copy the lecture notes") might come off as rudeness or thoughtlessness and perhaps be seen as a lack of concern for the students' success in the course.

Teachers must build rapport with students in order to be effective. In the case of problematic students, schmoozing is the key to getting their cooperation and attention on to the task at hand—learning. The good schmooze consists of bringing learning to students' common experiences. It entails encouragement, positive moralizing, humor, and sometimes even sarcasm.

We have seen how students can do the good schmooze and how teachers can recapture this lost art. We turn now to another important gatekeeping encounter, that of advising.

FOOT IN THE DOOR OR DOOR IN THE FACE?: SCHMOOZING IN THE ADVISING SESSION

Advising in higher education is the quintessential gatekeeping encounter where the good schmooze can make or break the results. It is a high-stakes verbal interaction for both advisors and students. Gatekeeping interactions are those where there is one party invested with institutional power who "keeps the gate." People in these roles have the decision-making authority to allow their interlocutors access or not. Knowing how to deal with others in gatekeeping encounters is important schmoozing. The art of talk in advising sessions can get one's foot in the gate, or door, or door in the face.[10]

In colleges and universities, advisors are employees whose role it is to use language to gain compliance on the part of their advisees. They must ensure that students abide by several rules, including registering for appropriate courses, paying fees, and meeting general requirements of their course work. However, little information is available to advisors in terms of the most effective way to *talk* to students in order to meet their goals. This often requires effective convincing or persuasive techniques—good schmoozing skills.

On the other hand, it would be of value to students to know what verbal strategies can be most effectively used to meet their own needs. These may include getting into a course when the class is full or getting an advisor to lift a financial hold. Students with good schmoozing skills are able to present themselves as they wish. The ultimate benefit is getting what they want or need—entrance through the metaphorical gate, or door. The question that arises is: What are the schmoozing features that contribute to a satisfactory advising encounter on the part of both parties?

The most important work on this subject looked at a phenomenon termed *co-membership* among advisors and advisees at a junior college.[11] Co-membership is, in essence, some commonality between student and advisor in ethnicity, race, or group membership or affiliation. Frederick Erickson and Jeffrey Schultz's groundbreaking finding was that co-membership opened doors for the students that might otherwise remain closed. When co-membership was absent, a lack of rapport was often evident that typically served to close the gate, resulting in "door in the face."

A few years ago, I undertook a rather large-scale study of how advisors and their advisees do the talk of good advising. I was interested in ascertaining what kinds of schmoozing techniques students use to get what they want or need; conversely, I also wanted to know what kinds of advisor talk makes for success. My research assistant[12] and I videotaped 37 advising sessions, each lasting approximately 15–30 minutes. We also interviewed the advisees after their session, and all of the advisors.

The results are most interesting. Students did little schmoozing with their advisors. That is, for the most part, they skipped any small talk and went straight to the business at hand. I concluded that this was undoubtedly due to the nature of the institution: a large, bureaucratic state university where it is difficult, if not impossible, to bend the rules. Students clearly felt that any attempt at schmoozing would be taken as disingenuous. There was only one student, from Australia, who tried to make small talk with his advisor, but it failed to get the advisor to open the gate. He made small talk at inappropriate junctures in the advising session. It quickly became clear that he was doing the schmooze of gaining favors. No success. In this context, the schmooze would need to be initiated by the gatekeepers—but how was this done?

Upon first glance, it seemed counterintuitive that the gatekeepers should be the ones doing the work of greasing the wheels of interaction. The analysis of the data yielded some insight into what exactly was going on. It became obvious that advisors took it upon themselves to humanize what would otherwise be cold, institutional interactions. It was up to them, as keepers of the gate. Most of the advisors studied made concerted efforts to establish co-membership with their advisees. They did this because they were there not only to keep the gate, but to help the students. In other words, while they took their role of gatekeeping seriously, they considered themselves counselors as well as advisors.

Co-membership does not have to be only about shared personal or demographic background. The rapport can be based on something as simple as agreeing on a similar like or dislike. In the following example, a female advisor set the stage for co-membership through a self-denigrating comment—her own lack of skills in math:

Advisor: They would yep they would increase it to you would be able to take it what is that um 9, no 6, 11 sorry, 11 credits though, I can't add at all. [whispers] Which is why I was an English major.

[student laughs]

Advisor: Yeah, um.
Student: I understand that. I hate math, too.
Advisor: It's not that I hate it, I respect it, but yeah I just can't do it.
Student: I'm the same way.

This advisor used the schmoozing technique of putting herself down, or self-denigration complaint. In so doing, she established equal footing with the student. They could commiserate with each other, both having the same gripe about math. The example illustrates how the skilled advisor builds rapport before conveying the rules, or what it

takes to get the foot in the door. It is a good news/ bad news strategy—
the good news is I'm a nice person. Now here are the rules. A skilled advisor
knows that this kind of schmoozing is an important resource that goes
with the territory of good advising.

"HERE'S WHAT YOU HAVE TO DO": ADVISORS' RESOURCES

The strategy of self-denigrating complaint/commiseration is a
valuable resource, as seen in this last example. While keeping the
gate, advisors have several other schmoozing resources available to
them to gain the students' compliance with their advice. In fact, the
advisors in this center were so good at the art of talk that students
came away from their advising sessions feeling satisfied, despite
not getting what they wanted! Students had higher levels of interactional satisfaction when advisors did several things while giving
students news that they might not want to hear. When the students
were interviewed after their advising sessions, most if not all of them
seemed unaware that they had not succeeded in getting their foot in
the door.

"Let's Figure It Out": Inclusiveness

The advisors often used inclusive verb forms as a way to gain compliance. In other words, instead of saying, "This is what you need
to do before you can. . . ," they included themselves in the effort to
brainstorm a solution to problems. This kind of inclusiveness gives
the interlocutor a sense of support—"we're in this together." It shows
that the advisor will participate in really helping to solve the problem
instead of simply conveying the rule and turning the student loose to
get the job done.

For example, a student came in who wanted to change his major. He
was not sure what to do. Advisors at this center are very familiar with
this problem and deal with such issues on a daily basis. This advisor
began by saying, "well **let's** figure it out." In so doing, she included
herself in a joint problem-solving task. It made the student feel like he
had an ally. He indicated a feeling of satisfaction in the post-advising
interview.

Changing the Subject

There were several instances where the advisors used the schmoozing technique of quickly changing the subject after giving the gatekeeping rule. The next example shows how effectively this can be done. The advisor was relatively young, female (early thirties), but experienced, having carried out this role for the past seven years:

> Advisor: The one thing I know for sure is that they definitely won't even consider it until you've met the minimum requirements. So, how are things going this semester?

She did not even give time for the student to mull over this bad news before plunging in with the good, personal schmoozing question. This is what we see as *bad news, good schmooze strategy*. In effect it is saying something like, "You have to make an effort to meet the requirements, but I'm interested in you and in counseling you." It draws the distinction between the gatekeeping function of advising and the counseling function. The latter is where the good schmooze lives.

Hedging and Softening

No matter what the context or sphere of interaction, the good schmooze always involves the ability to soften bad news. This is particularly noteworthy in advising encounters. Here are several examples, from three different advisors. The parts that soften or hedge the bad news are bolded:

> Advisor 1: You **know, I don't mean** to be the bearer of gloom and doom, but . . . [explains about transfer students] . . . it's gonna be really hard to change to psychology . . . I **just** want to be honest with you . . .
>
> Advisor 2: **I guess** honestly what I'm saying is probably it really looks like a long shot.
>
> Advisor 3: Well, **I mean, you know, I don't want to ever say anything is impossible**, but I think given our current climate with the whole transfer admissions and having to reduce our enrollment by 40 percent, **I mean** we're denying so many possible students that meet the minimum requirements for psychology, so I think it's gonna be pretty tough, um, but this would be the process.

Good advising entails knowing how to break bad news. Such phrases as "I mean" and "you know" serve to soften and hedge the negative. Of interest is that all three advisors in these examples were female. Indeed, hedging has been shown to be a linguistic strategy used more often by women than men. The same is true for other positive strategies.

"KUDOS TO YOU": POSITIVE TALK

The most-skilled advisors employed various kinds of positive talk in their student meetings. They commiserated, they encouraged, they complimented, and they used positive moralizing. For example, a student came in to find out if he was eligible to graduate. He needed the advisor's tally of courses that fulfilled the requirements. This particular female advisor began the discussion with a compliment to the advisee right at the start: "You have an excellent GPA, so kudos." The boost to the student's ego was a good schmooze technique. It set the stage for joint brainstorming of his record. This same advisor, a woman in her thirties, was highly sought out by the students. She came to the task naturally, with genuine warmth of personality suited to her task. When another student came in to complain that she had inadvertently taken courses that did not count toward her major, this advisor soothed her with positive moralizing: "Education is never wasted." Her manner of delivery was neither pompous nor authoritarian. It was conveyed in a most commiserative tone. The student was assuaged, and the discussion ensued about how to fulfill the requirements.

COMMISERATION AND ENCOURAGEMENT

By now it should be clear that a major strategy of rapport building in social schmoozing is the ability to show commiseration, especially in response to griping. Advising sessions frequently consist of gripes that students have. The advisors knew how to do the schmooze strategy of commiseration, as seen in the following sequence:

Advisor: So there are so many options. I know your head's probably spinning right now.
Student: A little bit.
Advisor: But what I'm trying to encourage you is there are plenty of graduate school options that don't necessarily apply to your undergraduate major in psychology, so don't get too fixated on that.

By saying "your head's probably spinning right now," the advisor indicated that she realized it was all a lot to take in. It is a good schmooze technique that was encouraging.

Consider two more examples:

A: How are you liking that developmental psychology class?
S: It's fun.
A: Good. [sing-song intonation]
S: It's definitely fun.
A: Found a better fit for you—sometimes that's all it takes, you know, for you to be able to do well.

This encouragement comes in the form of moralizing that is good schmoozing. Just like the distinction between good moralizing and lecture moralizing in families, moralizing in this type of interaction can be either encouraging or discouraging. It all depends on delivery.

Another example shows how advisors can be encouraging despite student negativity:

A: How are your courses going this semester?
S: [frowns] Not as great as I thought. I'm usually straight A's, overachiever, I don't see straight A's in my future.
A: Well, you never know, maybe you're not in the right major.

Timing Is Everything

In the advising encounter, small talk can reopen the conversation and provide a student with more information. Just when a student is about to leave with the door in his face, the advisor says:

A: So you're a Spanish major? So how's everything going this semester?
[Advisor and student chat for a bit, and the advisor suggests that the student check with the department and they might open a new section for a class that the student previously mentioned trying to get into but that was too full.]

Perhaps the advisor realized that the session had ended too harshly for the student. He took a step back just in the nick of time. The student, in a post-advising interview, seemed satisfied with the conversation. This was no doubt due to the way it was all wrapped up.

In fact, schmoozing on more personal issues often happened near the end of the sessions, after the gatekeeping obligations were taken care of. In the next example, a student came in to get advising on the paperwork needed to graduate. After all the business was done, the advisor reopened the more social schmoozing:

A: And you applied to graduate, so are you excited?
S: Yep-well, yeah, I guess it's a little of both.
A: Are you going to stay in the U.S. after?
S: No, going home.
A: Where's home?
S: Norway.

The encounter thus ended with a good schmooze chat. There was little to be gained in direct benefit for neither the advisor nor the student. It was all part of "shooting the breeze" that makes for warm feelings. After all, that is what it is all about—even in a high-stakes interaction such as the advising session.

"WHAT CAN I DO FOR YOU?": LESS SUCCESSFUL ENCOUNTERS

Not all of the encounters were successful, according to the interviews with the advisees. The few that left the students dissatisfied were the ones in which the advisor did very little schmoozing. In other words, even in sessions ending with the "door in their face" bureaucratically, students felt satisfied when advisors chatted with them on a more personal level. One advisor who did this less than the others was male. He was mostly interested in the business at hand. One clear indication was his consistent use of the kind of stock greeting heard in service encounters: "Hi, how are you. What's up, what can I do for you?"

This greeting is formulaic in nature and generally does not elicit a true response vis-à-vis how the student is actually doing. This kind of perfunctory opening conveys a tone of objectivity. The advisor is there to keep the gate. If advisees have met the requirements, they will get their foot in the door. If not, it will be door in the face. The gate will be kept closed.

Successful schmoozing on the part of advisors had several qualities: softening the bad news, changing the subject after bad news, ending with small talk, encouraging and commiserating, complimenting, positive moralizing, and using inclusive language. In highly bureaucratic institutions, it is the role of advisors to do the schmoozing to gain compliance. Advisees know that too much schmoozing can backfire. For students, schmoozing would only seem like "sucking up." The advisors' schmoozing in the study resulted from experience, good training in counseling, and sometimes just having the right personality for the job. The good schmoozers were the most successful in this role in the sphere of higher education.

CONCLUSION: THE GOOD SCHMOOZE IN EDUCATION

Schmoozing in the educational sphere is not unlike that of other domains of interactional space. For students, it sets the groundwork for doing well in courses—but it also opens up other, longer-lasting possibilities. We have seen how talk with teachers outside of class can have indirect benefits leading to life's opportunities. For advisors and teachers, good educational schmoozing has the potential to save lives, one student at a time. There is little that is more rewarding.

Higher education and even a graduate education are no longer rarities as they used to be several generations ago. More and more young people and older individuals are seeking a college degree or an advanced degree as either a credential for a career or simply for further learning. Because of this, the educational scene is becoming more and more diverse, with different ethnic and socioeconomic groups, more diverse age groups, and a more even gender distribution evident. This is particularly true in this sphere of interaction that has in the past been open to only whites, males, and middle-and upper-class individuals. Increased access to higher education will surely continue with the advent of new technologies, such as a possible iCollege. Schmoozing in the sphere of education is therefore increasingly important for helping those previously uninitiated into the appropriate norms of interaction in this domain. Knowing how to do the talk of educational settings can help open doors. Knowing why misfires occur can keep the doors from closing in your face.

NOTES

1. Bronislaw Malinowski, "The Problem of Meaning in Primitive Languages," in *The Meaning of Meaning*, eds. C. le Ogden and I. A. Richards (London: Routledge and Kegan Paul, 1923), 146–152.

2. Thomas Fuller, *Gnomologia: Adagies and Proverbs; Wife Sayings, Ancient and Modern, Foreign and British* (London: B. Barker, 1732).

3. Data collected by Lauren Musick, 2009.

4. Data collected by Caroline Kennelly Latterman, 2010.

5. 2008 University of Florida Teaching Assistant of the Year, College of Liberal Arts and Sciences.

6. Data collected by Edgar Rodriguez, 2009.

7. Data collected by Helen (Tzu Ting) Lin, 2009.

8. Data collected by Taylor Wilkinson, 2009.

9. Jodi Nelms, "A Descriptive Analysis of the Functions and Uses of Sarcasm in Higher Education Classroom Discourse" (unpublished PhD dissertation, University of Florida, 2001).

10. Foot in the door (FITD) and door in the face (DITF) are notions from the field of social psychology. See, for example, J. L. Freedman and S. C. Fraser, "Compliance without Pressure: The Foot in the Door Technique," *Journal of Personality and Social Psychology* 4 (1966): 195–202.

11. Frederick Erickson and Jeffery Shultz, *The Counselor as Gatekeeper* (New York: Academic Press, 1982).

12. Data for the study was collected by my research assistant, Caroline Kennelly Latterman.

CHAPTER 5

Schmoozing Cross-Culturally

I do not want my house to be walled in on all sides and my windows to be stuffed. I want the cultures of all the lands to be blown about my house as freely as possible. But I refuse to be blown off my feet by any.

Mahatma Ghandi

INTRODUCTION: WHY ARE THEY SO WEIRD?

A recent political cartoon in a national newspaper depicted a scene that most people today would find humorous. It showed two "natives" of a country faced with newcomers on the shore who had just alighted from what looked like a galleon. The newcomers were obviously invaders dressed in full armor. One of the natives turned to the other and said, "Don't worry. Cultural diversity is a good thing."

This is humorous because we all know that the invaders' intentions are probably not peaceful. Nonetheless, recent history and political trends tell us that we should take a positive attitude toward building a diverse society. The trouble is the paradox of knowing what should be the case and what really happens when people with different interactional norms come into contact.

If your rules or norms for what is appropriate language and behavior come into conflict with mine, I am naturally going to think you are at least weird. At worst, I am going to attribute characteristics to you that assign negative values to the whole group you represent. In other words, I may think your national, ethnic, or racial group is rude, offensive, or even dangerous.

It is hard to take the perspective that "I'm okay and you're okay" when we just do not communicate in the same way. We may both be well-intentioned people; but when in your cultural system it is okay to ask me how much money I make, but it is a taboo question in mine, a misfire naturally occurs. When this happens, I am likely to not want to interact with you again. Moreover, I am likely to think everyone from your group is to be avoided.

Schmoozing in cross-cultural encounters is an especially important endeavor in modern times. Our world is increasingly smaller as people from different societies interact with greater and greater frequency. The fact that at the time of this writing, there are now 12–15 million undocumented immigrants in the United States, is telling. That is not even taking into account the number of legal immigrants recently arrived in the United States. Much as some people would like this situation to change, it is not going away any time soon. More than ever before, we need to be able to recapture the lost art of the good schmooze with persons from other societies.

As mentioned earlier, we have lived under the myth that the United States is and has been a melting pot—a place where diverse peoples come, shed their languages and their interactional norms, and give up their cultural heritages to melt into one larger U.S. culture where we all speak English and are homogenous in cultural traditions. Clearly this is a myth and has always been so. All one needs to do is look at any one family's Thanksgiving table. If it is an Italian American family, there is pasta and "gravy" (aka sauce) to go with the turkey. Chinese? Perhaps wontons with the turkey. Jewish? Matzo ball soup, no doubt.

We are really a salad bowl with a myriad of flavors and textures, not a melting pot in which those flavors and textures are blended together into a uniform whole. We retain many of the differences that make culture interesting. True, the more we cook, the more blending takes place. But recent history has witnessed less cooking and more tossing together. Whether we like it or not, it is a fact. Newcomers may blend linguistically, but culturally speaking, it is another story entirely.

LANGUAGE, CULTURE, AND SCHMOOZING

Typically, children of newly arrived immigrants to the United States do melt, in some respects, at least in terms of language. If they are younger than early adolescence, they will come to speak English without a trace of a foreign accent. Many scholars of second-language acquisition have investigated just why this happens with young arrivals but not with older newcomers. But that is a subject for a different book.

Sadly, children of immigrants naturally shed languages. Most linguists consider this state of affairs unfortunate. Why not add languages without losing those that are native? On the other hand, while these immigrant children shed their mother tongue, they do not always shed interactional norms and values that may eventually conflict with those of native speakers. In other words, languages are easily shed, but norms of interacting are often retained. The result is language loss but cultural maintenance, to some extent. It is this latter fact, the cultural vestiges, that may eventually come to cause cross-cultural schmoozing difficulties.

When immigrants arrive, they are part of an out-group unless they learn our language and customs. However, it is not the language, per se, that causes the "us versus them" issue. It really is the cultural norms that are in conflict. When cultural norms diverge, it is the site where "us versus them" really comes into play.

A hypothetical example will help to clarify. Let us suppose that a young boy of Russian parentage grows up in a bilingual home. His home language is Russian. He soon starts watching American television and playing with English-speaking peers. As with most children, he rapidly acquires English, and perhaps even eventually refuses to speak Russian with his nuclear family. He may, in fact, completely lose his ability to speak Russian. This situation is not uncommon. The boy speaks English natively now, but his Russian norms of speaking may persist, as will be clear in a moment. This is despite his inability to speak that language. These norms mirror those of his parents because of the interactional patterns learned at home.

One wants to avoid stereotypes in such discussion; however, patterns of interaction do differ from culture to culture. The little boy may interrupt others too frequently when speaking in English, perhaps at an earlier point in the conversational turn than is the norm in English. He also develops a pattern of strongly disagreeing with others without hedging or softening. For example, when his friend says something he thinks is untrue, he does not wait until his friend finishes, but instead interrupts and says, "No, you're wrong."

The boy continues to do this into adulthood. When adults behave in ways that are not congruent with what is expected in a community, they are looked upon as weird and are consequently unable to successfully form relationships. The small talk elements that differ greatly from one place to another interfere with smooth rapport building. This phenomenon need not only be the fault of coming from different national origins. It can also come from diversity in ethnic, racial, and regional norms within one country.

Much of this chapter's discussion of cross-cultural schmoozing centers on getting it wrong. This is due to the fact that talk across cultural groups is fraught with the dangers of misunderstandings. The implications of doing the good schmooze cross-culturally derive from what does not work. Unfortunately, examples taken from real verbal interactions in all the spheres abound with misfires. We analyze here these examples, from public and private life, to derive conclusions on how to do it better. Never has the need for comprehension across languages and cultures been more salient than in these years following 9/11. Whatever our views may be about immigration, it is now a reality that the potential for misunderstanding permeates our everyday lives.

WORKPLACE SCHMOOZING: CULTURAL VALUES AND MISCOMMUNICATION

Many of us now spend a large portion of our waking lives in our places of work, and our workplaces are increasingly distant from our homes. Because of this fact, work relationships are more and more overlapping with social relationships. While a workplace is defined as a place where people come together to sell something, make something, and so on, it is a sphere of life of interacting with coworkers and, often, with the public. This may no longer be face-to-face contact, but even with Internet technologies, the faces may be there—albeit on the screen.

In any workplace, schmoozing misfires can do serious damage to a business's bottom line. When I first took up my university position,

I was in charge of the academic program of our intensive English program for foreign students. This is a job that requires good understanding of differing norms of talk across societies. One of the first tasks to undertake was to peruse our advertising literature sent out to countries around the world. A glaring problem immediately presented itself. Our expensive, glossy brochure contained several photographs depicting undergraduate students in various small groups in locations on the campus. I noticed that one of the photographs showed students lounging on picnic tables with their feet up on the benches. The soles of their feet were facing the camera when the shot was captured. Big blooper! In Muslim cultures, it is a serious insult to display the soles of one's feet or shoes. This is why George W. Bush's experience with having a shoe thrown at him by an Iraqi journalist was so insulting. At the time of the brochure blooper, we were recruiting many students from Middle Eastern countries. Once the mistake was recognized, we had to make sure the brochures were not sent to those countries. We trashed the whole lot and redid the brochure.

This is a good example of the inherent dangers of cross-cultural misfires in workplace schmoozing. In this case, the blooper was a possible threat to the bottom line of the institute. If we had lost enrollment from that particular part of the world, we risked a great potential loss in revenue.

"I CAN'T UNDERSTAND THEM": SCHMOOZING AND OUTSOURCING

Several good illustrations of cross-cultural schmoozing misfires are found in the 2007 film *Outsourced*. These exemplify the hazards of not getting it right. The situation of the movie is as follows: a young man from an American company is sent to India to set up an outsourced call center—the operation will no longer be conducted from within U.S. national borders. Most readers are no doubt very familiar with such call centers, and many complain bitterly about not being able to understand the other's accent. Despite this general misconception, the problems of misunderstanding go far beyond mere pronunciation. If accent were the extent of the issue, it would be a fairly easy problem to resolve. The problems are both linguistic and cultural (pragmatic).

A good example derives from a sequence when the new boss, Todd Anderson, introduces himself to workers at the call center. The boss starts talking about customer complaints:

Boss: Basically, you people need to learn about America. Things go faster if the customer feels they're talking to a native speaker.
Worker 1:   But we are native English speakers. English is the official language of the government. You got it from the British and so did we. We just speak it differently.
Boss: Next time you're on a call, try to listen to the customer's pronunciation, their slang, their small talk.
Worker 2:   What I want to know is, what is small talk?
Boss: Ya know, it's like, how're ya doin' today? How's the weather in Arizona? You can talk about sports—no, never mind. You want to sound American.

The boss indicates in the exchange that pronunciation is important in sounding American, but that small talk, or schmoozing, is equally, if not more important. He starts suggesting that they may want to do the good schmooze by talking about sports, but then stops short. He apparently comes to the realization that if they try to talk about sports it might backfire—they need to sound as American as possible. Given this, how are the workers to proceed with small talk, or schmoozing? We are left with the distinct impression that it is a sizable task, perhaps more of an obstacle than accent.

Beyond accent, the following sequence from the film illustrates different word meanings. The Indian workers in the call center are having another meeting with their boss to go over some of the ways in which they can ameliorate their communication problems with American callers:

Worker 1: A woman called and said, "I want to get school supplies for my grandson," and I said, "You need a rubber."

It is not explicitly elaborated that the American customer was confused, perhaps taken aback, and probably affronted. It would not be at all unimaginable that she did not successfully complete her call with this particular call center worker. That is left to the imagination of the viewer. In the ensuing discussion of the call, a humorous exchange ensued:

Worker 2: Yes, she wants a rubber.
Boss: No, it's an eraser. A rubber is a condom.
Worker 3: A flat?
Worker 4: No, it's an apartment.
Boss: No, a rubber is for birth control.
Worker 4: Does it work?

Here we have another mere linguistic issue rather than a cultural issue—easy enough to solve. The workers simply need to learn that certain vocabulary items in American English have different meanings from the British English (flat versus apartment) that was passed on to India. While the exchange is humorous, the predicament is not so serious. They just need to distinguish the colloquial American meaning of *rubber* from the English one. They also should distinguish *condom* from *condominium*, but that is another joke. When miscommunication is merely a matter of new definitions of terms, these can be learned.

A more serious issue—the kind that is the focus of this chapter—is when cultural values (and thus pragmatic norms) clash. Cultural values cannot be taken on as easily as new meanings of words. The following sequence illustrates one such clash in the same meeting between the call center workers and their new American boss:

Worker: I don't understand the purpose of [one of the products].
Boss: That's a burger brand. Americans eat a lot of beef, and some people like to burn their initials into their food before they eat it.
Worker: Why?
Boss: It's like a cattle brand, y'know the thing you use to burn a symbol into a cow. In America that's how you keep track of your cows—branding.
Worker 2: With a red-hot iron?
Boss: Yeah.
Worker: But wouldn't the cow run away?
Boss: We do it only to baby cows, when they're small enough to hold down.
Worker 3: A suggestion—you need to learn about India.

Worker 3 has an important recommendation: that the new boss should learn about Indian cultural values. Clearly, the boss was ignorant about the Hindu value of the sacred cow. Surely the Indian workers were more than just concerned about the cows escaping from the branding. They could not fathom wanting to brand these animals, let alone grill the meat and brand it before consuming it!

The suggestion that their new boss learn something about India is illustrative of *cross-cultural pragmatics* (CCP). In a CCP perspective, individuals from two societies or communities carry out their face-to-face interactions with their own rules or norms at work, often resulting in a clash in expectations and, ultimately, misperceptions about the other group. The misperceptions are typically two-way, that is, each group misperceives the other. However, in reality, the consequences of such a situation are scarcely two-way, since inevitably one group is always more powerful than the other in any specific context.

In the call center examples, the American values are more powerful despite the Indian setting. This is the case simply because the workers are trying to use and understand American English in order to sell products. Therefore, even though they are in India, it is the task of the Indian call center workers to develop an understanding of American cultural values and not the reverse. Because of this, Worker 3's assertion that the boss needs to learn something about India is true only because he is living in India—not because the company will derive any profit from his knowing about Indian cultural values. When the bottom line is sales and profit, CCP becomes a one-way endeavor. If they do not learn these new values, they risk job loss. In this context, "When in Rome, do as the Romans do" is somewhat turned on its head.

The examples from this film derive from workplace discourse. This chapter considers the various domains to illustrate the importance of cross-cultural schmoozing in all spheres of life.

CROSS-CULTURAL SCHMOOZING IN FAMILY INTERACTIONS

Knowing how to do the good schmooze with people from varied cultural/linguistic backgrounds can lead to general harmony in all domains of interaction, including the family. The sheer number of families in which individual members are marrying partners of racial, ethnic, and national groups outside of their own is clearly a natural consequence of transnationalism. Indeed, one could speculate from an evolutionary perspective that this is possibly the only thing that could turn the salad of our society into the soup that is the mythical melting pot.

ETHNIC AND REGIONAL DIFFERENCES IN FAMILY SCHMOOZING

While the family domain has traditionally been one of inherently shared norms for interaction and interpretation, this is no longer necessarily the case. The example at the beginning of this chapter told of the young Russian boy who stopped participating in the good family schmooze in Russian in favor of using English. Schmoozing misfires in families is a matter of interacting with children and with spouses and partners. It does not have to do only with partners from different parts of the world. Couples can run into trouble even when both partners come from different regions of the same country or different ethnic groups. I illustrate with a recent example related to me by a colleague.

A middle-aged woman, Angela, and her husband, David, are from different areas of the United States. It is a second marriage for both of them, and they met as adults when their interactional and pragmatic norms were already fairly set. David, from the Midwest, is of white Anglo-Saxon origin. Angela is an Italian American from Long Island in New York. Thus, while they are both Caucasian Americans, they come from different ethnic groups and different regions of the United States. They attribute a great amount of frustration with each other due to their different communicative styles and interactional expectations. This is true not only with each other, but also with people in service encounters.

The example related here is over how each said they would handle their dissatisfaction with a repair job on the couple's boat. They took the boat into a local marine mechanic for a yearly service. A week later, they received a call that the boat was ready to be picked up. When they asked over the phone what the bill came to, they were told $844.67. They were astounded! What they expected would be minor adjustments had turned into something major with deep financial repercussions. After all, many boats themselves do not cost much more than this.

Angela waited in the car while David went in to settle the bill. When he emerged Angela said, "Did you ask why it was so expensive?" David said no, he just paid up. Angela replied, "Please go back in there and have him explain each item." He did so, emerging a half hour later. He told Angela that he and the owner of the shop had a long discussion during which the owner explained the need to do what they did and why it cost what it did. Angela was furious:

Angela: Did you tell him he overcharged you and that you're dissatisfied?
David: No, I just had him tell me why it cost so much.
Angela: I wish you had told him you'd never use them again.
David: What good would that do? He's not going to lower the price.

Angela had wanted David to handle the interaction in a more confrontational manner. That is the way she would have handled it—it is the norm in the ethnic group from which she hails. David, however, was following his own midwestern norms for handling a touchy situation. It was a deeply ingrained part of his pragmatic system to manage these kinds of situations by doing the good schmooze. He firmly believed that would get him more in the long run. Angela just could not understand this. David could not understand why Angela wanted to fight about it.

During the next few days, they had a problem with the boat that they had not previously had. They took the boat back to the mechanic and it was a simple fix, no charge. David reiterated to Angela that he still would not use this shop again, since he felt overcharged and that they did not do a good job. He should not have had to take the boat back.

Angela: I hope you told him you were dissatisfied and that he not only lost your business, but that you would not recommend them.
David: You had suggested that originally. But I knew that I might have to rely on them to tweak something they hadn't done correctly. It's a good thing we didn't part acrimoniously when I picked the boat up the first time. They wouldn't have been willing to take another look at this problem without charge.

Angela would have given them a piece of her mind in hopes of getting the bill down. This is the interactional style she was brought up to use. David totally disagreed. In his view, just asking for an explanation is evidence of his dissatisfaction with how much it cost. He indicated that he was trying to stay on good terms with the shop's owner in case he would need to take the boat back. Indeed, he felt he proved his way was the correct one when there was a minor problem. After all, they did fix the problem and did not charge for it.

It is easy to see from this example that the spouses had their own view of how to handle a service disagreement. Angela would have chosen the confrontational route; David chose the schmoozing route. What was gained or would have been gained? David felt that he gained extra service. In David's estimation, you stick to politeness. Angela wanted to confront where confrontation was due—forget politeness!

There is no easy lesson in this interaction other than to illustrate how even two individuals from the same country, using the same language, are subject to different pragmatic rules that stem from different ethnic group or regional origin. Nobody is necessarily right or wrong here. It is simply different. Perhaps Angela, knowing the differences, should have settled the bill herself in the first place. Perhaps they should have done it together, with Angela voicing her displeasure at the bill and David smoothing things over. Good cop, bad cop. The fact is that this couple is in constant awareness of their differing norms and the potential problems therein.

"LET ME PUT IT THIS WAY, YOU'RE BUSTED": CROSS-CULTURAL FAMILY SCHMOOZING IN FILMS

Angela and David's scenario is mirrored in many media productions, including films, where cross-cultural family interactions are the focus. Examples abound from the film *My Big Fat Greek Wedding*. It was widely successful a few years back, and this was no doubt due to the hilarious way that cross-cultural interactions were highlighted. In one particular scene, the daughter, who is the focus of an intercultural romance, is in a room talking with her mother and aunt. Her father and boyfriend are on another side of the room. Two conversations take place in quick succession, one among the women and one between the two men. The camera angle flashes quickly from one conversation to the other.

The women: Aunt to niece (protagonist): Last night, Vicki Pavalopolis saw you sucking the lips off of his in the Denny's parking lot. She told her ma, who told

	my ma, who told your ma—let me put it this way, you're busted.
The men:	Father to boyfriend: You sneak around all over Chicago. But you never come here to ask me can you date my daughter.
Boyfriend:	I'm sorry, but to ask you if I can date your daughter—sir, she's 30 years old!
Father:	I am the head of this house.
Boyfriend:	Okay, may I please date your daughter?
Father:	[screams] No!

This film amassed wide critical acclaim due precisely to these types of cross-cultural schmoozing examples. Apparently, the American audience is fascinated by such potential pitfalls in communication across cultures. Clearly, as we can see, the issue is not one of language but one of cultural values. In the women's talk, we see the value placed on gossip, and that it is acceptable in their value system to relay the gossip to the subject of the gossip. Inherent in the gossip is the adult scolding of a family member, the grown daughter. Perhaps in many U.S. communities it would be much too confrontational to confront the young woman in this manner. To see this played out is humorous, indeed. The young female protagonist is caught between two cultural worlds.

While this may not be such a problem for her, it is for her boyfriend. He is an average American guy, with no background knowledge about Greek interactional norms. Consequently, he does not understand the importance of schmoozing with his sweetheart's father. We see this in their brief exchange. The father holds to the importance of a suitor's asking him, the head of the household, for permission to date his daughter. The boyfriend counters that she is already 30 years old—an adult in the eyes of our culture! Nevertheless, he relents and asks her father's permission, only to be flatly refused.

Examples of interethnic schmoozing misfires in families abound in films through the years. The 1977 Woody Allen film *Annie Hall* contained many scenes of this sort. One in particular stands out in memory. Alvy Singer, a Jewish man from New York, is having a romance with Annie Hall, a midwesterner. There is one split screen scene that depicts the cultural contrasts between Alvy's Brooklyn family having a holiday dinner and Annie's family doing the same in Wisconsin. The contrast is hilarious. In the New York half of the screen, Alvy's family is all doing simultaneous argumentative talk, everyone speaking their loudest and interrupting the others to get heard. In the Wisconsin half of the screen, Annie's family is doing polite, one-person-speaks-at-a-time turn-taking during dinnertime. The distinction could not be starker.

A more recent comedy film, *Meet the Parents*, is yet another such illustration of schmoozing problems across ethnic groups. In one scene, the engaged couple is visiting the future bride's parents, where they are introduced to the future groom (Greg, played by Ben Stiller). Similar to *Annie Hall*, Stiller's character is Jewish, while the bride is Protestant American. The first day visiting the bride's parents at their home, her mother enters the formal dining room as she begins to serve the food:

Groom:	Everything looks fabulous. It's such a treat for me to have a home-cooked meal like this. Dinner at my house usually consisted of everybody in the kitchen fighting over containers of Chinese food.
Bride's mom:	Oh, you poor thing! What, there wasn't enough food to go around?
Groom:	No, there was, we just never sat down like a family.
Mom:	Ugh.
Bride's dad:	Greg, would you like to say grace?
Bride:	Greg's Jewish, dad.
Dad:	Are you telling me Jews don't pray? Unless you have some objection?
Greg:	No, no, no. [he goes on to say grace, adopting lines from the Broadway play *Godspell*]

This scene is humorous because we see a clash of expectations due to differing ethnic/religious backgrounds. Albeit exaggerated, Greg's depiction of how his family had dinner at home is similar to Alvy's family dinner table interaction in *Annie Hall*. In both films, the characterizations are, of course, stereotypes. However, they do serve to draw very different pictures of familial schmoozing in different subcultures speaking the same language.

FAMILY SCHMOOZING IN PUBLIC LIFE

Examples of family schmoozing are rarely found in public life, since family interactions are by definition quintessentially intimate.

Having said this, we can take at least one example from political discourse. In June 2008, at the end of the Democratic primary race for U.S. president, Barack and Michelle Obama were caught on camera giving each other the fist bump, which is now widely known and used. Now, we know that this gesture is commonly used as a nonverbal message of congratulations. Some would say it started with African Americans and diffused to the younger generation of all races, which often appropriates language and behavior from this racial group. The press made quite a big deal out of the simple non-verbal familial interaction, with FOX News's E. D. Hill questioning whether the gesture could have been construed as a terrorist signal:

> Hill: A fist bump, a pound, a terrorist fist jab? The gesture every-one seems to interpret differently.

Keith Olbermann of MSNBC severely criticized this mistrust as "idiocy." He and TV journalist Rachel Maddow, both consummate liberal talk show hosts, had an ensuing discussion about FOX's portrayal of the Obamas as possible terrorists:

> Olbermann: This apparently springs from a comment on a right-wing blog. . . . But even Howard Kurtz on CNN on *Reliable Sources* asked the national correspondent from CBS News, Byron Pitts, who's an African American, he asked him, "Is this what all the brothers do?" And Mr. Pitts kept his composure and said basically, "Well, the younger generation, regardless of race, got what that gesture is." Is that really the sort of evil subtext that by now we all look for behind every stupid thing somebody on the Right says? Is that what this is? It's not that the Republicans want you to be afraid of Barack and Michelle Obama because they might be terrorists. They want you to be afraid of them because (jokingly) they might be black.
>
> Maddow: I mean, you go on in that E. D. Hill, in that FOX News clip today, and they try essentially to define this as something that is unalterably foreign to the American public. Hill goes on to say on FOX that,

you know, "What happened to the great pat on the back?" as if that's the only physical gesture, I guess, of affirmation that's appropriate in American politics. And this, what we're a week out of Bush doing that big awkward chest bump at the U.S. Air Force Academy in Colorado Springs?

[Image displays on screen of Bush and an unnamed member of the Air Force bumping chests against one another.]

Maddow: I mean Bush has that awkward habit of putting his hands on the heads of bald men. Right? There's all these sorts of weird physical gestures of affirmation that people do. The idea that you would somehow make this sort of "dap," the fist bump, to be something radical or something overly radically racialized—it's comical.

Olbermann: [jokingly] Whatever happened to the formal bow? Grover Cleveland used to bow all the time on the campaign trail. [seriously] There are the dangerous outliers in this here though, too. And again it's that same theme of maybe that's . . . we're not talking about foreign; we're not talking about terrorists. We're talking about race here and these just [are] rationalizations [by] people who are racist and don't want to admit that to themselves.

Their analysis effectively mocks what they see as FOX's attempt to cast serious aspersions on the presidential hopeful.

Olbermann and Maddow show their perspective on FOX's hint of terrorism as fearmongering about having an African American president. A simple suggestion that a nonverbal gesture of familial or friendly schmoozing can be foreign is dangerous. It hints that a family's interactional patterns indicate something negative about the group they represent. It is, essentially, xenophobic. Nonverbal features of interaction among close family and friends in one racial, ethnic, or even generational group can be seen as something to mistrust when viewed by an outside group. It may be part of the good schmooze for some, but for others it can be characterized as supremely dangerous—even potentially terrorist!

SOCIAL SCHMOOZING ACROSS CULTURES

As we have seen, fellow Americans who come from different regions, ethnic groups, and racial backgrounds can miscommunicate even when they assume mutual norms. Recall the discussion about speech acts in the chapter on social schmoozing. These are the small units of language interaction encompassing such linguistic exchanges as compliments, complaints, apologies, greetings, refusals, and so on. Different groups have vastly divergent ways to realize these acts. Any assumptions about what is acceptable and appropriate across cultural groups are fraught with hazard. For example, in one cultural group, it may be appropriate to ask people how much money people make, how old they are, or how much they paid for their home. A person from such a group might reasonably assume these are fine questions to ask regardless of one's interlocutor. This section examines several examples to illustrate schmoozing dangers in social talk across cultures. Avoiding these misfires is essential in successful social interaction.

"LET'S GET TOGETHER SOME TIME": INVITING

Most of us are all too familiar with the expression, "Let's get together some time," and we even joke about "Let's do lunch." This latter expression conjures up Hollywood producers trying to nail down a meeting for so-called schmoozing. It often happens that people from other cultures speaking in English wonder why Americans are so insincere. This perception is partly based on our propensity to offer invitations that do not specify time or place.

The chapter on social schmoozing discussed research[1] that analyzed perceptions of insincerity in the vague invitations that Americans offer. The researchers concluded that American fear of rejection is at the root of our hesitation to issue genuine invitations. Instead, we put out what they called "leads" that do not specify time or place. Hence, a lead such as "We really should have lunch someday" may merely be a person's initial step to find out if the other person would be willing. It is really a delicate dance of negotiation. One person takes two baby steps forward in a vague invitation in order to ascertain the other's desire to get together. The other's response may be two steps forward as well (or, conversely, a step or two back). Because of the difficulty in interpretation of someone's intentions, we assume these leads to be insincere.

If the analysis is correct, then we must all understand one important fact: that a lead deserves a positive response in order for an invitation to be carried out to its successful conclusion. A hypothetical exchange, then, might unfold as follows:

John is American and Ramon is his new neighbor, who just moved here to start a job in international business. He comes from another country but has spent the last few months in the United States studying English full time. The two men have bumped into each other in town and have a short conversation in English, perhaps on the run:

John: Hey, Ramon, how's it goin'?
Ramon: Okay. I've started the job and most of it is going well. We'll see how it goes when I have to get up in front of a group to talk.
John: I'm sure it'll be just fine. You sound pretty comfortable in English now.
Ramon: Yeah, it's getting easier.
John: Hey, it's great to see you. We should get together with the families some time soon.
Ramon: Okay. Well, see you later.

We might imagine that Ramon is left wondering why John has issued this disingenuous invitation. If we understand that John's "lead" is not insincere but merely a feeler, what is Ramon to do?

If Ramon tries to pin John down, he runs the risk of being rebuffed. In other words, he might try saying something like, "We'll be home all weekend and we'd love to come over." But that might be construed as too forward. To play it more safe, he might say, "We'd love to get together—just call us." That might give John just the feedback he needs to know that rejection is not forthcoming and that a get-together would be welcome. As is clear, the good schmooze is a delicate balancing act when socializing across cultural groups.

"Sorry I Can't Now, But Please Ask Me Again": Refusing

Refusing is a speech act that we typically think of as negative. This is precisely because it is, in essence, saying "no." In many cultures, such as the Japanese, it is too face-threatening to say no directly. In fact, more than 30 years ago, research came out describing "Sixteen ways to avoid saying 'no' in Japan."[2] In other cultures, however, refusals are, in certain contexts, a way of showing politeness. For example, in many Middle Eastern societies, a refusal of an offer of food is considered polite interaction. Because it is expected that the offer of food will be repeated after the first refusal, there is no danger of not eating enough. It is not difficult to imagine that this norm can cause misunderstanding and frustration. Some years ago, linguist Joan Rubin described just how this happened:[3]

> An anecdote was recounted about an Arab speaker's first encounter with some Americans. On his first visit to an American home, he was served some delicious sandwiches. When the hostess came to offer seconds, he refused. Much to his chagrin, the hostess didn't repeat the offer. Thus the Arab sat there, confronted by some lovely sandwiches which he couldn't eat.

We see in this anecdote how a refusal may, in certain cultures and in certain situations, be expected. When this is the case, a refusal is not so negative. Indeed, refusals can be carried out with finesse if one considers them a part of the good schmooze.

Columbia University sociolinguist Leslie Beebe[4] and her colleagues studied how North Americans and Japanese do the speech act of refusing. What they found was that the two societies have differing underlying systems for refusing. It is well known that elaborated refusals with many hedges and softeners work to make the refusal less negative; indeed, a softened, hedged refusal that gives an airtight reason why the refusal is necessary works best. Moreover, a refusal that requests another invitation or offer in the future can function positively toward the good schmooze. Something like the following, from Beebe's Japanese data on refusing invitations, just does not cut it:

Female professor to a graduate student:

Professor: Will you be coming to the party at my house this weekend?
Student: I have to go to a wedding.

The student's refusal was not only vague, it did not give any details about the wedding as a prior commitment. This goes along with the

Japanese value of avoiding direct refusal. Worse even is the absence of an apology or softener. In fact, only later did the professor find out that the wedding was the student's own! Most would agree that would have been a more airtight excuse.

That there are vastly different rules of interaction between U.S. and Japanese cultures is widely known. The previous sequence is a good example of the difficulty of getting it right in cross-cultural schmoozing. Another interesting difference is the Japanese norm that, while it is negative to refuse, it is permissible to refuse on principle. Japanese refusals such as the following were recorded by Beebe and colleagues:

> In refusing an invitation to dine at an expensive restaurant, a Japanese friend said, "I never yield to temptation."

> In refusing to try a diet that a friend suggested, the Japanese person said, "I make it a rule to be temperate in eating."

Apparently, stating a refusal on principle is an acceptable way to say *no* in Japanese, and Japanese speakers tend to assume this is also appropriate in English. But to the American ear, these refusals sound at the very least strange. Beyond that, they suggest possible conflict talk. Like vagueness, stating principles fails with American speakers. Clearly, something can be appropriate in one system but not in another. In order to avoid pitfalls, we must become educated citizens of the world in knowing something about differing norms for speech.

These examples from cross-cultural interactions ought to be illustrative to native speakers. If we begin to grasp other norms of interaction, the good schmooze has the potential to be realized. Of course, we must beware of not carrying assumptions too far. For example, if a person from the Middle East refuses our offer of food the first time, we might try offering a second time. But if we offer a third time, there is the danger of being perceived as too pushy. All that can be said regarding cross-cultural social schmoozing is that knowing that there are differing norms is a start. Understanding cross-cultural values in talk can ameliorate negative feelings about other national, racial, ethnic, and other groups. It is at least a beginning that is worth considering in the present state of globalization and transnationalism.

CROSS-CULTURAL SCHMOOZING IN
POLITICAL INTERACTIONS

Decades ago, near the end of the Vietnam War, it came time for the
United States to negotiate with the North Vietnamese. At the time,
President Richard Nixon was repeatedly recorded saying, "I'll talk
peace anywhere, anytime . . . ." Undoubtedly, the North Vietnamese
misinterpreted this to mean, "I won't negotiate." Given the research
on cross-cultural misperceptions of insincerity and vagueness, it is no
surprise that there was miscommunication across cultural expectations.
No doubt the Vietnamese interpreted Nixon's utterance as too vague,
indicating not a willingness to talk peace, but exactly the opposite.

The media is filled with examples from public and political life of
attempts at schmoozing that violate cross-cultural norms. They range
from nonverbal gaffes to verbal bloopers. One example of the need for
cross-cultural sensitivity derives from Secretary of State Hillary Rodham
Clinton's visit to Somalia in August 2009. A female in this important role
was meeting and greeting a Muslim head of this state. The issue was, to
shake hands or not to shake hands? Such a nonverbal feature of interaction can be fraught with the potential for miscommunication. In many
interpretations of the Koran, it is forbidden for a man to touch the hand
of any woman other than members of his family. Was Secretary Clinton
going to insult by offering her hand? Was it okay to do so?

In the end, after the ceremonies at the podium and questions answered,
the Somali president did shake Clinton's hand. Gestures such as shaking hands or bowing, in some cultures, are inherent parts of the good
schmooze. Failure to follow cultural norms for these types of rituals can
severely constrain social lubrication. In the case of our secretary of state
and the Somali president, whose norms were to be followed? While the
interaction took place on Somali soil, the diplomatic pressure was on the
Somali president to obtain the support he sought from the United States.
Because of this, he yielded to American norms rather than the reverse. A
similar incident occurred in the early days of Obama's presidency when
he was seen bowing to a foreign head of state. He was trying to display
cultural sensitivity, but the conservative news outlets were severely critical of this gesture. This is yet another example of the fallacy of "When
in Rome, do as the Romans do" in the current state of the world.

Many other examples of schmoozing blunders abound from the
2008 presidential election and the months leading up to it. During the

campaign in 2007, John McCain answered a question at a press conference on how we should deal with Iran:

> You know, that old Beach Boys song [Sings], "bomeran, bom,
> bom, bom, bom bomeran." [in other words, "bomb Iran"]
>   [Then he laughed and said] "anyway . . ."

McCain was using a play on the real words of the 1960's Beach Boys
song "Barbara Ann." Of course, this was McCain's attempt at a lighthearted humor despite the severity of the Iranian situation. To be sure,
the ability to joke is an important part of the good schmooze. This
was surely such an attempt to schmooze with the press—an effort to
establish rapport with them. But Iran poses a serious problem for U.S.
foreign policy, and joking about bombing that country is really no joke.
Some would say that attempt at schmoozing misfired.

To be sure, Republicans have no monopoly on cross-cultural misfires. Vice President Joseph Biden may in fact be the consummate flop
at schmoozing through attempted humor. Back in 2007, Biden was
recorded while discussing immigration with the press:

> In Delaware the largest growth of population is Indian American,
> moving from India. You cannot go to a *7-11* or a *Dunkin Donuts*
> unless you have a slight Indian accent.

Was this a cross-cultural schmoozing misfire? Biden was schmoozing
with the press and not with Indian Americans. This interaction is similar in nature to McCain's schmoozing with the press about bombing
Iran. Both examples are public, however. It is the public nature of the
interactions that make them potential schmoozing misfires.

Biden sent the wrong message to Indian Americans. Probably he did
not intend his statement to be insulting to immigrants from India. But
he could have said the same thing about the ubiquity of Indian American doctors in many U.S. hospitals (including Delaware, no doubt).
Biden's choice of those particular workplaces sent a message that could
be construed as a put-down.

Cross-cultural political bloopers need not be across languages, as
we have seen. Even members of different communities that ostensibly
speak the same language may have different norms or rules within that
language. Some have joked that the English and the Americans speak
different languages, with the only the former speaking "English" and

the latter "American." In the waning days of George W. Bush's presidency, he was recorded welcoming Queen Elizabeth to Washington:

> She helped us celebrate the bicentennial in 17 . . . 1976.
> [Bush looks at the queen] She gave me a look that only mothers can give.

Most of us who try to use humor in social schmoozing do it to establish a lighthearted good will. No doubt this was Bush's intention with this quip about the queen. But interacting with the queen of England has rules that go well beyond those of British/American differences in norms. Norms of bowing, curtseying, backing away, and so on relate to how one is to behave in the presence of this royal figure. Surely Bush's joke was construed as inappropriate schmoozing by the royal figure, just as was Michelle Obama's touch on the queen's back upon her their first meeting.

CROSS-CULTURAL INTERACTIONS IN EDUCATIONAL LIFE

At my own large state university, a walk through the corridors of the engineering or the physics building is revelatory—there are very few Anglo names on the doors of faculty and teachers. Most of the name plaques bear foreign names. The fact is, higher education is currently, by some reports, the number one export of the United States. This is to say that we train and educate young people from abroad, and most of them take their expertise back to their home countries. At the same time, the hope is that we also export goodwill.

At most large universities, where there are many internationals pursuing higher education, foreign graduate students are frequently funded through their advanced degrees as teaching assistants. While they are called *assistants*, many are in charge of their own undergraduate classes. The situation is ripe for cross-cultural schmoozing (and the misfires that accompany it). One of the issues that American students have with these international teaching assistants (ITAs) is that they frequently have trouble building rapport with foreign instructors.

I recently visited a class specifically focusing on ITA interaction with U.S. undergraduates. The course consisted of some dozen ITAs from various countries. On this particular day, the instructor, an American man with several years of experience in cross-cultural issues, had invited a panel of undergraduates to attend. Their function was to answer the ITAs' questions about their perceptions of foreign-born teachers. Here is how the exchange began:

The first question asked was by a male ITA from India:

ITA:	How do you like ITAs?
Female undergraduate:	Sometimes they have pronunciation problems.
Male undergraduate:	Fewer people ask questions.
Instructor:	If they like you, they won't complain as much about pronunciation.
First undergraduate:	We have a fear of cultural divide—we worry about communication issues.

At this point the instructor took the opportunity to teach about what he called *chit chat*:

Instructor: Americans [teachers] are really good at filling the space as students are coming into class. It's about approachability. Americans like to chat. We do it pretty naturally. You come from cultures where teachers are authorities. Here it's about diplomacy.

The instructor was trying to convey the importance of the good schmooze in teaching—undergraduates need to feel comfortable with their international professors, and one way for the instructors to ensure that comfort is to build rapport with them through small talk as they are waiting for the formal class to begin, or outside of the boundaries of the class time. This is easily done by teachers who know how to schmooze with students. The schmooze brings them closer to each other and creates the notion in the students that the teacher cares about them as individuals.

The instructor of this particular class in fact had modeled how this is done before the formal panel discussion ensued. He did it naturally, not knowing that the ensuing discussion would take chatting as one of the foci. As they were waiting for the rest of the class to arrive, he asked the small group already present, "Anything happening?" When there was little substantive reply, he persisted, "Is life working?" One of the ITAs answered, "Yeah." Then the instructor began a one-on-one chat with that ITA about a soccer match involving a team from his country.

Cultural difference in education is an issue not only in the United States, but also in other Western countries where immigration has burgeoned. One such country is France. A recent Oscar-winning foreign film, *Entre les Murs* (*The Class*), illustrates some of the dangers of teacher/student interaction when the students are a multicultural group. The setting is a French language class in Paris, where the students are from a diversity of national and thus racial/ethnic/religious backgrounds. He struggles to get these adolescents interested in the subject matter, but the students put up a lot of resistance, much of which stems from cultural clashes or lack of cultural sensitivity.

In one sequence, the students argue with the teacher about the fictional names that he uses when putting examples on the blackboard. He tends to use Western names. They ask him in a challenging way, "Why can't you use names like ours?" He is somewhat dumbstruck. After a bit of delay, he explains that it would not be fair to some in the group if he used names from the group of another. They are not appeased by this explanation. Clearly, they would feel less marginalized if the teacher used names like Suleiman in his hypothetical examples on the board. Something as simple as naming can cause alienation in a cross-cultural situation. This is especially true in educational settings in societies filled with immigrants from around the world.

CROSS-CULTURAL SCHMOOZING HIGHLIGHTED

"YOUR EYES ARE BEAUTIFUL": SCHMOOZING OR SEXUAL HARASSMENT?

In spite of the widespread acceptance that interactional norms vary from culture to culture, the prevailing attitude seems to be that "common sense" tells everyone what behavior and language is sexual. In other words, the tendency seems to be to assume that differences in cross-cultural interpretation do not extend to the area of what verbal and nonverbal behavior might have sexual implications and therefore what behavior might be perceived as introducing sexual behavior into a professional setting such as the university classroom.

This was the subject for a research project that I carried out in collaboration with colleague Andrea Tyler.[5,6] Tyler's work with international teaching assistants over several years and my own interest in gender and language sparked a series of discussions. These focused on actual incidents in which ITAs said certain things to undergraduates of the opposite sex that were construed by the undergraduates as highly inappropriate. It may be that behavior has some sexual implications in both cultures but that the degree of sexual content that is considered acceptable within particular relationships varies from culture to culture, so that the perception of doing something wrong or offensive or in violation of the cultural code differs.

Support for this hypothesis came from a female Korean graduate student who reported that a Chinese male student asked her for a date many times. When she asked him why he continued to ask her after several rejections, he voiced the belief that females say "no" even when they mean "yes." The Korean student reported that she thought he was a pest but did not consider his behavior as harassment. It was just part of his attempt at flirtatious schmoozing. However, when the same Chinese student repeatedly asked female U.S. graduate students for dates, they reported him to their department chair.

Indeed, because the issue of sexual harassment has been highlighted over the past decades in the United States, American women—and men—now have a heightened sense of what may or may not be construed as sexual in nature. A direct result is the attitude that sexually tinged language is no longer part of the good schmooze in our society. This is particularly true in professional settings such as the university classroom. Clearly, different norms prevail in different cultures, but one cannot be too careful when transferring one's cultural norms to a new setting where the rules—even the laws—may differ. Another example from real data in the educational setting illustrates:

> A foreign male ITA is in the classroom as students file in. A female
> student sits down and the ITA says to her:
>   I never noticed, but you have the most beautiful eyes. Eyes are
> a reflection of the soul. Your eyes are truly beautiful.

The undergraduate student was quite taken aback, as one can imagine. In her American system of appropriate speech, this sort of statement coming from a teacher was not acceptable. It was too forward. It suggested flirtation. Two possibilities present themselves here regarding the teacher's language. A first is that the use of a proverb such as "eyes are a reflection of the soul" is, in some cultures, appropriate language to use with a young person of the opposite sex. A compliment on appearance couched in terms of a proverb in that culture may be highly positive. As such, it is possible that no sexual innuendo was intended. A second possibility is that such innuendo was present, but that this was acceptable within this ITA's own cultural norms. That is to say, it may be that a male in a position of power (as teacher over student) has the right to talk with a female student in his class in such a way. Indeed, this kind of language was rampant even here just a few decades ago. Since then, we have been made aware of the legal implications of such language and behavior. It is no longer a part of the good schmooze.

Owing directly to the heightened awareness in the United States currently about sexual harassment, the teacher was found to have spoken inappropriately to the student in this U.S. context. When this student brought harassment charges against this ITA, he was removed from his teaching assistantship and lost his funding. He found out the hard way that this kind of schmoozing is forbidden. Not knowing the limits of the good schmooze cross-culturally cost him his ability to proceed with his graduate studies.

We had many examples similar to this one. This led us to wonder whether there was language and behavior that could be construed as sexual in U.S. contexts but not in other societies. But we also wanted to systematically study if certain sexually tinged language might be more tolerated in societies other than the United States. Given the heightened state of awareness of sexual harassment in the United States, this issue seems critical for the success of international graduate students teaching on U.S. campuses. While we realized that some men from cultures outside the United States bring with them negative attitudes toward women in universities and the workplace, we also suspected that some of these negative perceptions might be the result of cross-cultural misunderstanding.

In order to study potential differences in interpretation of appropriateness and sexual intent in various teacher-student interactions, our research took a two-pronged approach. We sought the reactions of both undergraduates and ITAs to 12 scenarios of naturally occurring (and potentially problematic) interactions. We asked ITAs and undergraduates of both sexes to comment on whether the interaction was appropriate or inappropriate. Here is a sample scenario:

> You have a class that meets three times per week. The TA borrowed a book from you two weeks ago. During the last class, which met on Friday, you asked if the TA happened to have brought the book to class. When the TA said, "No," you responded with, "Okay, no problem." At 9:30 P.M. Saturday night, the TA dropped

by your apartment to return your book. The TA asked what you were doing. When you said you were just reading, the TA said, "I'm not doing anything either."

Our research participants responded to each of the 12 scenarios, in each case indicating whether they thought it was appropriate or inappropriate.

The issue of cross-cultural perceptions of sexual intent is multi-faceted and many layered. The identity of the ITA, in terms of race, ethnicity, and gender, appeared to play an important role. Our participants often stated that their assessments would depend on who the ITA was and the manner in which the potentially offensive language and behavior was carried out. It was for this reason that we developed the video prompts for a second study. Each scenario was enacted twice, once with a female ITA and once with a male ITA and a student of the opposite sex.

The interpretations derived from these studies reflect culturally specific expectations for teacher-student relationships. For instance, while most U.S. undergraduates found it inappropriate for an ITA to stop by a student's apartment unannounced, many ITAs found this scenario quite acceptable. Some of the narrative comments indicated that this would be normal and neutral in their own cultures. Let's look at another example from the data:

It is the first meeting of a class with a new ITA. The ITA would like to get to know the students on an individual basis in order to better deal with their study of the subject. When you arrive at your first tutorial, the ITA begins to ask you the following questions: "What do you like to do on Friday and Saturday nights?" "Are you currently involved romantically?" "Does your social life leave you enough time for your academic work?"

The differences in judgments of the female undergraduates and the male ITAs surveyed on this scenario were very divergent—enough to be statistically significant. In other words, the male ITAs largely found the scenario just part of the good schmooze. The female undergraduates certainly did not. One female student termed the teacher's questions "beyond cheesy." Another called it "really tacky."

Gender and culture are intertwined here. The majority of the male ITAs judged it acceptable to ask students personal questions of this sort. It is part of what many foreign male teachers consider good schmoozing that can create rapport with undergraduate students, male or female. For the American female students, this was far from acceptable schmoozing.

Clearly, miscommunication involving conflicting cultural assumptions and linguistic cues is subtle and enduring. Forewarned, ITAs can make informed decisions about how they might avoid being misinterpreted and avoid cross-cultural misunderstandings concerning sexual intent. We see how role expectations determine what is or is not part of the good schmooze. Because ITAs are teachers, it is their task as nonnatives to understand the norms of the society in which they are teaching and work within them. Thus, the tables are somewhat turned around with ITAs as opposed to native teachers. While as instructors, these students wield power over undergraduates, having the responsibility of dispensing grades, as newcomers, they are placed in less powerful positions than that which ordinarily prevails among native-speaking professors. Undergraduates who pay hefty tuition fees complain to their parents about their inability to understand their teachers from other countries. Far worse are complaints about what are construed as violations of interactional norms, especially those that have a sexual nature.

The issue of power here is turned on its head. It is true that teachers are typically the more powerful group vis-à-vis. their students, holding in their power rewards and punishments. But when the teacher is international, schmoozing challenges abound, and their power is diminished. First, it is diminished by the fact of not being a native speaker of the language of instruction; second, it is diminished by parental pressure on the institution for teachers who are both comprehensible as well as appropriate. Thus, while cross-cultural understanding ought to be a two-way issue, we clearly see here that this is not the case. Invariably, the foreigner, despite playing a role that is traditionally more powerful in the institution of higher education, is cast in a less powerful position, and thus needs to more seriously understand the rules and norms of the U.S. students.

CONCLUSION: SCHMOOZING IN CROSS-CULTURAL INTERACTIONS

Nowhere is schmoozing more important than in cross-cultural encounters, where people may possess vastly divergent language and cultural norms. This is true in all spheres of interaction. The ability to acquire cross-cultural face-to-face interactional competence is increasingly crucial in an era of pluralistic workplaces, educational settings, and neighborhoods. A lack of schmoozing ability with people of diverse cultural backgrounds results in a decrease in social capital. For societies such as ours, where our neighbors, coworkers, and colleagues are likely to come from cultural backgrounds quite different from our own, we run the risk of prejudice, stereotyping, and ultimately alienation. The path to acceptance and inclusion is paved with realization that others' ways with language and nonverbal behavior are not necessarily inferior (deficient) but merely different. Understanding these differences opens doors, not only for those who are in less powerful positions, but for all of us.

I have attempted to demonstrate this in the preceding pages, where I have advocated cross-cultural interaction as a two-way understanding. This goes for interactions among people of different societies around the world (e.g., immigrants, students benefiting from higher education in another country) but also interactions with citizens whose backgrounds are different either ethnically or racially.

Anthropologists have long understood that cultural traditions are passed down for many generations, long after migration has taken place and societies are in a diaspora. Vestiges of communication styles persist long after settlement in new places. Because of this, we cannot merely hope to educate the newcomer into a new set of norms. We have seen this time and time again, starting with subcultures living in the same region, to different ethnic and racial groups interacting in schools and communities. Community norms will live on for generations, despite the best efforts of official policies to eradicate them.

An ability to carry on the good schmooze cross-culturally is a highly nuanced, but necessary skill in today's world. It is simply a fact that homogeneity is not only difficult to achieve but, in the rare cases where it prevails, is built on loss of language, ethnicity, and identity. We see this phenomenon unfortunately illustrated in places where diverse societies have been arbitrarily forced together into nationhood (e.g., the former Congo and the former Yugoslavia). The goal of striving toward homogenization results in serious consequences of in-group/out-group miscommunication and prejudice. Understanding other groups' norms of interaction has the potential to ameliorate hatred.

We need not stray as far from home to distant nations to witness such situations. Good cross-cultural schmoozing ought to start in our very families, neighborhoods, and communities. We may find that the people next door, our colleagues or coworkers, our teachers or fellow students, or even our in-laws have very different ways of speaking. We may then find that we will need to know something about these norms in order to benefit from neighborliness, workplace and educational satisfaction, and familial harmony that come with the good schmooze. Without understanding these differences, we set ourselves apart from important opportunities for social, educational, and workplace networks. This is true in all spheres of life.

NOTES

1. Nessa Wolfson, Lynne D'Amico-Reisner, and Lisa Huber, "How to Arrange for Social Commitments in American English: The Invitation," in *Sociolinguistics and Language Acquisition*, eds. Nessa Wolfson and Elliot Judd (Rowley, MA: Newbury, 1983), 116–128.

2. Keiko Ueda, "Sixteen Ways to Avoid Saying 'No' in Japan," in *Intercultural Encounters with Japan*, eds. John Condon and Mitsuko Saito (Tokyo: Simul Press, 1974), 185–192.

3. Joan Rubin, "How to Tell When Someone is Saying 'No' Revisited," in *Sociolinguistics and Language Acquisition*, eds. Nessa Wolfson and Elliot Judd (Rowley, MA: Newbury House, 1983), 10–17.

4. Leslie Beebe, Tomoko Takahashi, and Robin Uliss-Welz, "Pragmatic Transfer in ESL Refusals," in *On the Development of Communicative Competence*, eds. Robin Scarcella, Elaine Anderson, and Stephen Krashen (Rowley, MA: Newbury, 1985), 55–73.

5. Andrea Tyler and Diana Boxer, "Sexual Harassment? Cross-Cultural/Cross-Linguistic Perspectives," *Discourse and Society* 7 (1996): 107–133.

6. Diana Boxer and Andrea Tyler, "A Cross-Linguistic View of Harassment," in *Gender and Belief Systems*, eds. Natasha Warner, Jocelyn Ahlers, Leela Bilmes, Monica Oliver, Suzanne Wertheim, and Melinda Chen (Berkeley: University of California, 1996), 85–97.

CHAPTER 6

Conclusion: The Lost Art

⁓

Schmoozing saved my life many times. If I hadn't always enjoyed a good schmooze, I probably wouldn't be here right now at age 90, and neither would you.

Ben Boxer

Used to be, people would have conversations with each other for the simple joy of human interaction. It was not for any direct benefit. The activity of pure chatting led to a sense of well-being—harmony with others. It was not about networking. It was not about getting something out of someone, although it often resulted in favors, invitations, and actions that helped in one's life. But the good schmooze was not intended to reap such rewards.

To be sure, good schmoozing still exists among certain people in certain places. People in more rural places still chat with their neighbors over the fence, with the mail carrier, or with total strangers at the boat ramp—"Catch anything?" "Going fishing?" They wave to each other when passing by—in the car or on foot. They may not know each other, but perhaps they recognize one another at the local gas station. Older citizens still pass the time schmoozing in their assisted living facilities, and often the chat focuses on times gone by.

Most of us, however, have little time to spare out of our busy lives. Multitasking does not leave much room for the warm feelings that come from pure chatting for no direct benefit. There is no time to waste. We talk on the phone, text, check our e-mail on our smartphones, all while driving the long commute to work. Young adults are consumed with building a career, and networking takes priority. Those in middle years are overwhelmed with juggling demands of work and family—paying the bills, keeping their house from foreclosure, and ensuring that their loved-ones are fed.

Because we have so little time to sit and chat, the concept of schmooze has made friends with the notion of sucking up. This is indeed a sad place to be. One of the consummate examples of this new notion of schmoozing is Rod Blagojevich. An Associated Press story in June 2010 centered on his corruption trial. The article was accompanied by a photograph in which he sat in a chauffeured car pulling up to the courthouse, arm extended in a wave to the onlookers. The article states:

> The impeached former Illinois governor has drawn on his political skill to work the federal courthouse—from the sidewalk outside to hallways and the cafeteria to his courtroom—glad-handing bystanders and talking to reporters.

Blagojevich is described as the epitome of this new meaning of schmooze—from hugging a woman in the crowd of people hoping to attend the trial, to greeting a man with a running logo on his T-shirt, "Great to see you. Are you a runner too?"

Blagojevich was using some of the techniques of good schmoozing for the purpose of bad schmoozing. Perhaps, as the article suggested, he just could not stop himself from being a politician, in the worst sense of the word. Perhaps he was using it to get the jury to sympathize with him—showing himself as just a good guy, friendly, outgoing, and well-meaning, after all. But how could it possibly be "great to see" some total stranger with a running logo on his shirt? Do we normally hug total strangers? Is it really great to see a crowd of people waiting to see him skewered in court? Bad schmooze, indeed. This one is so very easy to pick out from good schmoozing. There is no fine line here. The difference is clear to any rational observer.

"LOVELY DAY, ISN'T IT?": TO SCHMOOZE OR NOT TO SCHMOOZE

A couple of years ago there was a segment on the NPR program *Fresh Air* in which the host interviewed Bob Morris, the author of a memoir titled *Assisted Loving*. In the book, Morris discusses his relationship with his elderly father after the death of his mother. In his early eighties, his father was still interested in finding a relationship with another woman. As a gay man who was also at the time seeking a relationship, Morris explained how he tried to assist his father in his quest while simultaneously seeking a partner of his own. So, he found himself sorting through the personal ads not only for himself, but also for dear old dad.

He describes how he and his dad were one day sitting on a park bench as a lovely looking older woman passed by. She was tall, attractive and well groomed, wearing a pearl necklace and sweater set. He was thinking that she looked like a good candidate for a man such as his father; however, he was not inclined to talk to her as she passed by, thinking it would be too brazen to stop a stranger in this context. But his father did just that. He called out, "Lovely day we're having, isn't it?" The woman stopped and replied, and they had a chat. Morris discusses how his father's willingness to put himself out there opened a conversation and a possible friendship with a very nice and attractive stranger.

Morris knew the line between the good schmooze and the self-serving schmooze. Therefore, he hesitated talking to the woman, knowing full well that it might be construed as crossing a line of appropriateness. But his father, at the age of 80-something, probably felt that he had nothing to lose. After all, what would be the harm in a passing comment about the weather? If a person so elderly wants to flirt, it will probably all be taken in good spirit. Such was the case.

"RENT-A-FRIEND": SCHMOOZING AND THE INTERNET

The unfortunate fact nowadays is that people find it difficult to make simple human connections. The problem has been noted in the print and the media, for it is all-pervasive in our modern culture. An Associated Press article that appeared in *The Gainesville Sun* in June 2010 was titled "Rent-an-Everything—Internet Culture Now Offers Friendship." The article described a new Internet service where, for $34.95 a month or $69.95 a year for a login and password, 2,000 new members paid to read the profiles of 167,000 potential pals. These Internet friends serve the purpose of accompanying them on such activities as touring, dining, and movies at the cost of on average $20–30 per hour. The article goes on:

> In a world where friend is a verb and you may never meet some of yours from *Facebook* in real life, where research indicates chronic loneliness can lead to depression, suicide, high blood pressure, and viral infections, where roughly 20 percent of all people—60 million in the United States alone—say they feel lonely at any given moment, is renting a friend a solution or stopgap?

The sad fact that it is difficult to make real friends today is in sharp contrast to days gone by—the days of the good schmooze. In earlier times, we lived in dense networks.[1] We shared several aspects of life with the same circle of people. We worked with them, married their siblings, worshipped together, went to the local pub together, and shared each other's celebrations and grief. Nowadays, our networks, particularly in urban living, are more open and loose. We may know one person from our apartment building, another from work, and yet another from school. Chances are these people do not know or interact with each other. We have a lot of so-called "friends" on *Facebook*. But these friends are not friends of each other—not real friends anyway. We have not built up a shared relational identity with a close circle of real friends. Our schmoozing consists of tweets and updates that report snippets of our unfolding lives—hardly the same as good old schmoozing.

TEXTING, TALKING, AND SCHMOOZING

Instead of schmoozing, we text, we tweet, we blog, we post updates. We are writing more, at least in these truncated versions of writing. This new writing is an intermediary between the written and spoken word. It is indeed a new genre about which much has been written and reported.

As anyone who has a teenager at home well knows, teens are all about texting. They text at the movies, they text during meals at restaurants, and they even surreptitiously text in class. According to my stepson Zach (just emerging from his teens), they text because they fear that calling will interrupt whatever their interlocutors may be doing. If they text, they can expect an immediate response, regardless of the prevailing goings-on. But it is not only teens who are into texting. A recent report indicated that 50 percent of adults have been known to text while driving!

In April 2010, *All Things Considered* on NPR had a segment on what is now going on among teens. According to a University of Michigan study funded by the Pew Center, teens send on average 50 texts daily—some even double that or more. Some high schools have outright bans on texting. In Los Angeles, a history teacher lamented that as her students are more and more immersed in texting, they are increasingly shy and awkward in person:

> They can get up the courage to ask you for [a deadline] extension on the computer . . . but they won't come and speak to you face-to-face about it. And that worries me, in terms of their ability—particularly once they get out in the workplace—to interact with people.

The workplace already has less and less face-to-face interaction. Even people who share office space find themselves e-mailing each other to find out information. The landscape of work has changed, and it will continue to evolve as teens enter the workplace.

As for family interaction, the scene is somewhat different, according to this study. When it comes to communicating with their parents, most teens prefer to speak with them by phone. Why should this be so? The study found that teens are strategic about which form of communication to use. When they want to ask permission for something, they know they will get more of the results they desire with in-person, or at least phone requests. This way, they can more readily plead and cajole. As one of the researchers stated:

> We heard from teens who said, "When I want the *yes*, I'll go to the phone because my parents can hear my voice, and I can wheedle and charm them, and that's how I'm going to get what I want."

These teens know instinctively that there is nothing better than talk. But once again, the cajoling is not about the good schmooze. Teens have learned their life lesson—that schmoozing is all about direct benefits. The good schmooze is an endangered species of talk.

"Schmoozing Saved My Life": Up Close and Personal

The quote that begins this concluding chapter is, as you may have guessed, from my father, Ben Boxer. As scholars, we do the work we do for reasons—sometimes reasons that are below the level of consciousness. My parents have inspired the issues that I study. Growing up in an immigrant family surrounded by a swirl of languages, I noticed early how people talk. Sometimes the talk of my family differed in dramatic ways from the talk of native English speakers around me. This was not only linguistic, but also cultural.

One aspect of talk that was always most interesting to me as a young child (and a painfully shy one at that) was my father's ability to engage in the good schmooze. He schmoozed with neighbors; he schmoozed with coworkers; he schmoozed at home. It was the beginning of a lifetime of sociolinguistic research for me, his middle child. It always fascinated me how a good schmooze would lead to nothing concrete—for him it was just an enjoyable interval of time chatting. My father's story is all about the good schmooze. It was recorded and transcribed a few years ago by a local oral historian[2] at my request.

Dad was born Binem Bokser on September 13, 1920, in Warsaw, Poland. He left Poland when the Germans began to attack in the fall of 1939. It was with the help of a Polish-born German woman, a stranger, who had a pass that allowed her to take people to work on the border. He went to see the woman, had a chat, and told her he wanted to leave with her on her next convoy. She took a liking to him, and though there was some danger in helping him, she readily agreed. The woman conveyed him 20 kilometers away, just two kilometers from the Russian border.

After dropping him off, German border guards detained him at the border crossing. They kept him all day, confiscating everything he had brought along for the journey. He schmoozed with a border guard into the night. Finally, very early in the morning, the guard opened the gate and let him go into what was then a no-man's-land on the bank of a river separating Poland from Russia. But the Russian border guards were not about to let him cross. He was finally caught and arrested and subsequently made to walk for many miles to a little town on the other side of the border, in Russia.

It was Friday night and he could see the Sabbath candles lit in the windows of the people's houses in the town, so he knew that there were Jews there. Soon he saw the people walking to the synagogue for the Sabbath service. As the guards were taking him to jail, he dared to speak to these local townspeople, telling them that he was running away from the Germans. Apparently, because he was speaking in the *lingua franca*, Yiddish, the guards let the schmoozing pass.

These Russian Jews in that border town said that they would speak to the rabbi about visiting him the next morning, on the Sabbath.

He remained in jail overnight. In the morning the rabbi showed up with two Russian officers—Jewish officers! He was freed. The rabbi assigned him to stay with some people as guests in the town. But it was too dangerous to let him stay for any length of time. After the Sabbath, they put him in a horse-drawn carriage that dropped him 30 kilometers away, at the nearest railroad station. He hopped on a train and went deeper into the Ukraine to a large city near Kiev.

By this time, he was very hungry. He was just 19 years old. There was no food; he was homeless. He soon met some other boys escaping the Nazis, too. He made friends with them, forming a pack. One of the boys had a brother who lived in the area between White Russia and the Ukraine. They traveled to several towns and stayed there for a few months. They met a man, and after schmoozing awhile with him, the man took them all in. He had horses, and he hired them to work with the animals.

That city was 80 miles from the border. While my dad was there, the Russians declared that no one who had escaped the Germans was allowed to live any closer than 100 kilometers from the German border. On the road again, homeless, he headed toward Pinsk. There, by happenstance, he started schmoozing with a local shoemaker. After chatting for a while, the shoemaker said that my father looked familiar. It turned out, after much back-and-forth conversation, that the man had been a good friend of my father's father in school. What a small world! Here he was, all the way from Warsaw in Pinsk, Russia. Who should he meet but someone who knew his father!

The activity of making informal conversation to establish common ground with another is pure social schmoozing. We used to call it "Jewish geography." But it is not limited to Jewishness. It is the same as *co-membership*. It is give-and-take of information that seeks commonality of identity. Based on some sharedness, whether it is regional, ethnic, racial, religious, political outlook, and so on, a mutually beneficial relationship is often built. If my dad had never stopped to chat, he would not have met this person.

The shoemaker was a Soviet citizen, but my father was not. Because of this, he could only do so much to protect my father. At the time, the Russians declared that whoever wanted to obtain Soviet citizenship should register; whoever did not should state reasons for declining the offer. My father (bravely or foolishly) declined. He did not want to hide out for the duration of the war. But he did not want Soviet citizenship, either. He wanted to return to Poland after the war. Consequently, he was detained and sent to Karelia, on the Russian/Finnish border. Once again he was a prisoner. He was sentenced to five years in jail—five years because he refused to become a Soviet citizen. He had no lawyer, no trial. They just sentenced him, and that was that.

So there he was by himself in prison. He made a few friends, schmoozing all the way. But it was a hard labor compound. He was put to work as a lumberjack. It was very cold and the food was very scarce. Prisoners had to cut many meters of forest per day. If they were unable or unwilling, they would not be fed. One day my father, fed up with all of this, decided to play a joke—he went out to the gate in just his underwear. He thought that they would see the humor in this prank and not send him out to work. It backfired. They shoved him outside in the dead of winter and made him work that whole day wearing only his underwear.

He got very sick. By the end of the day, he could not walk or even stand. They put him in a little two-man clinic. No one thought he would make it. The doctor was also a prisoner—a Russian physician. Dad began a running schmooze with the man as he recovered day by day. The doctor took a shine to him. He treated him with everything at his disposal and got him back on his feet again. Once again, my father returned to the forest and to lumberjacking. The doctor was instrumental in saving my father's life. He might have done so regardless of the schmoozing, of course. After all, as a physician, he had an ethical obligation to heal. One cannot help but wonder to what extent, if any, good schmoozing played a part.

In the meantime, the war got closer to the border. It was 1942, and the Germans began attacking the Russians. My dad was still in prison. By now he had been in there for almost three years, working off the five-year sentence. The Soviet Party people, who were in charge of the prisons, evacuated them at that point. The prisoners in Karelia were considered dangerous because they had refused Soviet citizenship. They were all put on a boat and sent across Russia into the Ural Mountains. From there they headed to the salt mines.

At one point, they ordered my dad off the boat to go into the city for supplies. He took a Russian newspaper with him for the purpose of wrapping the fish and meat he was to acquire. But as he was walking along, he read something in the paper that caught his interest. An article reported that Polish citizens were going to be given amnesty and freed. Russia had asked the Allies for help, but the Allies made them a deal: if they wanted the Allies' help, they would have to free the Poles.

Unfortunately for my father and two of his buddies, they were not among those allowed to go. My father showed the authorities the paper where it said, "Amnesty for Polish Citizens." "Yes," they said—"but you are Jewish. It doesn't count for you." He replied, "I'm Jewish but I was born in Warsaw and I'm a Polish citizen and I'm still considered a Polish citizen. That's why I'm being detained—because I didn't want to take the Russian citizenship."

Three nights later, they called him in the middle of the night and said, "Hey Bokser, how much money did they take from you when they took you?" "Thirty rubles," replied my father. So they gave him 30 rubles and said he could go. But they did not give him his birth certificate or passport. They told him they did not have them because everything had been burned. He was free, but had no papers and no place to go. He was told to go to a nearby city and that new papers would be sent to the city hall. They told him someone would meet him there and find him a job. He was homeless once again.

It was an industrial city and there were factories—clothing factories, and he was a tailor by trade. They would not hire him because he was just a young lad without papers. He stayed three days and three nights on the city hall steps until they called him in to give him his "papers."

"What are you?" they asked. "What do you do?"
"I'm a tailor," he said.
"A tailor? How old are you?"
"I'm 22."
"What can you do as a tailor?"
"I can't show you now with nothing in front of me, but you put me in the shop, you give me material and you give me a person and I can make any garment you want . . . A suit, a coat. Anything you want. Just try me."

[My father had left home when he was 13 years old to learn a trade. He had been a tailor for six years before the war started.]

The authorities took him to the factory. The men in charge took one look at him and said, "You're just a kid, what can you do?" He was dirty, unwashed after three days of homelessness. Lice were crawling all over him. They led him into the factory with a sewing machine, gave him three yards of material, and he began to sew. An old Russian man came in and started to chat with him as he was sewing away.

Seeing that the young tailor was so friendly—and so hungry—the man shared his food. As he left, the man said, "I think you're a good kid. Tomorrow I'm going to bring you good news."

The next morning the man came around again. He said that when the factory closed that night, my father should go with him. The man said, "I have a neighbor, and you can stay with her. She has a child and she will take care of you." She took him in. In my father's words:

> It was like an angel came to me. She put up a wooden washtub and I took a bath and she washed my clothes and ironed them. I looked like a brand-new dollar bill. When I came into work the next day, everyone began clapping.

That did not last long. A few weeks later, some government people appeared. They took everyone who was working at the shop out to dig trenches for their Soviet tanks to be able to pass. It was winter and very cold: "We were near Moscow. The earth was frozen a foot deep—it was such hard work, I felt like I broke my back." He continues:

> One day I looked around and saw a Russian guy in a uniform. He looked Jewish, and so I turned around and I said to him in Yiddish, "*Am eju?*" (my compatriot? my landsman?) to see if he understood. He did, and he turned around and said, "Yes I am." I asked him if he could help me. I told him that I was a tailor and I was put there in hard labor and I needed help. Although we weren't prisoners, they had taken the whole factory and put us to work. They didn't care that they had made us their slaves overnight. He told me he would go to the headquarters and talk to his colonel. Then he told me that if I saw him coming back, I should just drop my shovel, stop everything and come with him. Well, he did come back, and I followed him quickly.
>
> He took me to his headquarters, and there sat the colonel. He asked in Yiddish right away, "Are you Jewish?" and I said, "Yes." And he started to talk to me in Yiddish just like my father. He was surprised that a young boy like me hadn't been taken to the front line. I told him my story of how I was jailed and just released. He turned around to the other two guys. They were both captains. Then he put a Russian uniform on me that had medals on the uniform showing that I had fought.

Of course, my father had not fought at all—he was just a simple tailor. He ended up in the Russian army! He averted trouble by schmoozing, in Yiddish, with the right person at the right time. Once again, the "Jewish geography schmooze" saved him, just in the nick of time.

When the war ended, my father asked permission to go into Warsaw to see if any of his family was still alive. As he headed to Poland, he met my mother, Renee. She had just been released from the concentration camp in which she had been imprisoned for the past four years. She too was looking for any surviving family. They found each other on this difficult journey. Neither of them found any family survivors. They were all gone. My mother was one of eight children; my father was one of six. So there they were, two homeless people.

My father asked her if she would go with him to the American side of Germany, where they could be given sanctuary in a displaced-persons camp. She agreed. A Russian truck picked them up, and they headed for the border of Poland and Czechoslovakia. My father was still in uniform and was sitting in the front in the cabin with the driver. She was in the back with several other people. He had given her some things to hold that he had in his rucksack. It included $15,000 of Russian money that he had saved while in Russia. When they crossed over into Czechoslovakia, a border guard stopped them. He thought my dad was a driver, too; therefore, he did not bother him. They took everyone else to a holding area, including my mother.

My father, another man, and the drivers of three trucks in the convoy left and continued on a short distance. My father asked them to stop in front of a tavern. The fact is that he had schmoozed during the ride with the one fellow who was not a driver. At this point, he said to this new acquaintance, "Get the drivers drunk and distract them while I go back to the border, because they have my stuff. They have my money and all my worldly goods in my bag."

He got out of the truck and walked back to the border. Taking on the persona of, in his own words, "a Russian big shot," he asked the border guards:

"Where are those people you took?"
"They're in the back," said one of the guards.
"Well, I need to see them. They stole my backpack."
They showed him the way to those just detained. When he saw my mother, my father whispered to her in Yiddish, "I'm heading for the

American side to Camp Fahrenwald, in Munich. Just play it cool and meet me there when you can."

Five weeks later, he arrived at the displaced-persons camp in Fahrenwald. When he got to the camp, there was a message waiting for him. It said that there was someone in Munich looking for him. Of course, it was her. She came out, extending to him a small mirror. She said, "Here's the $15,000 you gave me to keep for you."

When my dad had gone back to talk to her at the border, he had asked her to take the money with her and keep it hidden. That is exactly what she had done. While she was in the holding area, she took the $15,000 and hid it in the back of her mirror. At one point, they tried to take the mirror, but she started crying and said it was the only thing she had left from her home. My father says of that moment, "Right then I knew I could trust her. And so I said, 'Are you coming with me?' And she said, 'Sure.'"

They went from Munich to the camp. That was October 26, 1945. They stayed in that relief camp from October 1945 to 1949. During that time, they married and had two children, all the while trying to emigrate:

> There were hundreds of people who lived in that camp. They were survivors of concentration camps and people who came back from Russia alive. Everyone was trying to get out. Some people were registered to go to Australia, some to Israel. I had no permit to go anywhere. I was trying to find somebody.

One day he was schmoozing with a man, his barber, in the camp. He told the barber that his father's uncle lived in Argentina and that he wanted to contact him. The barber told him that he had a brother who lived in Argentina, and that he kept writing to this brother, but his brother never wrote back. My father asked him what language he was writing in. He said that his letters were written in Yiddish. My dad exclaimed, "Well no wonder you haven't heard back. These letters get censored." He told the barber that he would write a letter for him in Russian. Russian would go through, like English, French, and German. But Yiddish would never go through.

So my father wrote to the man's brother in Argentina. In the letter, he said that he had a cousin, Lazarus Bokser, in Buenos Aires. He asked the man if he would try to find this distant relative. The barber's brother received that letter because it was written in Russian. When the man wrote back, he said that he had been walking past a store, and the name Lazarus Bokser was written on the door. He went in and spoke to Lazarus and told him about the letter. Soon afterward, my father received a letter from his cousin. Eventually, Lazarus sent papers so that the family could immigrate to Argentina via Paraguay.

This was all before my parents had had any children. By the time those papers arrived, my brother had been born. So my father sent the papers back, asking his cousin to add the child. By the time he got the papers with his son's name on it, his daughter (yours truly) had already been born. And so he sent back the papers again and asked him to add the new baby . . . That was the last time he heard from his Argentinean cousin.

How we got to this country is another schmoozing story. One night, a fellow came around and was shooting the breeze with my father. He happened to mention that in Munich there was an American embassy and they were signing up 10 or 20 tailors from the camps to work in a factory in the United States. They were getting help from the United Jewish Appeal. They gave him a test, and after he passed, they put him on a list. In the middle of May 1949, we boarded an American military transport ship—a young, penniless couple with two small children and speaking no English—and crossed the Atlantic Ocean. It took 11 days to cross. We reached New York on Memorial Day.

My parents were married for 57 years when my mother died in 2003. This is my father's coda to the memoir: "This is just one story in my life. It has all been very full and really very lucky."

THE LOST ART OF THE GOOD SCHMOOZE

Yes, indeed, this is really a story of luck. Beyond luck, however, it is also a story of talent; and beyond luck and talent, it is a story of the good schmooze—a lost art. The good schmooze will get one only so far. But it is a foot in the door. A series of good schmooze episodes can do more than just prevent the doors from slamming in one's face. One never knows. It might save your life.

Bookstore shelves bulge with literature aimed at guiding people through modern life. Thousands of books are available urging us to step back from our busy lives, take some deep breaths, relax, become mindless for brief periods, renew, and recharge our batteries.

Let us also try to recapture the lost art of the good schmooze. It is never a waste of time.

NOTES

1. Leslie Milroy, *Language and Social Networks* (Oxford: Blackwell, 1980).

2. Barbara Esrig, oral historian, Gainesville, Florida.

Glossary

Co-membership: Common membership in any group—ethnic, regional, racial, and so on.

Communicative competence: Knowing what is appropriate to say, with whom, and in what situation.

Cross-cultural pragmatics (CCP): Understanding (or misunderstanding) of each other's norms of speaking. For example, in one culture, it may be appropriate to ask how much money one makes, but not in another. Understanding the differences in rules of speaking is a two-way endeavor in CCP.

Discourse analysis: The study of what people say and how they say it in order to ascertain how meaning comes across.

Domain: A sphere of life in which verbal and nonverbal interactions occur. Examples: social, family, work, school, and religion.

Face-threatening act: A speech act that either (1) interferes with the positive self-image of an interlocutor, or (2) oversteps a boundary of privacy, for example, saying "move out of the way" instead of "excuse me." Thus, *face* refers to the self-image that one wishes to project.

Gatekeeping: The context of being responsible for granting access, giving permission, or fulfilling a request or denying it. The *gatekeeper* makes the decision (e.g., advisor).

Interaction and transaction: Interaction is give-and-take talk among people who are simply chatting without real need for information. Example: *How was your vacation? B: The weather was great.* No real information is sought. Transaction is an exchange of information. Example: *A: What time does the movie start? B: 8 P.M.*

Interlocutors: Co-conversationalists.

Lingua franca: Language in common.

Phatic communion: Making personal connections through small talk.

Pragmatics: What is actually meant by what is said or written. Example: *It's hot in here* (may be an indirect request to open a window).

Semantic derogation: Evolution from a positive to a negative meaning. Example: *Hussy*—in older versions of the English language, it meant *housewife*. It now means a woman of questionable sexual morality.

Speech act: A sociolinguistic term referring to such verbal phenomena as greetings, requests, refusals, compliments, apologies, praise, and so on.

Bibliography

Albright, Madeline. *Read My Pins*. New York: Harper Collins, 2009.

Bateson, Gregory. *Steps to an Ecology of Mind*. Northvale, NJ: Jason Aronson, 1987.

Beebe, Leslie, Tomoko Takahashi, and Robin Uliss-Welz. "Pragmatic Transfer in ESL Refusals." In *On the Development of Communicative Competence*, eds. Robin Scarcella, Elaine Anderson, and Stephen Krashen, 55–73. Rowley, MA: Newbury, 1985.

Boxer, Diana. *Complaining and Commiserating: A Speech Act View of Solidarity in Spoken American English*. New York: Peter Lang, 1993.

Boxer, Diana, and Andrea de Capua. "Bragging, Boasting and Bravado: Male Banter in a Brokerage House." *Women and Language* 22 (1999): 5–22.

Boxer, Diana, and Andrea Tyler. "A Cross-Linguistic View of Harassment: Chinese and Hispano-American ITAs." In *Gender and Belief Systems*, eds. Natasha Warner, Jocelyn Ahlers, Leela Bilmes, Monica Oliver, Suzanne Wertheim, and Melinda Chen, 85–97. Berkeley: University of California, 1996.

Boxer, Diana, and Florencia Cortes-Conde. "From Bonding to Biting: Conversational Joking and Identity Display." *Journal of Pragmatics* 27 (1997): 275–294.

Boxer, Diana, and Florencia Cortes-Conde. "Humorous Self Disclosures as Resistance to Socially Imposed Gender Roles." *Gender and Language* 4 (2010).

Brown, Penelope, and Stephen C. Levinson. *Politeness: Some Universals in Language Use*. Cambridge: Cambridge University Press, 1978.

Carey, Benedict. "Video Project Holds up Mirror to Families." *Gainesville Sun*, May 23, 2010.

Coates, Jennifer. *Women Talk*. Oxford: Blackwell, 1996.

D'Amico-Reisner, Lynne. "Avoiding Direct Conflict through the Co-Construction of Narratives about Absent Others: Gossip as a Positive Speech Activity in the Talk of Close Female Friends." Paper presented at the American Association of Applied Linguistics conference, Stamford, Connecticut, March, 1999.

Danziger, Jeff. "CartoonArts International." *New York Times*, May 16, 2010.

Eisenstein, Miriam, and Jean Bodman. "'I Very Appreciate': Expressions of Gratitude by Native and Non-Native Speakers of American English." *Applied Linguistics* 7 (1986): 167–185.

Erickson, Frederick, and Jeffery Shultz. *The Counselor as Gatekeeper*. New York: Academic Press, 1982.

Fraser, Bruce. "Insulting Problems in a Second Language." *TESOL Quarterly* 15 (1981): 435–441.

Fuller, Thomas. *Gnomologia: Adagies and Proverbs; Wife Sayings, Ancient and Modern, Foreign and British*. London: B. Barker, 1732.

Freedman, J. L., and Fraser, S. C. "Compliance without Pressure: The Foot in the Door Technique." *Journal of Personality and Social Psychology* 4 (1966): 195–202.

Girard, Joe, and Robert Casemore. *How to Sell Yourself*. New York: Warner Books, 1988.

Goffman, Erving. *The Presentation of Self in Everyday Life*. New York: Doubleday Dell Publishing Group, Inc., 1959.

Goffman, Erving. *Interaction Ritual: Essays on Face-to-Face Behavior*. Garden City, NY: Doubleday, 1967.

Goldschmidt, Myra. "For the Favor of Asking." *Working Papers in Educational Linguistics* 5 (1993): 35–49.

Goldsmith, Daena J. "Content-Based Resources for Giving Face Sensitive Advice in Troubles Talk Episodes." *Research on Language and Social Interaction* 32 (1999): 303–336.

Goodwin, Marjorie H. "Tactical Uses of Stories: Participation Frameworks within Boys' and Girls' Disputes." In *Gender and Conversational Interaction*, ed. Deborah Tannen, 110–143. New York: Oxford, 1993.

Johnson, Rebekah. "Discursive Practices in the Family Context: Negotiating Identity, Guilt and Acknowledgment in Family Discourse." Paper presented at the American Association of Applied Linguistics conference, Atlanta, March 6, 2010.

Lewis, Michael. *Liar's Poker*. New York: Norton and Company, 1989.

Malinowski, Bronislaw. "The Problem of Meaning in Primitive Languages." In *The Meaning of Meanings*, eds. C. le Ogden and I. A. Richards, 146–152. London: Routledge and Kegan Paul, 1923.

Maltz, Daniel N., and Ruth Borker. "A Cultural Approach to Male/Female Miscommunication." In *Language and Social Identity*, ed. John J. Gumperz, 195–217. New York: Cambridge University Press, 1983.

Milroy, Leslie. *Language and Social Networks*. Oxford: Blackwell, 1980.

Moyna, M. Irene. "'Nosotros los Americanos': Humorous Code-Switching and Borrowing as a Means to Defuse Culture Shock." Unpublished manuscript, University of Florida, 1994.

Nelms, Jodi. "A Descriptive Analysis of the Functions and Uses of Sarcasm in Higher Education Classroom Discourse." Unpublished PhD dissertation, University of Florida, 2001.

Norrick, Neal. *Conversational Joking: Humor in Everyday Talk*. Bloomington: Indiana University Press, 1994.

Organes, Rachel. "'If You Do That I'm Going to be Heartbroken': The Language of Jewish American Guilting." MA thesis, University of Florida, 2009.

Rubin, Joan. "How to Tell When Someone is Saying 'No' Revisited." In *Sociolinguistics and Language Acquisition*, eds. Nessa Wolfson and Elliot Judd, 10–17. Rowley, MA: Newbury, 1983.

Tannen, Deborah. *You Just Don't Understand: Women and Men in Conversation*. New York: William Morrow, 1990.

Tannen, Deborah. *I Only Say This Because I Love You*. New York: Random House, 2002.

Tyler, Andrea, and Diana Boxer. "Sexual Harassment? Cross-Cultural/Cross-Linguistic Perspectives." *Discourse and Society* 7 (1996): 107–133.

Ueda, Keiko. "Sixteen Ways to Avoid Saying 'No' in Japan. In *Intercultural Encounters with Japan*, eds. John Condon and Mitsuko Saito, 185–192. Tokyo: Simul Press, 1974.

Wolfson, Nessa, Lynne D'Amico-Reisner, and Lisa Huber. "How to Arrange for Social Commitments in American English: The Invitation." In *Sociolinguistics and Language Acquisition*, eds. Nessa Wolfson and Elliot Judd, 116–128. Rowley, MA: Newbury, 1983.

Index

About the Author

DIANA BOXER is professor of linguistics at the University of Florida. She is the author of *Applying Sociolinguistics: Domains and Face-to-Face Interaction* (John Benjamins, 2002), *Complaining and Commiserating: A Speech Act View of Solidarity in Spoken American English* (Lang, 1993), and co-editor, with Andrew D. Cohen, of *Studying Speaking to Inform Second Language Learning* (Multilingual Matters, 2004). She has published in the areas of discourse and pragmatics, sociolinguistics, gender and language, and second-language acquisition in such journals as *The Annual Review of Applied Linguistics, Discourse and Society, ELT Journal, Gender and Language, Journal of Pragmatics, Multilingua, TESOL Quarterly, Text,* and *Women and Language.*